Research-Based Instruction that Makes a Difference in English Learners' Success

Research-Based Instruction that Makes a Difference in English Learners' Success

Mayra C. Daniel and Kouider Mokhtari

ROWMAN & LITTLEFIELD
Lanham • Boulder • New York • London

Published by Rowman & Littlefield
A wholly owned subsidiary of The Rowman & Littlefield Publishing Group, Inc.
4501 Forbes Boulevard, Suite 200, Lanham, Maryland 20706
www.rowman.com

Unit A, Whitacre Mews, 26-34 Stannary Street, London SE11 4AB, United Kingdom

British Library Cataloguing in Publication Information Available

Library of Congress Cataloging-in-Publication Data
Research-based instruction that makes a difference in English learners' success /
edited by Mayra C. Daniel and Kouider Mokhtari.
   pages cm
Includes bibliographical references and index.
ISBN 978-1-4758-1865-9 (cloth : alk. paper)—ISBN 978-1-4758-1866-6
(pbk. : alk. paper)—ISBN 978-1-4758-1867-3 (electronic) 1. English language—
Study and teaching—Foreign speakers. 2. Interdisciplinary approach in education.
I. Daniel, Mayra C., 1950– editor of compilation. II. Mokhtari, Kouider,
1955– editor of compilation.
PE1128.A2R463 2015
428.2'4—dc23   2015028280

Printed in the United States of America

Contents

Foreword

English language learners (ELLs) continue to outpace the non-ELL population in K–12 school enrollment. "New destination" states such as Georgia, North Dakota, and South Carolina have experienced a more than 200 percent increase in their ELL population, which has put unprecedented demands on schools (Mikow-Porto et al., 2004; Shin & Kominski, 2010; Uro & Barrio, 2013). These ELL enrollment increases combine with political, economic, and other educational trends to create a situation where many ELLs are placed full time or for most of the day in mainstream rather than specialist language programs. In 2003, nearly 50 percent of all ELLs received minimal (fewer than ten hours) or no special services, compared to 32 percent a decade earlier (Zehler et al., 2003). It is likely that these percentages are even higher today, particularly in rural districts (Flynne & Hill, 2005).

These trends do not imply that instructional time that is dedicated to specialized language and literacy development or the need for specialist language teachers and programs has lessened. In fact, a recent report of the Council of Great City Schools (Horwitz et al., 2009) identified the presence of specialized ELL expertise at all decision-making levels as a major feature of successful school districts. However, given the exponential growth of the ELL student population in the country and an awareness of the high level of unpreparedness of most teachers to work effectively with ELLs, there is great urgency in reforming teacher education at the inservice and preservice level (Ballantyne & Sanderman, 2008). In response, several conceptual frameworks have been developed that outline the knowledge and skill base of mainstream teachers of ELLs, such as the culturally and linguistically responsive teaching framework described in Lucas and Villegas (2013). While differing in perspectives and focus, a common thread among these frameworks is an emphasis on the importance of understanding the role of language and

vii

culture in schools as it specifically pertains to bilingual learners who are at various proficiency levels and come from diverse backgrounds; and teachers' ability to organize their classroom instruction effectively for these students (de Jong & Harper, 2005). These frameworks have been key in framing the discussion about mainstream teacher preparation, but there is a clear need for coherent set of studies and understandings to inform practice. Mayra Daniel and Kouider Mokhtari's edited volume makes a significant contribution to furthering this goal.

Research-Based Instruction That Makes a Difference in English Learners' Success provides a comprehensive overview of literacy and language-related theoretical understandings and practices for ELLs that teachers, literacy coaches, teacher-educators, and others involved in professional development of mainstream teachers working with ELLs. The scope of the book facilitates a comprehensive approach that considers not only general understandings about academic literacy development but also specific foci on vocabulary, writing development, and the use of literature. The book responds to the current demands of the twenty-first century by including a specific chapter on digital spaces and data-driven decision-making. Collectively, the four sections in the book effectively weave together theory and effective practices for ELLs in the mainstream classroom.

Mainstream teachers who work with ELLs within the broader educational movements toward standards-based instruction (e.g., Common Core Standards), inclusion, and accountability need the knowledge and skills to understand their instruction from the perspective of the bilingual learner. They need to be able to articulate, practice, and advocate for practices that, while perhaps not necessary for their monolingual learners, are a must-do for their ELLs (de Jong, Harper, & Coady, 2013). This volume is an important step to providing them with the conceptual and practical tools to accomplish this and work toward creating equitable learning environments for their ELLs.

May 2015
Ester de Jong
Professor and Director
School of Teaching and Learning
University of Florida

Introduction

Research, Policy, and Practice Insights to Support the Teaching of English Learners in the Mainstream Classrooms

Kouider Mokhtari and Mayra C. Daniel

The contributors of *Research-Based Instruction That Makes a Difference in English Learners' Success* consist of classroom teachers and teacher-educators representing a broad array of subject matter expertise and experiences in the fields of first language acquisition, second language learning, and literacy development. For the past several years, each has been working on different yet shared issues, questions, and challenges pertaining to the education of all students, including English learners (ELs), in K–16 instructional settings. These issues, questions, and challenges focus predominantly on three closely interrelated priorities: (1) improving students' language proficiency levels, (2) advancing their literacy development, and (3) making disciplinary content comprehensible for all students in the mainstream classrooms.

In *Research-Based Instruction That Makes a Difference in English Learners' Success*, our aim is to share collective insights about supporting students' language, literacy, and content learning across the curriculum. While these insights can be found in dispersed published research, policy, and practice documents, they are rarely found in a single volume such as this one. We anticipate that these insights will be particularly helpful for language arts and academic subjects teachers who already know how to teach their subjects to native speakers of English, but who wish to learn how to teach them to ELs in the same instructional K–12 settings. Our goal, however, is not to explain how to teach language, literacy, and content subjects, but rather to provide new and experienced teachers with important research, policy, and practice insights that will help them design, implement, and evaluate instruction aimed at reaching and teaching ELs in the mainstream classrooms.

The research, policy, and practice insights highlighted in *Research-Based Instruction That Makes a Difference in English Learners' Success* draw on several key areas including what we know about students as learners of English as a second or foreign language, the nature of language acquisition and language learning processes, the roles of language proficiency and first language literacy in second language reading, and various related educational, social, and cultural influences on student academic achievement and school success. Examples of key research, policy, and practice insights the book contributors draw upon include, but are not limited to, the area discussed next.

EL ENROLLMENT HAS DRAMATICALLY INCREASED IN U.S. SCHOOLS

In practically every state in the United States, primary, elementary, middle, and high schools are experiencing expanding enrollments of students whose primary language is not English. Recent demographic data show that linguistically and culturally diverse students constitute an increasingly strong presence in our schools and communities. There are approximately five million ELs in the United States, and this number is on the rise. It is estimated that two-thirds of these students are in at least one course taught by general education teachers. Growth in K–12 EL enrollment has skyrocketed in the past twenty years. One in twenty public K–12 students was an EL in 1990. In 2008, it was one in nine. Projections suggest that in twenty years it will be one in four (Goldenberg, 2008).

ELs CONSISTENTLY UNDERPERFORM ON TESTS OF ACADEMIC ACHIEVEMENT WHEN COMPARED TO THEIR NATIVE-BORN PEERS

Historically, it is hard to ignore the reality that many ELs tend to perform less well on standardized tests and drop out of school at higher rates than their English-speaking peers. National report cards indicate that ELs have historically achieved lower levels of success on key academic achievement tests than their native-speaker peers, in part due to difficulties associated with reading, writing, and learning academic content in a new language. For several decades, national literacy achievement tests such as the National Assessment of Educational Progress (NAEP) show significant achievement gaps for historically underperforming subgroups of students in fourth and eighth grades. The 2007 NAEP report indicates that ELs in fourth and eighth grade scored thirty-six and forty-two standard-scale points, respectively, below the performance of their native speakers of English peers (Grigg, Donahue, & Dion, 2007; Lee, Grigg, & Donahue, 2007). Academic achievement gaps indicate that many ELs may not have attained the English language proficiency or subject matter content needed to participate fully in mainstream classrooms.

ELs ARE HELD TO THE SAME STANDARDS AS NATIVE ENGLISH SPEAKERS

In recent years, federal legislation such as the No Child Left Behind (NCLB) Act of 2001 and the 2008 reauthorization of the Higher Education Opportunity Act contain provisions holding public schools, state departments, and higher education institutions accountable for the education of culturally and linguistically diverse students. For instance, under the NCLB Act schools, districts, and state education agencies are held accountable for ELs' progress through Adequate Yearly Progress (AYP) reports for reading and mathematics, and Annual Measurable Achievement Objectives (AMAOs), documenting students' satisfactory progress in learning English and attaining English proficiency. Given current policy trends, teachers of ELs are held accountable for their year-to-year achievement.

COMMON CORE STATE STANDARDS PRESENT CHALLENGES AND OPPORTUNITIES FOR ELs

In addition to the NCLB accountability measures, the implementation of the Common Core State Standards (CCSS) presents opportunities and challenges for ELs and their teachers. On one hand, we believe the standards will present these students with an opportunity to gain equal and greater access to rigorous instruction along with higher expectations for academic success. On the other hand, they will require teachers to make the challenging new standards accessible to ELs regardless of English proficiency. These opportunities and challenges will, in turn, require a change in how teachers view and implement English language instruction in the mainstream classroom, and how students and other stakeholders perceive ELs' educational needs.

ENGLISH LEARNERS ARE QUITE DIVERSE IN TERMS OF SCHOOLING, LANGUAGE PROFICIENCY, AND FIRST LANGUAGE LITERACY

ELs come to school with diverse prior schooling experiences, varying levels of oral language proficiency levels, and differing literacy abilities in their first language. This diversity in schooling experiences, language proficiency, and first language literacy are important factors in their school performance and academic progress. It is worth noting that a high proportion of students classified as ELs were born in the United States.

Many enter early grades as beginner English speakers and continue to receive English language support as their levels of language proficiency and grade levels increase. The good news is that in the early grades, these students do almost as well as monolingual peers on acquiring early grade reading skills. In two related studies, Nonie Lesaux and her colleagues reported that primary grade ELs and non-ELs typically perform at similar levels on measures of basic reading skills such as phonological processing, word reading, and spelling. However, they conclude, "the findings of studies on reading comprehension paint a very different picture, yielding highly consistent results that, in comparison to their monolingual peers, reading comprehension is an area of weakness for language minority learners" (Lesaux, Rupp & Siegel, 2007; Lesaux, Crosson & Pierce, 2010).

On the other hand, many ELs who arrive to the United States as adolescents or adults, enter school at later grades with oral English proficiency levels ranging from beginner to advanced. Research has shown that if ELs have no prior schooling or have no support in their native language, it may take seven to ten years for them to catch up to their peers' proficiency in academic English (Cummins, 1991; Thomas & Collier, 1997). Teachers have double or triple duties when working with these students in the mainstream classrooms: they have to consciously address the language and literacy gaps to help ensure content is comprehensible for these students.

ELs USE WHAT THEY KNOW ABOUT THEIR FIRST LANGUAGE AND LITERACY TO HELP THEM READ AND LEARN IN THE TARGET LANGUAGE

ELs make use of the cognitive and linguistic skills they attained while learning to read and write in their first language to read and learn in the target language even when the languages have different writing systems (August & Shanahan, 2006; Benson, 2008; Koda & Zehler, 2008). Studies of bilingual literacy development and cross-linguistic transfer indicate that there is a high level of transfer of skills and strategies from the first to the second language.

An example of cross-language transfer is represented by cognates, words in two languages that share a similar meaning, spelling, and pronunciation. It is estimated that 30–40 percent of all words in English have a related word in Spanish, which makes cognates a great tool to support English language acquisition for these students. The similarity between the first and second language, including the number of cognates, affects the amount of exposure and study required to become proficient in English.

Cross-linguistic transfer enables second-language learners to accelerate academic learning in the target language. For example, once students develop word decoding skills in their first language, they will most likely not need to relearn these in their second language. A student, therefore, will learn to read in the new alphabet quickly and can then focus on learning the new vocabulary and grammar of the second language. The consensus appears to be that the greater the similarity in the writing systems of the two languages, the greater the degree of transfer, thus reducing the time and difficulties involved in learning to read the second language (Snow, Burns, & Griffin, 1998).

FOR ELs THE QUALITY OF INSTRUCTION IS MORE IMPORTANT THAN THE LANGUAGE OF INSTRUCTION

When teaching all students, research indicates that teacher expertise and the quality of instruction matters for all students, including ELs (Darling-Hammond, 1999). In a recent synthesis of research on English reading outcomes for various types of programs for Spanish-dominant ELs in elementary schools, Cheung and Slavin (2012) found that the outcomes for elementary-aged children taught in Spanish and transitioned to English were no different from the outcomes for those taught only in English. What mattered most across the various reading interventions that proved to be effective for these learners was the use of "extensive professional development, coaching, and cooperative learning." These findings support the conclusion increasingly being made by researchers and policymakers concerned with optimal outcomes for ELs and other linguistically diverse students: Quality of instruction is more important than language of instruction (351). Learning to read and write in a second language requires formal language instruction in an academic setting as well as teachers' pedagogical practices and methods that facilitate language acquisition, literacy development, and content learning.

OVERVIEW OF THE BOOK

The contents of *Research-Based Instruction That Makes a Difference in English Learners' Success* are based on key insights from research, policy, and instructional practices that classroom teachers will find helpful when addressing ELs' instructional needs in language, literacy, or content area classrooms.

The book is organized in four parts. Part I, which comprises chapters 1 through 5, focuses on research, policy, and practice insights aimed at supporting ELs' language and literacy development across the disciplines.

In chapter 1, "Enhancing English Learners' Access to Disciplinary Texts through Close Reading Practices," Zhihui Fang and Suzanne C. Chapman discuss how to enhance ELs' access to disciplinary texts through close reading practices. With visionary planning, careful consideration of resources, and keen awareness of individual needs, teachers can use close reading and other evidence-based methods to meet the requirements of the CCSS while also creating an environment that fosters access and promotes equity for ELs across content areas.

In chapter 2, "High Expectations: Increasing Productivity and Complexity in English Learner Writing," Kathleen A. J. Mohr, Sylvia Read, and Alayne Leavitt make the case for improving writing instruction for ELs by placing an emphasis on increasing productivity and complexity as critical aspects of writing achievement. They then provide instructional recommendations to promote more writing across the disciplines with the goal of strengthening subject-matter learning while increasing students' academic language proficiency.

In chapter 3, "A Middle School Mathematics Workshop for Multilingual Classrooms: Lessons Learned from a Highly Effective Teacher," Mayra C. Daniel and Billy Hueramo describe how Andy, a middle school mathematics teacher, effectively reaches and teaches ELs by helping them bridge the gap between their language proficiency and disciplinary demands in a mathematics workshop.

In chapter 4, "Using Art and Literature to Enhance Critical Thinking and Vocabulary Development for English Learners," Chris Carger shares a success story involving the use of Reaching Out through Art and Reading (ROAR), an initiative aimed at advancing university students' instructional practices and improving ELs' language and literacy achievement outcomes.

In chapter 5, "The Case for Young Adult Literature: Using Narratives in the English Learner Classroom," Melanie D. Koss addresses the contribution of young adult literature to adolescent ELs' reading experience and then provides useful resources for teachers and students.

Part II of the book, which includes chapters 6 and 7, provides practical guidance for using assessment data to document student performance and inform instruction.

In chapter 6, Kouider Mokhtari describes a metacognitive assessment survey that teachers of ELs can use to help identify students' reading comprehension strengths and needs. Teachers have an opportunity to learn how to administer the metacognitive assessment survey, how to interpret the results obtained, and how to use assessment data to inform reading instruction for ELs in middle, high school, and college classrooms.

In chapter 7, Paul Boyd-Batstone describes a new assessment tool, Classroom Assessment for Language Levels (CALL), which helps teachers to rapidly assess the language level of an EL and use the information gained to plan and deliver instruction aimed at enhancing students' language and literacy achievement outcomes.

Part III of the book, which is made up of chapters 8 and 9, provide research, policy, and practice insights and guidance for supporting students' language, literacy, and content learning in digital spaces.

In chapter 8, Ian O'Byrne and Martha Castañeda examine how digital literacies can be used to support the language and literacy needs of ELs in mainstream classrooms.

In chapter 9, Dong-shin Shin describes how a second grade teacher uses Web 2.0-based social media to support her ELs' language and literacy development. She also shares challenges teachers and students encounter when using social media in K–12 classrooms, and offers examples to show how these media can be used to promote and support students' academic literacy development.

Part IV of the book, which comprises chapters 10 through 13, focuses on how key understandings about language and literacy can help teachers support ELs in mainstream classrooms.

In chapter 10, John Evar Strid shares insights gleaned from recent research, policy, and practice reports pertaining to various aspects of language and literacy development that have important implications for teaching ELs in mainstream U.S. classrooms.

In chapter 11, Fabiola P. Ehlers-Zavala discusses key components of reading instruction that are critical to the language and literacy development of ELs. She then offers recommendations for action and resources for supporting the reading comprehension challenges of these learners in mainstream classrooms.

In chapter 12, Joan Wink and her colleagues offer recommendations about how teachers can engage ELs in deep levels of reflection to support their language development, literacy acquisition, and academic achievement outcomes.

In chapter 13, David Schwarzer introduces the concept of "transliteracy" as an alternative ideology to the traditional notion of literacy development and shows how this reconceptualization can more effectively support the language and literacy development of ELs in mainstream classroom.

Each chapter of the book includes insights from research, policy, and practice pertaining to the education of ELs, practical guidance to help teachers incorporate these insights in their instruction, and suggested resources for further study, which are helpful for ongoing teacher professional learning and growth. We collaborated on the content of each of the chapters with the goal of addressing important and timely issues, questions, and challenges facing teachers of ELs in mainstream classrooms. We hope the insights provided will offer support and guidance for all teachers who are responsible for the education of all students, including culturally and linguistically diverse learners.

Part I

SUPPORTING ENGLISH LEARNERS' LANGUAGE AND LITERACY DEVELOPMENT ACROSS THE DISCIPLINES

Chapter 1

Enhancing English Learners' Access to Disciplinary Texts through Close Reading Practices

Zhihui Fang and Suzanne C. Chapman

In this chapter, we illustrate how teachers can enhance English learners' (ELs) access to disciplinary texts through close reading practices. We suggest that close reading is a valuable pedagogical tool that can support ELs' language/ literacy development and content learning at the same time.

THE CHALLENGES OF SCHOOL LEARNING

The educational knowledge that school children are expected to learn becomes increasingly specialized over the span of their K–12 schooling. This knowledge is presented to students primarily through written texts in language that becomes progressively more technical, dense, abstract, and complex (Fang, 2012a; Schleppegrell, 2004). For example, in the early years of schooling, history is typically presented to students as story-like representations of the past (in genres such as autobiographical recount, biographical recount, and historical recount), where events are organized chronologically as they unfold in real time. By contrast, in later years of schooling, history is often presented to students as abstract interpretations of the past (in genres such as historical account, historical explanation, and historical argument), where events are embedded as part of a causal/consequential explanation or an argument about the significance of an historical event (Coffin, 2006). This shift from narrative genres to expository genres is also found in science, where a similar knowledge path exists to apprentice students into the social practices of science— from doing science (with procedures and procedural recounts) to organizing science (with descriptive and taxonomic reports) and explaining science (with sequential, causal, factorial, and consequential explanations) to challenging science (with persuasion and discussion) (Veel, 1997). These shifts involve

3

transition from the grammar of the mother tongue (speaking) to the grammar of writing and disciplinarity, with increased use of abstract and metaphoric language (Chrisite & Maton, 2011; Fang, 2012b). The transition can be illustrated with two excerpts (see table 1.1) from *Getting Away with Murder* (Crowe, 2003, pp. 17–18), an award-winning social studies trade book about the killing of a Black boy named Emmett Till and the trial of his white killers in the racially tense period of the 1950s in the United States. Text 1 is distinct from Text 2 in that the former tells the story in verbs using everyday language with which students are familiar, whereas the latter interprets the story in nouns using language that is symptomatic of written academic discourses featuring density, abstraction, and generalization.

It is this grammar of writing and disciplinarity, often referred to more generally as academic language, that presents challenges to all students. These challenges are especially significant for ELs, who currently constitute about 10 percent of public school population (roughly 4.7 million). In 2011, for

Table 1.1 Two Representations of the Past

Text 1 (Elementary-Like)	Text 2 (Secondary-Like)
Before they stepped into the yard, Milam turned and asked Wright if he recognized them. "Nosuh, I don't know you." "Good, Preacher. How old are you?" "Sixty-four." "Well, if you decide later that you do know any of us here tonight, you'll never live to be sixty-five." "But where are you taking him?" asked Wright. "Nowhere if he's not the right one," said Milam. Mose Wright and his wife watched from the porch while the two men walked Emmett into their car. Bryant forced Emmett close to the back window and asked, "Is this the boy?" "Yes," said the woman from the backseat. Bryant shoved Emmett into the front seat, sat next to him, and pulled the door closed. Milam got behind the wheel, and the car, its lights still off, moved into the dark, taking the boy from Chicago with them.	The kidnapping and murder of Emmett Till and the trial of his killers became one of the biggest news items of 1955. The viewing of his disfigured corpse at Rainer Funeral Home and his funeral at the Roberts Temple of the Church of God in Christ in Chicago attracted more than ten thousand mourners. The grisly open-casket photo of Emmett that appeared in Jet magazine horrified and angered hundreds of thousands more. The National Association for the Advancement of Colored People (NAACP), other civil rights organizations, and political leaders expressed outrage at the cold-blooded murder of this boy from Chicago. In an interview, Roy Wilkins, Executive Secretary of the NAACP, labeled the crime a racist act, saying, "It would appear that the state of Mississippi has decided to maintain white supremacy by murdering children." Newspapers across the country, especially those in the Northern states, condemned the killing and the racist attitudes that led to it.

example, ELs trailed their non-EL counterparts in the reading portion of the National Assessment of Educational Progress by thirty-six points at the fourth grade level and forty-four points at the eighth grade level (National Center for Education Statistics, 2013). A lack of proficiency with academic language on the part of ELs was frequently cited as a main reason for this achievement gap (August & Shanahan, 2006; Schleppegrell & O'Hallaron, 2011; Snow & Uccelli, 2009). Unlike those from the previous waves of immigration, today's ELs "tend to be people of color, limited education, and low socioeconomic backgrounds and to settle in urban centers with limited human and material resources" (Haneda, 2014, p. 88). Many of them have little or no experience with academic ways of using language. Unfamiliarity with academic language prevents ELs from effectively accessing content and participating productively in subject area learning, ultimately resulting in their academic underperformance and school failure.

What is it about academic language that makes content area learning in particular challenging and schooling in general alienating for ELs? We will answer this question by analyzing Text 3, an excerpt from an environmental science trade book written by Edward O. Wilson, two-time winner of the Pulitzer Prize. The book is about the destruction and restoration of the complex biodiverse ecosystems in Gorongosa National Park in Mozambique. Texts like this one are valued by the discipline because they are the primary vehicle through which disciplinary content is produced, communicated, stored, critiqued, and renovated.

Text 3: Disease organisms are especially dangerous. The establishment of a single alien pathogen of uncertain origin can be catastrophic to the new hosts it invades. The accidental introduction of a chytrid fungus (possibly African) into Australia, New Zealand, Europe, Africa, North America, and the American tropics has resulted in the loss or reduction of scores of species of frogs. During the past one hundred years, human modification of rivers, streams, and lakes in North America alone (mostly through damming and pollution) has caused the extinction of at least sixty freshwater fish species. Our environmental domination of the land and sea has reduced Earth's biodiversity through the extinction of at least 10 percent of its plant and animal species, mostly in the last century. It is driving species at an accelerating rate through conservation biology's descending categories of "threatened," "endangered," "critically endangered," and finally, "extinct." (Wilson, 2014, pp. 125–26)

This explanation text uses language in uncommonsensical, unfamiliar ways. First, it draws on a set of technical terminology, such as *organisms*, *alien pathogen*, *chytrid fungus*, *species*, *biodiversity*, and *conservation biology*. These terms are essential to the discussion of environmental issues; without them, the discussion would be neither precise nor complete. Second, the text is populated with nominalizations, such as *establishment, introduction, loss, reduction, modification, pollution, extinction, domination,* and *biodiversity.* These are abstract nouns that derive from verbs (*establish, introduce, lose, reduce, modify, pollute, dominate*) or adjectives (*extinct, biologically diverse*). They enable the author to build technical taxonomies, synthesize previously presented information, infuse ideology and value, and develop a cohesive chain of reasoning (Fang & Schleppegrell, 2008). At the same time, they bury concrete processes (realized in verbs) and qualities (realized in adjectives), as well as the grammatical participants (realized in nouns) that engage in these processes or possess these qualities. This information will have to be recovered by the reader to ensure full comprehension. For example, in "the establishment of a single alien pathogen," it is not clear what (or who) establishes a single alien pathogen. The information can sometimes be inferred from the preceding text, but at other times it is assumed by the writer and can only be retrieved by those with adequate background knowledge about the topic. Third, the text uses long noun phrases, such as *the establishment of a single alien pathogen of uncertain origin; the accidental introduction of a chytrid fungus (possibly African) into Australia, New Zealand, Europe, Africa, North America, and the American tropics; the loss or reduction of scores of species of frogs; human modification of rivers, streams, and lakes in North America; the extinction of at least sixty freshwater fish species; our environmental domination of the land and sea; the extinction of at least 10 percent of its plant and animal species;* and *conservation biology's descending categories of "threatened," "endangered," "critically endangered," and finally, "extinct."* These noun phrases enable the author to pack a heavy load of information into sentences, making the text exceedingly dense and taxing to process. Fourth, the text uses pronouns whose referents can be challenging for inexperienced readers to identify. For example, "it" in the second sentence refers to "alien pathogen" earlier in the sentence, "its" in the fourth sentence refers to "Earth" earlier in the sentence, and "it" in the last sentence refers to "our environmental domination of the land and sea" in the sentence prior. Finally, Text 3 realizes causal relations not through the usual means of conjunctions (*because, so*), but through verbs, such as *can be, has resulted in, has caused, has reduced,* and *is driving.* This way of using language can obscure the true causes and effects of environmental problems, preventing students from fully understanding the text and becoming actively involved in solving these problems (Chenhansa & Schleppegrell, 1998).

These linguistic features—technical vocabulary, nominalizations, long noun phrases, referential opacity, and logical metaphors—rarely occur in everyday spoken contexts. However, they tend to co-occur with regular frequency and for functional reasons in disciplinary texts. A concentration of these linguistic features in a single text can make the text simultaneously technical, dense, and abstract, creating a stumbling block to reading comprehension. For ELs, texts like Text 3 can present an insurmountable challenge, in both content and the language through which this content is presented. Thus, in subject area learning, students must not only learn the content of academic disciplines but also develop the language proficiency that enables them to access this content. This is a tall order for ELs. Although many of them have little trouble acquiring basic interpersonal language for purposes of social interaction with family members and peers, most struggle mightily with developing academic language proficiency (Cummins, 2008). This is likely due to a lack of sufficient exposure to, deep engagement with, and effective instruction in how to handle academic texts. As Snow and O'Connor (2013) pointed out, ELs tend to experience inequities in their literacy education because they are often given oversimplified texts and have few opportunities to work with and through texts of sufficient richness, depth, and complexity.

TEACHING CLOSE READING

The Common Core State Standards (CCSS) (www.corestandards.org) clearly recognizes this problem, calling on teachers to provide ample opportunities for students to interact with academic language and richly complex texts. It underscores the need for students to develop new language capacities that enable them to read, write, talk, think, and reason like scientists, historians, mathematicians, and other disciplinary experts. These language capacities are to be developed "through first-hand disciplinary experience, as language and thought-in-use, in content-area classes" (Langer, 2011, p. 4). An important avenue for developing these capacities is close reading. Originated in literary criticism, close reading is recommended by the CCSS as a method for reading both literary and informational texts that requires detailed analysis of language and images in the text. It typically involves a brief text segment, such as one to two short passages, that is of sufficient richness and complexity. Proposed to "help students strengthen their ability to learn from complex texts independently, and thus to enhance college and career readiness" (Snow & O'Connor, 2013, p. 2), close reading encourages students to grapple with complex texts by examining their words, sentences, and visuals thoroughly and methodically through deliberate reading and rereading.

Several models of close reading have been suggested for classroom implementation. One such model is articulated by Shanahan (2012) on his blog, *Shanahan on Literacy.* Believing that rereading is essential because complex texts do not give up their meanings easily, Shanahan advocated conducting close reading through a series of three readings of the text. In the first reading, students read with the intent of being able to retell or give the key ideas about the text. In the second reading, students take a step further to consider how the text works, answering questions such as "How did the author organize the text?" "What literary devices were used and how effective were they?" "How were data presented?" "Why did the author choose this particular word?" and "Was the meaning of a key term consistent or did it change across the text?" Finally, in the third reading, students go even deeper to consider the message the author is conveying, how the message connects to other works or to the reader's own life, and the quality of the evidence presented. Students are expected to be able to answer questions such as "What does this text really mean?" "What does it have to say to me about my life or my world?" "How do I evaluate the quality of this work?" and "How does this text connect to other texts I know?" This model, as Shanahan himself put it, features "an intensive analysis of a text in order to come to terms with what it says, how it says it, and what it means."

Like Shanahan, Brown and Kappes (2012) also viewed close reading as involving an investigation of a brief piece of text with multiple readings. Drawing on literacy research and practice, they described a model of close reading that aims at helping readers of all abilities grapple with texts of varying complexities, engage in thoughtful conversation about these texts, and develop knowledge, skills and strategies to become critical, independent readers. The model, which may vary slightly based on the content of the text, includes the following steps: (a) students are provided a short but complex text, (b) students independently read through the text, (c) students participate in a group read-aloud, (d) teacher provides students with text-based questions to assist in closely examining the text, (e) students engage in a group discussion of these questions, and (f) students write about the text. According to Brown and Kappes (2012), this model needs to be modified when working with struggling readers, who may include ELs. For example, during the initial independent reading of the text, ELs may be placed with another student or within a group to partner read the text. ELs are further supported in the third step, a group read-aloud in which they have the opportunity to hear the text again and listen to a fluent reading of the text. ELs may again be placed in small groups as they work through their text-based questions and work in small discussion groups.

Fisher and Frey (2012), who viewed close reading as a way to build students' capacity to cope with challenging texts, identified several key features of close reading related to text selection, teacher behaviors, and student behaviors based on observation of close reading practices in secondary classrooms. Specifically, they found that (a) the text selected for close reading is typically brief (ranging from a few paragraphs to a couple of pages) but challenging; (b) the text is read several times; (c) the teacher provides limited preteaching of the text prior to students actually reading it; (d) when students reread the text, the teacher asks students text-dependent questions that require them to provide evidence from the text and that may relate to main ideas, key details, vocabulary, text structure, author's purpose, inferences, and intertextuality; and (e) students annotate the text as they read by taking margin notes, underlining, or using sticky notes. They emphasized that the teacher should preread and gain familiarity with the text prior to its use for instruction so as to identify elements of the text that make it challenging and worth close reading, determine the appropriate amount of frontloading, develop text-dependent questions to pose to students, and choose the right strategies that support students' interaction with the text (e.g., using shorthands or wiki sticks for note taking).

These models offer concrete classroom routines for getting students to engage directly with complex texts right from the start. They are particularly helpful for those who are capable of processing complex texts but may need guidance in focusing on what is important in the text. However, they offer few details on how teachers can provide linguistic support that is often needed in the reading and rereading of complex disciplinary texts. For example, while each model suggests sample text-dependent questions to answer during reading and rereading, little information is furnished on how to go about answering these questions. Simply reading, rereading, and discussing a text multiple times does little to help those who are already struggling with complex texts. ELs and other struggling readers need tools for independently unpacking the often dense, abstract, and metaphoric language of disciplinary texts in order to gain access to the ideas, concepts, and arguments that are encoded in these texts.

Other models of close reading fill this gap by foregrounding the role of language in meaning-making. These models promote explicit attention to the lexical and grammatical patterns in disciplinary texts and offer concrete strategies to help students cope with these patterns. In a recent paper addressing language and literacy issues found in the CCSS, Fillmore and Fillmore (2012) described a method for providing ELs instructional support that enables them to learn how language works in complex texts. This method recognizes that the language used in the complex texts of academic disciplines differs in many ways from the language of everyday, ordinary talk. It involves close reading of complex texts on topics in such content areas as science, social studies, history, and English language arts. Central to the method is a daily instructional session (fifteen to twenty minutes) in which the teacher leads students in analyzing and discussing one "juicy" sentence drawn from the text the class is working on. This sentence is usually "so complex it begs for explication, is grammatically interesting, and is focused on an important point in the passage" (p. 6). Through unpacking the sentence, one word or phrase at a time, students are expected to develop an awareness of the relation between specific lexis or grammatical structures and the functions they serve in texts.

For example, in a multiethnic and multilingual kindergarten class in a Manhattan, New York, public school, where Lily Fillmore has been working with teachers to improve literacy instruction for ELs, students were studying the life cycle of butterflies. They observed and recorded the changes taking place in a cage as butterfly eggs hatched, caterpillars (butterfly larva) turned into chrysalides (pupa), and chrysalides transformed into butterflies. In class discussion, students shared their observations, such as "Butterflies pump their wings . . . so their wings could dry," "Butterflies have long proboscis . . . so they could drink nectar," and "Butterfly drink nectar from the flower and then the chrysalis not coming out, then the water coming out now."

As part of the study, the teacher and her students also read and discussed Irene Kelly's (2007) *It's a Butterfly's Life*. Each day, the teacher selected a sentence from the book and engaged the children in conversation about it. For example, when this complex sentence was chosen, "The most awe-inspiring event in a butterfly's life is its metamorphosis, as it transforms from egg to caterpillar to chrysalis, emerging as a creature of delicacy and grace, filling our sky with color," the teacher and her children read and reread the sentence, drawing on what they had learned from the firsthand experience of observation to help them identify, clause by clause, the ideas packed into the sentence. These ideas were transcribed on strips of paper and taped onto a poster board for display. Sample strips include "Butterflies lay eggs on a little leaf"; "The caterpillar hatches from the egg"; "Inside the chrysalis the caterpillar turns into a pupa. The chrysalis is the cover to protect the pupa"; "The butterfly is beautiful like a flower"; "The butterfly has colors like a rainbow"; "The butterfly comes out of the chrysalis"; and "The butterfly is graceful like a dance". The teacher then engaged students in reading and rereading these strips, discussing their meanings and comparing them to the original sentence to highlight wording differences. Subsequently, students acted out words and phrases for describing the changes that occur during the butterfly's life cycle, such as *growing inside the egg, cutting a circle, wriggling to get out, nibbling the eggshell, chewing more leaves, bending/ twisting/turning, molting and stretching, spinning silk pads, attaching to a branch, hanging upside down, emerging from the chrysalis*, and *pumping the wings*. Lessons like this sensitize students to the way ideas are packed in informational texts and give students "a sense of purchase on the complexity that confronts them" (Fillmore & Fillmore, 2012, p. 8).

Unlike Fillmore and Fillmore (2012), whose model is based in traditional grammar, Fang and Schleppegrell (2010) described a model of close reading, called functional language analysis (FLA), that is informed by "functional grammar" (Halliday & Matthiessen, 2004). Seeing grammar as

use idea

a creative resource for making meaning, FLA promotes systematic exploration of meaning through detailed analysis and discussion of language patterns in the text. It offers a set of linguistically informed strategies that helps readers answer three questions important to both literary and informational reading: (1) what is the text about? (2) how is the text organized? and (3) what is the author's perspective? To answer the first question, which relates to main ideas and key details, students analyze each clause by sorting it into processes (realized in verbs of different kinds such as *doing, being, saying,* and *sensing*), participants (realized in noun phrases of varying complexities), attributes (realized in adjectives), and circumstances (realized in adverbials or prepositional phrases). To answer the second question, which concerns the way meaning is stitched into a coherent message, students analyze what begins each clause, how clauses are combined (i.e., through embedding, subordination, or coordination), and how cohesion is created (e.g., the use of reference, ellipsis, conjunction, and repetition). To answer the third question, which is about how the author infuses judgment and points of view, students analyze each clause in terms of mood (i.e., declarative, interrogative, and imperative), modality (e.g., probability, obligation, seriousness), and word choices (e.g., nouns, verbs, adjectives). Teachers can observe the following procedure when teaching FLA (Fang & Schleppegrell, 2008, p. 111):

a. select a text that is short, contains important or worthy content, and presents comprehension challenges to target students
b. identify the specific content goals (related to disciplinary knowledge and concepts) and language and literacy objectives that are to be accomplished through FLA
c. decide on which FLA strategy (or strategies) to use and what metalanguage terms are needed in order to conduct the analysis
d. engage students in the analysis as a whole class, in small groups, or individually, depending on the amount of experience they have had with FLA

FLA gives teachers a powerful tool for engaging students in thoughtful, analytical reading. It helps students more effectively access and critically evaluate the information they are expected to learn from disciplinary texts. At the same time, it illuminates the ways language is used as a creative resource for making discipline-specific meanings and for constructing texts valued by discipline insiders. The discursive insights students gain from intensive lexical and grammatical analyses make them become more critical readers and effective writers.

For example, in a tenth grade environmental science class, students were reading and discussing Wilson's (2014) *A Window on Eternity* as part of their study on ecosystems. The goal of the unit is, on one hand, to deepen students' understanding of the interdependence of species and factors impacting the balance of nature and, on the other hand, to develop students' facility in the grammatical resources functional for constructing effective explanations. Recognizing that ELs need support in working through the dense language of the book, the teacher conducted small group reading conferences on a weekly basis. During one of these conferences (each lasting approximately thirty minutes), the teacher engaged students in close reading of an explanation text (Text 3) through application of FLA. Having already developed with students the metalinguistic constructs associated with FLA such as *clause, participant, process, circumstance, attribute, actor, goal, attributor*, and *beneficiary*, and having reviewed the text himself to identify what the analysis can offer, the teacher engaged students in discussion about how the author has constructed the text, focusing on how they can unpack the dense meanings.

First, to explore what the text is about, he guided students to construct a visual like table 1.2 that identifies the processes used in the text and attendant participants, attributes, and circumstances. As students partitioned each clause, they had to think about the meaning of each clause constituent in the context of the text, such as "Is the author chronicling events (*doing* process), describing or defining an organism (*being* process), telling what is said (saying process), or reporting what is felt or thought (*sensing* process)?" "Who or what is involved in each of these processes?" "What roles do these grammatical participants play—carrier or attributor of an attribute, initiator of an action (actor), recipient of an action (goal), senser or phenomenon of a mental activity, or sayer or message of a verbal exchange?" and "What do 'its' in clause 5 and 'it' in clauses 2 and 6 refer to?" Identifying the processes gives readers a sense of what is going on in the text. Identifying the participants and their roles gives readers insights into who or what is represented, what their relationships are, what is being defined or described, and how definition or description is constructed. Identifying the circumstances provides readers information about the when, where, why, and how of a process.

Through these analyses and discussion, students discovered that the author used two types of verbs, *being* and *doing*. The *being* verbs in clauses 1–2 (*are, can be*) describe the effects of disease organisms and alien pathogen as *especially dangerous* and *catastrophic*. The *doing* verbs in clauses 3–6 (*has resulted in, has caused, has reduced*, and *is driving*) construct a series of causes (actors) and effects (goals and beneficiaries). These causes and effects (e.g., *the accidental introduction of a chytrid fungus, the new hosts it invades, the loss or reduction of scores of species of frogs*), like the "things" being described earlier (*disease organism, the establishment of a single alien pathogen of uncertain origin*) and the manner through which natural or human actors exert their influences (*the extinction of at least 10 percent*

Table 1.2 Sample of Functional Language Analysis

Clause	Circumstance	Participant	Process	Participant	Attribute	Circumstance
1		Disease organisms [carrier]	are [being]		especially dangerous	
2		The establishment of a single alien pathogen of uncertain origin [attributor]	can be [being]	the new hosts it invades [beneficiary]	catastrophic	
3		The accidental introduction of a chytrid fungus (possibly African) into Australia, New Zealand, Europe, Africa, North America, and the American tropics [actor]	has resulted in [doing]	the loss or reduction of scores of species of frogs [goal]		
4	During the past one hundred years	human modification of rivers, streams, and lakes in North America alone (mostly through damming and pollution) [actor]	has caused [doing]	the extinction of at least sixty freshwater fish species [goal]		
5		Our environmental domination of the land and sea [actor]	has reduced [doing]	Earth's biodiversity [goal]		through the extinction of at least 10 percent of its plant and animal species, mostly in the last century
6		It [actor]	is driving [doing]	species [goal]		at an accelerating rate through conservation biology's descending categories of "threatened," "endangered," "critically endangered," and finally, "extinct."

of its plant and animal species; *conservation biology's descending catego-*
ries of "threatened," "endangered," "critically endangered," and finally,
"extinct."), are constructed in technical, dense, and abstract noun phrases
that will need to be deconstructed to facilitate understanding. To help students unpack these noun phrases, the teacher used a strategy called "noun
deconstruction and expansion" (Fang, 2010), which involves building a
noun train by adding as many pre- and post-modifiers as possible to a head
noun or conversely, deconstructing a long noun phrase by identifying its
head and pre- and post-modifiers as well as the function each of these constituents serves. The exercise helped students gain insights to the structure
and logic of noun phrases.

Having answered the first question of what the text is about, students
now had a good understanding of the overall meaning of the text as well as
the meaning of individual clauses. With this knowledge, they moved on to
examine how the text is structured. They recognized that the text provides an
explanation of both natural and human causes of environmental problems.
The first three clauses focus on the natural factor, with the first sentence
serving as the topic sentence. The last three sentences address the human
factor, albeit without a topic sentence. Further, with the exception of clause
4 that begins with a prepositional phrase indicating time (duration), each
clause begins with a technical or dense noun phrase, suggesting that the text is
organized around abstract causes. This is unlike in, for example, a chronicling
text, where clauses typically begin with prepositional or adverbial phrases
that realize time, place, and manner of an event.

To explore the author's perspective, the teacher had students search for
words that indicate attitude, judgment, or evaluation. Students noted that
words like "especially" (clause 1) and "at least" (clause 4) add force to the
claims the author makes. These, along with other choices—such as *domi-*
nation, *extinction*, *accelerating*, *dangerous*, and *catastrophic*—underscore
the severity and urgency of the environmental problems that the author
intends to highlight. They suggest that the author is gravely concerned with
the devastating effects of both natural and human causes of environmental
problems. Students also mentioned that the author used a modal verb *can*
(clause 2) to indicate the possibility (not certainty) of an alien pathogen
doing harm to the new hosts it invades, an adverb *possibly* (clause 3) to indicate the likely source of chytrid fungus, and another adverb *mostly* (clauses
4 and 5) to qualify the statements on the kind of human activities that are
primarily responsible for the extinction of freshwater fish species and the time
period when serious environmental problems occurred. These word choices
suggest that the author is using language in a cautious, responsible way.
The teacher then initiated a discussion on why the author uses only sentences
in the declarative mood and long noun phrases that are technical, dense, and

abstract. Students agreed that these language patterns enable the author to present information in an authoritative, scientific manner.

Finally, the teacher guided students to rewrite Text 3 using language that is more familiar and comfortable to them. Students shared their writing and talked about how their language choices differ from those of the original text and the impact of these choices on clarity, style, and understanding. Students then independently wrote an explanation of an environmental issue impacting the local community, drawing on the rhetorical resources of explanation exemplified in Text 3 and other similar texts they have worked with.

The analysis and discussion of language patterns focusing on three key questions of content, organization, and style/perspective enabled ELs to develop a deeper, more complex understanding of text. It also gave them insights into how the author uses language as a creative resource to present information, embed value, structure text, and develop argument. As students talked about and applied these resources, they were learning both about science content and about how language works in discipline or genre-specific ways.

TAKING ACTION

Close reading can be applied in any school subject where text reading constitutes an integral part of disciplinary learning and socialization. Although there is still a dearth of empirical evidence regarding the efficacy of close reading in helping students reach the goals established by the CCSS, recent discussions (e.g., Boyles, 2012/2013; Shanahan, T., 2013; Snow & O'Connor, 2013) suggest that the method has the potential to assist students in both building content knowledge and developing discursive insights about language and text.

When implementing close reading practices, teachers can follow the seven guidelines Hiebert (2014) proposed for using texts to increase students' capacity to comprehend increasingly more complex texts. These are: (1) select texts with content that furthers the goal of instruction, (2) establish how the knowledge in a text relates to students' proficiency and how knowledge demands change over a text, (3) establish the vocabulary demands of the text, (4) examine the text for unique uses of language, (5) examine the variation in the complexity of a text's sentences, (6) determine how the length of the text (and the length of the task with the text) will influence students' engagement in the text, and (7) determine how the features of the task and context may influence students' comprehension and engagement. At the same time, it is important to bear in mind that close reading is only a small, though important, part of the total reading instruction. Other evidence-based routines, strategies, practices, and resources—such as promoting literacy engagement and identity affirmation (Cummins, 2014)—need to be simultaneously in place if close reading is to be successful in achieving its end. In fact, close reading is most effective when used regularly within the context of disciplinary experiences in which students engage in doing, observing, reading, writing, talking, inquiring, and reflecting.

Effective implementation of close reading practices ultimately depends on the teacher's capacity. From this perspective, teachers need to develop deep, robust understanding of content, language, text, and literacy related to their discipline, as well as an intimate knowledge about their students, so that they are equipped to engage students of all ability levels and backgrounds in close reading practices. Given the many complex ways ELs use language outside of school, teachers need to value and build on the linguistic resources students bring to school when scaffolding their learning of academic language and disciplinary literacies. Because close reading takes time and can be challenging to implement, teachers need to make long-term commitment to the practice. They also need to provide ongoing support to help ELs and other struggling readers develop the skills and strategies needed to take up close reading practices. In these efforts, it may often be necessary for content teachers and language/literacy teachers to collaborate. Such collaboration will be most productive if the partnership is established on an equal footing without either party feeling marginalized. This means that the two parties must share common goals for students, recognize that both content and language/literacy are integral to disciplinary learning, and respect and value the expertise that each side brings to the table.

The CCSS expects all students, including ELs, to exhibit "with increasing fullness and regularity" such literate capacities as (a) independently comprehending and evaluating complex texts across a range of types and disciplines; (b) building strong content knowledge base across a wide range of disciplines; (c) responding to the varying demands of audience, task, purpose, and discipline in spoken and written communication; (d) understanding the author's points and evaluating the veracity of claims and soundness of reasoning; (e) making evidence-based arguments or decisions; (f) using technology and digital media strategically; and (g) understanding other people's perspectives and cultures (NGA & CCSSO, 2010, p. 7). These goals require that students have ample opportunities to work with and through texts of different types and sufficient richness and complexity and at the same time be supported in these interactions. It is through frequent encounters with—and regular close readings of—these texts in disciplinary contexts that students are able to learn rich content knowledge and develop critical reading and writing skills, both central to disciplinary learning and enculturation. There is little doubt that the CCSS has influenced—and will continue to influence—what we teach and how we teach in the years to come. Teachers can prepare for their roles in the CCSS era by harnessing the freedom afforded by the CCSS and drawing on the growing number of instructional and assessment resources available, both in print (e.g., Fang & Schleppegrell, 2008; Fisher, Frey, & Lapp, 2012; Hiebert & Grisham, 2012; McLaughlin & Overturf, 2013; Morrow, Shanahan, & Wixson, 2014) and online (e.g., ell.stanford.edu; www.achievethecore.org; ldc.org; www.engageny.org; www.textproject.org; www.cde.ca.gov/re/cc/; www.parcconline.org; and www.smarterbalanced.org). With visionary planning, careful consideration of resources, and keen awareness of individual needs, teachers can use close reading and other evidence-based methods to meet the requirements of the CCSS while also creating an environment that fosters access and promotes equity for ELs across content areas.

Chapter 2

High Expectations

Increasing Productivity and Complexity in English Learner Writing

Kathleen A. J. Mohr, Sylvia Read,
and Alayne Leavitt

In this chapter, we make the case for improving writing instruction for English learners by placing an emphasis on increasing productivity and complexity as critical aspects of writing achievement. We then provide instructional recommendations to promote more writing across the disciplines with the goal of strengthening subject-matter learning while increasing students' academic language proficiency.

INTRODUCTION

The goal of developing writing proficiency by providing effective writing instruction has challenged educators and researchers over the years. Knowing which writing skills to expect and how to teach them are again controversial topics and various stakeholders have joined the debate for very good reasons. There is now a stronger emphasis on writing throughout the Common Core State Standards (CCSS), with more balance expectations for consuming and generating fiction and nonfiction genres. The expectation of more analytic writing will require significant changes in how schools and teachers plan writing topics and provide writing instruction, especially for lower achieving students. As noted in a recent federally sponsored report:

> The Standards ask that teachers move away from primarily assigning writing projects that rely largely on students' personal reflections and responses. Personal writing, at best, captures only what a student already knows and is thus less likely to prepare students for writing that requires analysis or interpretation—the type of writing that leads to academic success in high school and college. (Baker et al., 2014, p. 47)

Furthermore, for the first time, the 2011 National Assessment of Education Progress (NAEP) (National Center for Education Statistics [NCES], 2012) included a computer-based writing assessment under a new NAEP Writing Framework. This framework, guided by the National Assessment Governing Board, describes the specific competencies expected of eighth and twelfth grade students according to three broad communicative purposes (i.e., to persuade, explain, or convey experience). The twenty-two NAEP writing tasks are daunting and expect sophisticated use of texts, video, photographs, and animation to support synthetic responses composed on laptops. With this and other assessments being administered via computer, basic keyboarding is again a priority in many writing programs, complicating what teachers need to accomplish.

In an already crowded curriculum with teachers feeling less confident about writing instruction (Draper, Barksdale-Ladd, & Radencich, 2000), many schools are looking to writing programs to deliver big assessment results from their diverse student populations. Whether commercial or computerized writing programs can solve the problem remains to be seen, but supporting writing development, especially among students learning English in school is getting much-deserved attention (August & Shanahan, 2008). The newly released IES Educator's Practice Guide (Baker et al., 2014) summarizes recent EL-literacy research with four key recommendations. Interestingly, although the "What Works Clearinghouse" document was written to update the 2007 Educator's Practice Guide (Gersten et al., 2007) with regard to EL literacy, two of the most recent recommendations target writing as important aspects of content area learning:

Recommendation 2: Integrate oral and written English language instruction into content-area teaching.
Recommendation 3: Provide regular, structured opportunities to develop written language skills.

This focus on writing with goals for better outcomes, especially among ELs, is warranted. The mean score of the 2011 NAEP Writing was 150 of 300, which established a baseline for subsequent administrations. Discouragingly, only 27 percent of all eighth graders scored above "basic" on the 2011 assessment. The average score for Latinos was 136, compared to 158 for whites, and 165 for Asians. For eighth grade ELs, the average score was 108 compared to 152 for non-ELs. Once again, this is public pronouncement of a significant achievement gap, separating ELs from non-ELs. Under the CCSS and given research-based recommendations, teachers should reconsider the kinds of writing, as well as the sophistication of writing, that they develop in their students. The 2014 Educator's Practice Guide (Baker et al.,

2014) emphasizes four areas of effective EL teaching: academic vocabulary, content area instruction, writing instruction, and small-group intervention for ELs who are struggling in school (p. 3). These recommendations provide an opportunity for educators to re-envision appropriate instruction and to incorporate these key recommendations into their writing programs.

To ameliorate the writing skills of students, especially ELs, teachers need to reconsider their instructional practices and find ways to enrich students' writing processes and direct their learning. Put simply, "an important ingredient in ensuring that students become skilled writers involves teachers' use of effective writing practices" (Rogers & Graham, 2008, p. 898). But, do teachers generally understand effective writing practices well enough to employ them with diverse groups of students? Interestingly, research indicates that primary grade teachers tend to make few or no adaptations for struggling writers (Graham, Harris, Fink-Chorzempa & MacArthur, 2003). In fact, even well-intended teachers tend to allow weaker students to write less, perhaps because the teachers don't know what else to do or they hope that writing will develop over time if students are not discouraged. However, lofty writing outcomes will not be met without rigorous instructional goals for all students.

oh no!

I have thought this ...

EL WRITING

Essentially, the 2011 NAEP writing assessment provides a target to which other assessments and instructional programs can, and will likely, aim. According to the NAEP, at the basic level, the texts written by eighth graders should be coherent and effectively structured with many well-developed ideas. As noted on the NAEP website (NCES 2012),

> Supporting details and examples should be relevant to the main ideas they support. Voice should align with the topic, purpose, and audience. Texts should include appropriately varied uses of simple, compound, and complex sentences. Words and phrases should be relevant to the topics, purposes, and audiences. Knowledge of spelling, grammar, usage, capitalization, and punctuation should be made evident; however, there may be some errors in the texts that impede meaning.

Doing well on standardized assessments, such as the NAEP writing, is a challenge, but just one outcome expected of ELs. Well before eighth grade, these students struggle to actively participate in school, achieve grade-level curricular benchmarks, and communicate proficiently in writing. As noted previously, teachers often fail to support these efforts, in part due to lower expectations for ELs. In many cases, ELs are simply not required to do a lot of writing, *basic ideas*

Propositions?

are not expected to write lengthier compositions, nor encouraged to make their writing more complex. Complexity in writing usually refers to the number of propositions, the use of polysyllabic words, and the length and structure of sentences. Productivity focuses on amount of text produced and can include the following measures: (a) number of words (Hopman & Glynn, 1989; Van Houten & McKillop, 1977; Van Houten, Morrison, Jarvis, & McDonald, 1974; Wolfe, 1997), and (b) number of words plus number of adjectives (Weygant, 1981), and number of sentences, words, and syllables (Mohr, 2014).

For the most part, youngsters begin school believing that they can write (Calkins, 1983). Soon thereafter, they get negative messages about being writers that influence their efficacy as writers (Pajares, 2003). Interestingly, although boys in general tend to be more self-congratulatory regarding their competencies than girls, when asked whether they were better writers than their peers, girls were more positive in their self-reports than boys across grade levels (Pajares, 2003; Pajares, Miller, & Johnson, 1999; Pajares & Valiante, 1999, 2001). Therefore, in addition to a difference between ELs and native speakers, there is a gender gap in writing perceptions and skills. It is a challenge for teachers to communicate writing as relevant and valuable to both genders and that writing contributes to students' sense of selves and their identities as learners.

To add to the challenge, beliefs about English abilities tend to decrease starting in middle school. Thus, it is important that teachers work to build writing skills and confidence among students that will sustain them from the primary grades, before the content area reading and writing that predominate the intermediate grades. Abedi and Herman (2010) found that EL students report a lower level of opportunity to learn (OTL)—defined as content coverage—than their native English-speaking peers, even within the same classroom. Thus, when academic reading and writing demands increase, ELs, especially EL males (Mohr, Robles-Goodwin, & Wilhelm, 2009), tend to become less positive about themselves and their futures. Indeed, research has demonstrated that there are Matthew Effects for writing—that those who write tend to gain skills and positive dispositions, while those who struggle tend to fall further behind (Glasswell, 2001). In this chapter, we present ways for teachers to elevate their writing instruction, especially with regard to their expectations of ELs to produce more and increasingly more complex text, with the hope that improved instruction will contribute to student success and more positive writing dispositions.

Promoting Writing Productivity

First and foremost, teachers should expect students to write more and more often. If most every lesson were to include some writing in support of the learning objectives, ELs would certainly get more opportunities to communicate in writing. Moreover, teachers can set clear and specific goals to increase students' writing productivity. Although it may seem contrived, telling students to count the number of sentences and to add a few more sentences can improve writing. The number of sentences tends to correlate with more propositions or basic ideas, which in turn make a written text more substantive. A study by an instructor at MIT has shown that even success on the SAT essay is closely correlated with length: the more words pile up, the higher the score (Winerip, 2005).

Another recommended practice is that teachers reinforce students for their writing productivity (Rogers & Graham, 2008). In a study with second graders, Mohr (2012) counted both the number of words and correctly spelled word parts as a source of information to ELs about their writing samples. Providing a score for the number of words and word parts to the students was one kind of feedback about their efforts to communicate in English, which motivated many, especially the boys, to write more than they would otherwise in twice-weekly modeled writing activities. When trying to add more, these second graders considered ways to "enlarge the writing" with personal experiences, searched for additional English vocabulary that fit the topic, and took risks in their writing that may have built more writing stamina—the willingness to keep writing and to work out writing difficulties. It seems appropriate that students should be able to write more in May than they did in the previous September, so depending on the topic and format, teachers can expect and set goals for longer compositions as their students progress through the school year.

Promoting Complexity

When writers work to add more to their texts, one desired outcome is that the writing becomes more complex. The number of related ideas increases and explaining or connecting the stated propositions can make the writing more interesting to read and more substantive in content. While having more to say is one goal, making one's writing more sophisticated should be a high priority for writing teachers. Experienced teachers know that students have "something to say" but they may not feel comfortable or want to do the work to get their thoughts on paper. Therefore, it can be powerful if teachers give more instructional attention to generating ideas and for grooming those ideas for an intended audience. The brainstorming and revising portions of writing units are key aspects for ELs. Yet, writing instruction for planning and revising tends to be brief, according to self-report, occurring less than ten minutes per day (Cutler & Graham, 2008). Thus, teachers need to plan ways to engage students in prewriting activities for gathering and organizing ideas in advance of writing so that the cognitive work of ideation precedes the challenging transcription work that ELs must do when writing in English. Indeed, the 2014 Educator's Practice Guide (Baker et al., 2014) suggests two means for accomplishing these goals: the use of small-group discussions and graphic organizers. Group discussions can encourage the talk to generate and consider ideas, while graphic organizers can be used as tools for organizing the ideas into an appropriate format that will facilitate the actual writing process. The following section delineates instructional ideas that add to these key recommendations.

WAYS TO INCREASE WRITING PRODUCTIVITY AND COMPLEXITY: GENERATING IDEAS FOR WRITING

Mentor Texts

Teaching students how different texts are structured and formed (Troia & Olinghouse, 2013) is a strong first step for enhancing student writing. Researchers recommend having students read and analyze exemplary texts so that they can determine what patterns or forms the texts follow and then having students emulate those patterns or forms in their own texts (Englert, Berry, & Dunsmore, 2001; Troia & Olinghouse, 2013).

Analyzing texts for what they have to show writers is sometimes called "reading like a writer," and the texts are referred to as mentor texts. Mentor texts can show writers how to do basic tasks, such as punctuation or choosing vivid nouns or strong verbs. Texts also have structures that can be discerned and used as patterns for students to follow. When teachers help ELs take a patterned text, such as *Cat the Cat, Who Is That?* (Willems, 2010), the students can follow the pattern but choose their own characters and situations. The main text is fairly simple: "Cat the Cat, who is that? It's Mouse the Mouse. Hello, Mouse the Mouse!" But each character Cat the Cat encounters the answers differently: "Hello there!" "Hey, dude!" and "A pleasure, as always!" Similarly, students might find it useful to write their own story about Henry and Mudge (Rylant, 1987), which allows them to create new adventures for well-known characters.

Students can also analyze texts and find larger structural features, such as chronological order, and then find the corresponding transition words. For example, in *Owl Moon*, Yolen (1987) uses temporal terms, such as "then," and phrases such as "all of a sudden" to signal the passage of time. But, she also uses repetition to give a reader a sense of time slowing down: "For one minute, three minutes, maybe even a hundred minutes, we stared at one another." Young writers can borrow this use of emphasis in their own writing. A focus on time words can be very helpful to ELs who often need help to use common vocabulary in effective ways in their compositions and borrowing language to make their own is a reasonable step of EL writers.

One suggestion is to identify a number of books that have something to teach students about writing and to read them early in the school year, and then use them again and again to illustrate different strategies that writers use and different structures that are available (e.g., question/answer structure, problem/solution) (Ray, 1999). Students can then be asked to use these strategies and structures in their own writing. If students' nonfiction texts are deadly dull, then it's time to point out the features of well-written nonfiction that keep readers engaged. Brenda Guiberson's informational books begin with scene-setting sentences, not dry facts. In *Cactus Hotel* (1991), before we learn the details of the life cycle of the saguaro, Guiberson writes: "On a hot, dry day in the desert, a bright-red fruit falls from a tall saguaro cactus. Plop. It splits apart on the sandy floor. Two thousand black seeds glisten in the sunlight." Fruit? In the desert? Two *thousand* seeds? The variety and details in these sentences can inspire ELs to be more detailed in their own descriptions of science-based writing.

Patterned Poetry

Another use of mentor texts is to explore the patterns in popular poetry formats and use them as writing skeletons for students to complete or adapt. One common example employs Judith Viorst's "If I Were in Charge of the World," (1987) which lists things in life that the narrator thinks should be changed to suit a child. But, the poem has a skeletal structure that can be borrowed to allow students to make their own suggestions without generating a new format. The same is true for many other poetic patterns. Denise Fleming's *Where Once There Was a Wood* (1996) relies on an adjective-noun-verb format that ELs can leverage for their own descriptions:

Where once there was a wood, a meadow, and a creek,
Where once the brown snake slithered and slipped out of sight.
Where once the (adjective), (noun), (verb) and (verb), prepositional phrase.

Modeled Writing with Anchor Sentences

Modeled writing is typically an interactive process in which the teacher demonstrates writing for, or co-constructs writing with, students (Mohr, 2012). The teacher seeks to show via think-aloud ways to generate ideas and get them down on paper, with the goal to help students understand how writers work and the various elements that they must consider. In most situations, this think-aloud process can generate a few sentences that help get student writers started on a topic. In a sense, the modeled writing sentences become an anchor for the students as they write more to extend the co-constructed portion.

Anchor sentences serve as prompts that start the cognitive flow. Using the Language Experience Approach (Mohr, 1999), teachers can present a shared experience, such as closely examining bluebonnet plants to note the parts and structure of the stem, leaves, flowers, and seed pods. The teacher can introduce new vocabulary during the experiential discussion, and then build knowledge and ideas via conversation or progressive discourse (Cazden, 1998). Once the open discourse has helped students know and understand the shared experience, the teacher can solicit ideas for sentences that would describe the situation. For example, teacher and students may co-construct the sentences: "Lupines are plants that have seed pods. Bluebonnets are a kind of lupine and are the state flower of Texas. They grow wild in the early spring and create beautiful blue oceans across the Texas prairies." Students can be encouraged to reread and discuss the co-constructed anchor sentences, noting the spelling of words and sentence structure. Then, the teacher can dictate or have students copy or adapt the anchor sentences for their own writing. They should be encouraged to add more sentences and provide more details. In this way, the anchor sentences help students get started on a writing task, but allow students to make the writing their own as they revise and extend the starter sentences. Well-known cognitivists (Berninger & Richards, 2002) recommend "teacher-provided cognitive tasks that channel the idea flow for mindful mental work in which ideas and knowledge are transformed through problem-solving writing activities into new knowledge" (p. 260). Anchor sentences provide "explicit cueing . . . in a highly supportive social context" (p. 261) and can be very productive for less-skilled writers. Using mentor texts, patterned poetry, and anchor sentences can encourage risk-taking behavior that is a highly significant predictor of writing competency, more than SES status or reading performance (Pajares, 2003).

WAYS TO INCREASE WRITING PRODUCTIVITY AND COMPLEXITY: SUPPORTING THE DRAFTING AND REVISING PHASES

Graphic Organizers

A key finding of recent research is that graphic organizers can be valuable tools for organizing one's thinking in preparation for writing (Baker et al.,

Table 2.1 Dreamer Biography Frame

Dreamer	Goal	Attempt	Obstacle	Reaction	Outcome
Christopher Columbus	Wanted to sail west across the Atlantic to reach the Orient.	But when he tried to find a sponsor, he was turned down many times.	For years no one would help him try his plan.	He convinced the King and Queen of Spain to sponsor his trip.	Christopher Columbus sailed west and claimed the new land he found for Spain. His dream was partly fulfilled.

2014). To meet the recommendation for more informational writing, teachers should consider the thoughtful use of graphic organizers to help students make sense of content, take notes, and organize their thinking. A well-done organizer can greatly facilitate the completion of various writing tasks. Timelines, Venn diagrams, flow maps, plot charts, and the like, can go a long way in helping students organize what they know about various subjects or topics. To support ELs, teachers can customize organizers to include key vocabulary and language structures that students may need to communicate their ideas clearly. The 2014 Educator's Practice Guide (Baker et al., 2014) includes numerous examples of instructional plans and viable organizers that could benefit teachers and students, but table 2.1 is an example that helps students take notes before writing a more detailed biography.

Table 2.1 is a simple format that helps ELs take notes that could be elaborated upon in a more detailed composition. When they include the spelling of some key terms, graphic organizers enable students to work more independently in their writing.

Collaborative Writing

Research on collaborative writing, when peers write together and engage in dialogue, clearly points to its effectiveness: "Working with peers helps students externalize covert processes, making them transparent to the implementor and to the other participants in the interaction" (Englert, Mariage, & Dunsmore, 2006, p. 210). All phases of the writing process—planning, drafting, revising, and editing—benefit from collaboration (Troia & Olinghouse, 2013). In addition, feedback from peers can be quite helpful, if the students are adequately taught how to give specific, descriptive feedback (Beach & Friedrich, 2006).

Working with a peer can distribute the writing task so that cognitive capacity is maximized, allowing the students, in turn, to focus on meaning rather than transcription (Englert, Berry, & Dunsmore, 2001). Conversely, when one student is transcribing, he or she can focus on issues of conventions of text such as spacing, spelling, and punctuation while the other student monitors overall construction of meaning. Together they can better approximate the literacy practices of skilled writers. Indeed, when writing, two heads are better than one.

ELs can be partnered with other ELs or with native English speakers. Working together, two fourth grade girls, both ELs, took notes from texts and wrote paragraphs to represent their acquired knowledge about the chuckwalla, including one paragraph about its tail, written in the voice of the animal: "Where did my tail go? Did you know if you grab a chuckwalla by the tail, my tail separates from me? And it's like my tail is still alive because it keeps on moving (just to distract my enemy). Then I grow a new tail in its place." As they took notes and wrote their paragraphs, they continually negotiated with each other regarding what information to include, how to phrase ideas, how to make the text engaging to a reader, how to word the subheadings so they would hook the reader (Where did my tail go?), as well as how to spell, punctuate, and to use their graphic organizer to group similar ideas into paragraphs (Read, 2005). The EL students were engaged and productive, and the texts they produced were as or more complex than those of their native-English peers.

Sentence Combining

Sentence combining is a teaching strategy that demonstrates how to take short simple, or kernel sentences and combine them to make more syntactically complex sentences. Research on sentence combining clearly demonstrates it efficacy (Hillocks, 1986; Troia & Olinghouse, 2013) for increasing the sophistication of student writing. Sentence combining need not rely on grammatical terminology or finding errors, but should focus on learning new skills. The studies that support sentence combining as an effective strategy have occurred in classrooms as low as second grade, and some studies have emphasized its special advantages for struggling students (Hillocks, 1986).

In sentence combining, kernel sentences are provided and students are taught guidelines for combining them. For example, this set of sentences based on an Aesop's fable illustrates the notion of "kernel" sentences:

- Fox saw Crow.
- Crow was flying.
- Crow had cheese.
- Her beak held the cheese. (Strong, 1994)

The guidelines, or processes, for combining are that you can delete unnecessary or repeated words, rearrange words, add a variety of connectors, and change word forms (Strong, 2001). Using these guidelines, many sentences could result, including the following combinations:

Fox saw Crow flying with cheese held in her beak.
Crow was flying, holding cheese in her beak, and Fox saw her.
Fox saw Crow flying while holding cheese in her beak.
With cheese held in her beak, Crow flew and was seen by Fox.
Crow was flying with cheese held in her beak; Fox saw her.

The goal is to help students see and experiment with different options for acceptable sentence construction (Strong, 2001). ELs generally have less awareness of English syntax and may need explicit modeling of word order and sentences types, such as compound and complex structures. Older students can be instructed to talk through options with a partner and then write their sentences, whereas young children can be instructed entirely through oral practice or chanting (Strong & Strong, 1999). For example, when presented with the following sentences, many children will recall the combined version of the following sentence set.

Jack went up the hill.
Jill went up the hill.
They went to fetch a pail.
Water was in the pail.

Specific chanting exercises can be used to prompt specific ways to combine that will nudge students along the developmental ladder of syntactical maturity. For example, students could combine the following sentences into the accompanying sentence frame:

Mona is a mouse.	_____
You can't hear her.	that_____ .
She roams the house.	_____
The coast is clear.	when _____ .
She eats many treats.	_____
She is without any fear.	without_____ .
Mona is a mouse.	Oh,_____
You can't hear her.	that_____ .

newcomers

After chorally reading the uncombined sentences together, the teacher models how to combine the first two sentences both orally and in writing (i.e., Mona is a mouse that you can't hear). Then the students can chant the combined version with the teacher for two or three repetitions. After

Polysemy: a coexistence of many possible meanings for a wd. or phrase.

continuing this pattern for the remaining pairs of sentences, the students can perform the chant chorally several times as a group. Chanting sentence combinations supports both oral language fluency and syntactical awareness.

Mona is a mouse that you can't hear.
She roams the house when the coast is clear.
She eats many treats without any fear.
Oh, Mona is a mouse that you can't hear.

This chant approach also allows teachers to determine vocabulary targets so that exposure to polysemous words, homonyms, figurative expressions, synonyms, and antonyms can become instructional objectives along with syntactic complexity (Strong & Strong, 1999).

Show, Not Tell

One means of promoting complexity in narrative texts is to communicate that good writers "show, not tell" the reader by using descriptive language. Other ways to phrase this writing technique is to "paint a picture" or "make a movie" with the words. Teachers can start with reading aloud examples from books where authors "show, not tell." For example, in the picture book, *The Relatives Came*, Rylant (1993) paints a picture with her words to help us understand what the relatives are feeling. She could just tell what was happening by saying, "The relatives were excited to see us." Instead, she writes,

> Then it was hugging time. Talk about hugging! Those relatives just passed us all around their car, pulling us against their wrinkled Virginia clothes, crying sometimes. They hugged us for hours. Then it was into the house and so much laughing and shining faces and hugging in the doorways. (p. 10)

The difference, as shown here, is using sentences to describe, rather than declare. Detailed descriptions can help ELs "see" the scene and encourage them to add more details in their writing. ELs and novice writers may need help to identify places where they could revise "telling" sentences into "showing" sentences. Teachers can initiate this process by encouraging them to "make a movie" in their minds and then write what they see in one or two places in their writing until they begin to do so on their own.

Another basic option that helps to "complexify" compositions is to teach ELs to add adjectives to their drafted sentences during the revision phase. This may require that teachers post and review lists of interesting adjectives and synonyms for common descriptors that pertain to the writing topic. Students may need to close their eyes and "see" in order to "show, not tell" and to add adjectives. Drawing pictures to go with the writing can also help in the visualization process. Once a text is drafted, the teacher should show ELs how adjectives add detail and make sentences more interesting. (Remember that ELs may need to be shown how adjectives generally precede nouns in English.) Like all students, ELs have something to say and effective teachers get them to think and talk and then elicit more ideas by talking about their thinking. If it makes sense for the task, teachers can give students bonus points for how many adjectives are added to their compositions. Making the inclusion of details and adjectives or adverbs a criteria in the assessment process can motivate some students to revise their work and communicates the value of more description.

Teacher, Peer, and Student Feedback

It is common in the writing process for teachers and peers to give students suggestions for revision, and both forms of feedback have been found to be effective in improving the quality of final drafts (Karegianes, Pascarella, & Pflaum, 1980). The research on peer feedback shows that when peers are trained to ask questions about other students' writing, instead of just "assessing" it, students are provided more opportunities to improve their writing (Hyland & Hyland, 2006). Giving peer feedback also helps the students to look more critically at their own writing. Using peer feedback in the classroom gives ELs opportunities to engage in academic discussions about their writing, and helps them construct knowledge with their peers (Richards, 2010). Peer feedback is a form of collaboration that affords conversations and elevates the writing task as something to think about and improve, not just to complete for the teacher.

While teacher and peer feedback is an important part of revision, it is even more important to teach ELs to reread and revise their own writing. As Young (2005) states, "We often neglect the most useful resource we have available to use when trying to understand student learning, the students themselves" (p. 23). Teaching students how to think critically about and revise their own writing can help increase the complexity and quality of their writing (Fitzgerald, 1987). When revising, writers "operate from an internal dialogue, activate their prior knowledge, draw on their awareness of genre and audience, and put themselves in the position of readers" (Richards, 2010, p. 90). For most students, operating from an internal dialogue needs to be taught explicitly with lots of modeling. The internal dialogue for some ELs will be in their first language, not English, so more English modeling may be necessary. If a teacher creates opportunities for students to investigate their own and each other's writing during each step of the writing process, students can explore the possibilities for revision and improvement and verbalize those internal thoughts (Richards, 2010). Teachers can model how writers work to improve their writing by thinking out loud while writing, and encourage students to do the same (Faigley & Witte, 1981). This think-aloud strategy is an essential part of teaching revision to ELs and incorporates oral language at the same time. While challenging, the revision process is critical to improving writing. ELs need to understand that the goal is not just about pleasing the teacher or completing an assignment. The message that writers revisit and rework their texts can help ELs understand that writing in English is a process, rather than product or performance. Again, teachers cannot afford to just accept the written work from ELs; they must communicate high expectations and authentic processes, including the real work of revision.

Audiences

The ability to read and write from a reader's perspective is also integral to revision (Bartlett, 1982). One strategy that can help them see their writing through the eyes of a reader is to give them an audience other than the teacher. The majority of students view the teacher as the audience for their writing, but there are many other audiences that students can write for to give them more purpose and meaning (Richards, 2010). For example, a second grade class writing fractured fairy tales could go into a kindergarten or first grade and read their stories to the younger students. Students in the same classroom can be the audience via "author's chair" when students read their writing pieces to other classmates, or have an "author's shelf" in the classroom or school library for students to share their finished writing pieces. This can encourage and motivate students to revise and write more complex pieces because they know someone will actually hear or read their writing, rather than it just sitting in their journal or being graded and sent home.

CONCLUSION

This chapter makes a case for improving writing instruction for ELs. Students who are not yet proficient in English are academically vulnerable and at risk for school failure and lifelong disadvantages (Baker et al., 2014). In an effort to help teachers focus on the needs of ELs, we have argued for an emphasis on increasing productivity and complexity as critical aspects of writing achievement. We then provided instructional recommendations to promote more writing and encourage more elaboration in ELs' writing. These recommendations align with recent research reports that stress more inclusion of writing across the curriculum as a way to strengthen subject-matter learning and increase the academic language proficiency of students. Teachers who understand the critical need and role of effective writing instruction to support EL achievement should consider ways to adapt the instructional ideas available and would do well to incorporate the following broad-based principles:

- Plan for regular writing as a tool for learning across content areas.
- Consider ways to include informational writing with a focus on academic language.
- Use texts as models for good writing and of various genres.
- Employ think-alouds to model the writing process and to get ELs to talk and visualize before writing.
- Explore the use of various graphic formats to organize ideas for writing.
- Utilize small group and peer-pairing configurations to promote collaboration.
- Focus on revision to help students improve their writing.
- Find audiences for students' writing that give purpose and meaning to the writing process.

Chapter 3

A Middle School Mathematics Workshop for Multilingual Classrooms

Lessons Learned from a Highly Effective Teacher

Mayra C. Daniel with Billy Hueramo

In this chapter, I describe how Andy, a middle school mathematics teacher, effectively reaches and teaches all of his EL students by helping them bridge the gap between their language proficiency and disciplinary demands in a mathematics workshop.

The way we interact today is ever changing due to the mobility of the world's populations and the ease with which we communicate using new technologies such as tablets, smartphones, and other devices and applications. Yet in spite of how speedily and easily we reach out to folks across continents, English learners (ELs) in U.S. schools and students throughout the world who enroll in schools where their home language is not the one used in schooling, face problems achieving academic success in content area classrooms. Of particular interest to researchers and educators are the struggles of students in mathematics (Allexsaht-Snider & Hart, 2001; Boaler, 2008; Chval & Khisty, 2009; Flores, 2007; Moschkovich, 2010). Many researchers have attributed this challenge to the increased linguistic complexity of math in the higher grades (Abedi & Hejri, 2004; Ma & Singer-Gabella, 2011; National Governors Association Center for Best Practices & Council of Chief State School Officers, 2010) and the difficulties ELs face learning the content of math at the same time they are first exposed to the everyday English the teacher uses to teach math (August & Shanahan, 2006; Short & Fitzsimmons, 2007). What can we do, as teachers, to bridge the gap between EL students' language proficiency and the content demands of mathematics?

In this chapter, I will share insights learned by observing Andy (pseudonym), a highly skilled middle school mathematics teacher, over a period of five months. These insights provide powerful guidelines for teachers willing to make mathematics comprehensive for their EL. I spent this time with a teacher whose student test scores increased when he taught them. I wanted to know why. I wanted to try to explain what went on in his classroom that made the difference in student achievement. I asked myself why because as an educator I feel we need to do everything we can to prevent ELs from falling behind in middle and high school math classrooms (Abedi & Lord, 2001; Lager, 2006).[1]

RESEARCH AND THEORETICAL BACKGROUND

For middle school students, or those in early adolescence, development of their bi-, multi-, or plurilingualism, literacy, and cultural identities takes place in worlds of different cultural norms. They spend their days juggling culturally shaped definitions of what makes up acceptable behavior in their home environment as contrasted to the norms of the larger community and school personnel. They interact in more than one language and often do so simultaneously. They awaken at home, walk through the streets of their neighborhoods to school, spend their days with teachers whose expectations and language they may not fully understand, and then at the end of the day once again return to the familiar home environment. Their teachers, too, face issues. The mismatch between home and school is problematic for teachers, their students, and their families. Teachers who live and work in different neighborhoods are less likely to be privy to the realities of their students' lives. Thus for them, the workplace provides compounds that separate them from their students.

What do we know about teaching ELs? How has research informed us? We know a great deal but we still don't have all the answers. We are certain that students are empowered when they know their voices and perspectives are valued (Freire, 1998). We also know that when teachers pay attention to the knowledge and beliefs that learners bring to school, use this knowledge to scaffold instruction, and monitor students' changing conceptions, academic achievement increases (Donovan & Bransford, 2005).

One of my goals in this chapter is to convince all teachers who read this that they can be effective educators of ELs. I know that all teachers can teach ELs well even when they do not share the students' first language. All math teachers can be literacy brokers! I saw Andy implement the same pedagogy successfully with students from different cultural and linguistic backgrounds. I am sure that all teachers can eliminate the cultural and linguistic mismatches between home and school that prevent students from achieving academic success just as this teacher does. I am certain that the trenches are the setting to discover better ways to teach math and that culturally competent teachers hold the power to open the right doors so that ELs come to understand math. I believe that, *Together, we can do this!*

When planning content area instruction, I encourage you to first learn about your students' lives and backgrounds. We can agree with Thomas and Collier's (2002) research when they tell us that the sociocultural context of schooling is as important as the discipline a teacher is teaching. Who students are and what they know extends far beyond their prior formal schooling. Their identities develop and they grow into lifelong learners through their daily interpersonal interactions, and with the help of the role models (parents, friends, and teachers) within their circles of influence (González, Moll, & Amanti, 2005; Khisty, 1995).

Immigrants schooled in other countries frequently find that the way mathematics is taught in the U.S. educational system is different from the way they were taught. Even in the lower elementary grades, simple computation is approached in ways unique to each culture. Students learn the concepts of addition, subtraction, and division in different ways across the world. This is a fact but we cannot assume it is an insurmountable obstacle. We need to make sure that every educator believes that *All ELs can get math because all ELs need math!* Math classrooms must offer intriguing worlds for students so they will be able to go from not understanding to mastery. The teaching that helps ELs succeed and visualize ideas in their minds begins with culturally responsive teachers like you and Andy who address ELs' backgrounds and lived experiences within their pedagogy (Lee, 2007).

Why do ELs struggle to understand mathematics? First, they are working to acquire English, the dominant language of U.S. society and schools. Meanwhile, they are trying to grasp sophisticated content area material just as all other students at their grade level (August & Shanahan 2006; Short & Fitzsimmons, 2007). This intersection of language and content learning creates a high cognitive load that cannot be overlooked (Marsh, 2008). ELs are at a disadvantage because they do not have the language base that allows them to focus on the content and specialized language unique to the discipline of mathematics (Echevarria, 2012; Lesh, Galbraith, Haines, & Hurford, 2010). Researchers estimate that readers need mastery of at least 95 percent of the words in a basic narrative text to understand its basic message (Schmitt & Carter, 2000). If this is true of narrative text, imagine how tough it must be for the non-native English speaker to understand expository text. Abedi and Lord (2001) documented that ELs' success in mathematics tests with word problems highly correlates to their reading scores and thus it is not surprising that when ELs reach the higher grades, the gap between them and monolinguals' achievement becomes markedly visible (Kanno & Cromley, 2013).

What else makes math difficult for ELs? Mathematics requires ELs to be able to read a word problem and grasp what they are being asked to do to solve the problem. When they begin this task, they first have to access the language in the problem and decontextualize its meaning. They have to abstract the situation being posed and represent it symbolically so that it is possible for them to manipulate the representing symbols. This requires deep understanding. When students are engaged in this process not knowing even a single word or the way words are used to convey meaning in a phrase can be the stumbling block that stops comprehension and prevents their grasp of a new concept. We need to remember that when students lack sufficient English to be able to comprehend what they read, their efforts may be so taxing, thus affecting their ability to access content and learn (Krashen, 1981).

CREATING A MATHEMATICS INSTRUCTIONAL TEAM

This chapter is about Andy, a middle school grade mathematics teacher and first generation Mexican American. His life is a heartwarming tale of bicultural identity development and the academic achievement of a child born to a family of immigrants. Andy and Natalie (pseudonyms), his teacher aide, form a winning baseball team with their students. They are role models and collaborators in an ever-developing yet smoothly running system. We know that effective professional learning teams within schools and districts contribute much to students' academic achievement (NCTAF, 2010). This research has shown that teachers who collaborate in learning teams hold themselves to higher standards, improve their practice, and accelerate learners' achievement beyond what individual teachers can accomplish working on their own. Andy's pedagogy is a well-planned sequence of instructional steps that require the collaboration of all involved parties. He and Natalie make sure the ambiance of the class has the dynamics of a family that gets along. The students consult with them as they would a beloved aunt or uncle. Together they strive to make home runs a reality for every learner. At daily practice the ELs are out in the field becoming mathematicians as they develop their knowledge and acquire skills. Andy is the pitcher who progressively makes instruction more and more challenging. When he senses student frustration, he adjusts the input he offers to a more manageable level. Natalie is the catcher. She is ready when Andy throws a strike. They both smile when there are no strikeouts and everyone gets on base and contributes to the score.

Andy models for students how to think and how to express themselves as mathematicians (Gutierrez, Sengupta-Irving, & Dieckmann, 2010). He makes sure the ELs see, hear, and say what they think and are learning in math terms (Thompson, Kersaint, Richards, Hunsader, & Rubinstein, 2008). He teaches math together with academic and everyday English because he knows that for ELs the discipline is complex conceptually and linguistically (Abedi & Lord, 2001; Lager, 2006). Andy takes the language in the math problems and uses it in conversations the students understand. Math problems become logically presented narratives based on the lives of the students in the classroom. Andy also demands the student to engage in abstract thinking. He teaches them to reconstruct the sentences in the math problems as a way to get to the gist of the questions. He uses the Smart Board to model ways to take apart the noun phrases within math problems and works with the students to conceptualize a solution. He leads the students to develop the skill of reordering words and paraphrasing. As needed, he and Natalie freely change between languages to clarify concepts. The students are encouraged to do the same in whatever languages they speak (Cummins, 2009).

Andy's teaching results in improved scores for the ELs on the state achievement test. In the year of this study, students who had been in Andy's class for two years increased their academic achievement in math; almost 50 percent of the eighth graders met and 9.1 exceeded expectations (an increase from zero).

THE MATHEMATICS STANDARDS

Math teachers can look to the National Council of Teachers of Mathematics (NCTM) for guidance. The council recommends equitable mathematics education requiring that teachers hold high expectations, respect, understanding, and strong support for all students. The Common Core State Standards (CCSS) in mathematics emphasize that fostering the development of mathematicians begins with classroom tasks that engage learners in high levels of abstract thinking. The CCSS put the power in teachers' hands and supports their working to foster students' ability "to justify, in a way appropriate to the student's mathematical maturity, why a particular mathematical statement is true or where a rule comes from" (National Governors Association, 2014, p. 4). We want to help our ELs to successfully navigate this road. Table 3.1 highlights what NCTM stresses students have to be able to do within a

Table 3.1   Mathematics Tasks and Language

Task	Type of Task
Contextualize what is being asked in word problems; pause during the manipulation process to probe into the referents of the symbols used	Language
Understand and use mathematical assumptions, definitions and results to construct arguments	Math Language
Justify and communicate conclusions clearly	Math Language

Handwritten margin notes: Students moving in. School system.) Mobility rate. Of the school system and out.

mathematical task. As we can see, these tasks include both language and content goals.

THE CONTEXT

The observations that I am sharing in this chapter are based on the four hours a day for a period of five months that I spent in Andy's classroom. I was a participant observer in his seventh and eighth grade math classes and also spent a study hour and lunch period with the eighth graders. Higgins School is located in a town that houses a state university in a rural area approximately one hour from the city of Chicago. The district has a 24.9 percent mobility rate, 24–36 percent of the students are ELs, and low-income figures total from 46.4 to 62.8 percent.

The seventh grade students were one each from Nepal, India, Pakistan, two from Malaysia, and nine long-term ELs (students born in the United States who appear to speak English well yet struggle academically) of Mexican descent. The eighth graders were all of Mexican American heritage. The group included one student who had arrived to the United States nine months prior to this study, and two others who were in their second and third year of school in this country. The remaining students were immigrants from Mexico who had attended school in the United States for a period of three to five years.

FROM RESEARCH TO PRACTICE: ANDY'S SAFE HAVEN

As a participant observer and researcher in Andy's classroom I noted that besides knowing how to teach math he knows how to reach the ELs in a very effective way. My time in Andy's classroom allowed me to see that he takes his students to academic success because he is more than a math teacher. He is their acknowledged mentor, friend, and parent. I also credit Natalie's advocacy and deep commitment to the ELs because what she does for them extends beyond her job description. She is there helping them at recess, at lunch, and in the afterschool club that she leads.

My conversation with you will be based on our joint acknowledgment that there has been a shift in mathematics education to theoretical perspectives that acknowledge identity, power, and learning are intertwined and co-created within social discourses (Gutierrez & Rogoff, 2003). I will share what makes Andy's instruction effective and identify what he and Natalie do that helps the ELs succeed in math.

In Andy's classroom every moment is an opportunity to explore and use the students' funds of knowledge (González, Moll, & Amanti, 2005). This is why he enrolls them! Expectations for participation are clear because he provides predictable routines. His approach makes a difference because his math workshop offers a recursive pedagogy that continually involves every student (see figure 3.1, Layers of Andy's Workshop). Yes, we all know that good teachers do this but please keep your minds open to the possibility that the differences in his teaching are very subtle. He is very tuned in to what each student knows and he senses and delivers what the ELs need to get a hit! He does not let the students off the hook or accept being a *slacker* when learning becomes hard. He requires outputs and accepts errors as part of learning. He asks the students themselves to select what they write down in their math journals and requires that they each explore how to solve the

Language	• Provides bridges for understanding. • Contextually introduces language students will need to understand lessons. Presents this in a concrete manner using visuals, examples from the students' lives. • Provides explanation at a language level the students can understand. • Asks students to write things down in their notebooks, to share and explain how they arrived at their answers to each other, and to volunteer to write how they solved the problem on the Smart Board. • Plans lessons that consider the ELs are learning new concepts and the language needed to understand these. • Points out when a word has one meaning in everyday life and a different meaning in mathematics.
Content	• Offers recursive presentation of concepts. • Checks student comprehension repeatedly during instruction.
Content / Language	• Asks the right questions to find out what students know. • Prepares and shares guides to help the students with the day's lesson. These can be examples, explanations of terms in sheltered English and/or Spanish, drawings, and diagrams. • Uses students first and second languages to explain concepts.

Instructional Technology and Methods

- Incorporates the Smart Board in instruction.
- Sequences/scaffolds instruction well.
- Engages students in an ongoing predictable system of comparison and contrast.
- Makes it safe for students to ask questions.

Student Role

- Listening
- Asking questions that reflect thinking
- Working well with classmates
- Justifying their answers
- Creating sentences that explain how they solved the word problems
- Not giving up when they do not understand

Figure 3.1 Layers of Andy's Workshop

math problems. When he presents concepts as a simplified narrative, it is his version of an anticipation guide that is followed by an in-context explanation of new vocabulary.

Andy's classroom provides a safe haven that to the ELs is a home within a U.S. school. His instruction focuses on two related components: developing the students English language proficiency through a purposeful consideration of language and students' cultural capital as well as assuring the ELs understand, use, and are able to explain the math concepts to themselves, to each other, and to him. In figure 3.1, Layers of Andy's Workshop shows the layers of teaching occurring in this classroom. Andy provides multiple levels of instructional techniques. First he uses language, literacy, and content strategies to influence his students' learning. One thing that is evident in his teaching is that he does not just focus on one or the other at any given moment. This is true to the extent that there are distinct language and content strategies and also strategies that use language and content in an intertwined process so that strategies addressing both issues simultaneously are being synthesized at various points throughout the lesson. He also uses some supportive strategies. At the same time, he advises students of their role in the process as is evident in figure 3.2, Cyclical Teacher Math Workshop, so that there are really four distinct layers of teaching forming a strong infrastructure for learning. In some cases, it is the lack of understanding of this intertwined process that may prevent teachers from being able to serve ELs because they think they have to completely divest their language teaching from the content teaching. Andy's success shows a very concrete process by which the two can be addressed at the same time.

One of the strengths in Andy's pedagogy is the way he uses the Smart Board to add concreteness and reinforce the language and content in his lessons. He also asks his students to volunteer to write their answers and the way they arrived at these on the board. He models for the students how to think, accept responsibility, and own the learning through their participation. He meets his responsibilities in the learning and the students can identify and meet theirs (see figure 3.2).

Activity on a day when students were working in small groups to prepare for the Illinois State Achievement Test (ISAT) serves to demonstrate the benefits of Andy's math workshop. One triad consisted of Gladys, who had come to the United States from Mexico four years ago; Doris, who arrived from Mexico less than one year before; and Mariana, who had completed two years of schooling in the United States (all names used are pseudonyms). The question to be solved asked the students to list all the possible combinations of pizza that could be made using one type of crust, one topping, and one kind of cheese from three lists of possibilities. I observed the group using Spanish to work through the problem and write a narrative in English that justified

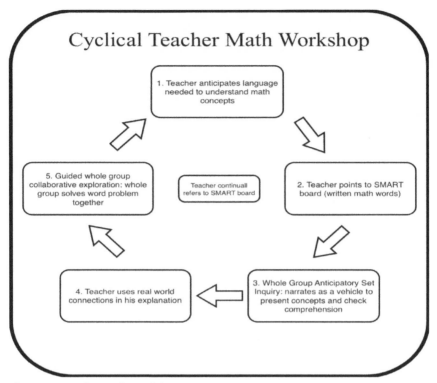

Figure 3.2 Andy's Math Workshop

how and why they arrived at the solution. They were helping each other to understand the question by explaining the meaning of the words to each other using both languages. I noticed that as they were composing their answer they did not use some of the words in the problem that might have made their explanation clearer. Gladys and Doris talked to me about the vocabulary that they encounter in math. Gladys said, "Words like vertex. I don't know them in Spanish and I don't know them in English. Now I know the words because *el maestro*/the teacher taught them to me." Doris told me *"En esta pregunta no entiendo la palabra* crust/In this question I don't know the word crust."

The girls zero in on the way the question is written. At this point their focus is not on solving the problem correctly but on the reasons they can't do it. This example demonstrates why it is important that teachers join their students in their explorations into the language of instruction. The triad plays with writing what they label "easier to understand questions." One of their efforts reads "List how many kinds of pizza you can make with _____ ." Another example is longer and reflects how speakers of Spanish express themselves. It is "List the pizzas that you can make with different ingredients by not using them at the same time, by not repeating the ingredients." They share how the question would be written in Spanish. They are baffled that the word ingredient is not in the question. In their examination and critiquing of the math problem, the girls demonstrate that the question evaluates both their English and mathematics expertise. I agree with the students' decision about the way the question is written. They tell me that "It's a bad question." I see why not understanding just part of a question is the wall that prevents an EL from demonstrating math knowledge.

THE MATH WORKSHOP: A RESEARCH-BASED PRACTICAL APPLICATION

One of Andy's goals is for the ELs to develop metacognitive awareness. He makes sure they come to understand their thinking and their roles in his math workshop. In the past we have used the term code-switching to acknowledge the ways students mix their languages. Teachers have always asked if this is a natural part of second language acquisition and whether this should be encouraged or discouraged. Now, Garcia's (2009a) work has allowed us to see that there is much more to what students do in their interpersonal communications as they develop a new language. Andy knows that the students' language behaviors are part of the process of acquiring English and helps them to make sense of the language that is new to them. Andy's conversations with the students show them that he accepts their colorful use of language because he knows they are making meaning. His students know they have the teacher's respect. They freely engage in what Garcia labels translanguaging. Andy works within a controlled and welcoming lively noisy room. The result is that in Andy's classroom the students feel free to communicate in whatever way helps them to understand and so they succeed at *getting* the math. He takes sample problems from the achievement test manual and clarifies these for the students. He begins all lessons using the Smart Board so that the students begin by reading what he terms background knowledge. He presents the information in simpler terms (sheltered English). He follows with culturally appropriate examples that offer students definitions they can understand. Every day the students look at a modified example from the training manual that addresses their funds of knowledge, explore what they know, come up with questions, and explain to classmates and to themselves why the sample problems the teacher is using can be solved the way he is teaching them is possible. Andy tells me that as he works with the ELs and they collaborate with each other, they provide each other additional language supports. He guides the students to identify key points in the lessons in order to engage them in an exploration of language and in high levels of processing.

Another of Andy's objectives is for the students to adapt to U.S. society while keeping their pride in their families and backgrounds. He shares personal stories with students as a way to help them look to the future. He tells them how he struggled as the oldest and first person in his family to go to college. He also interacts with students in a way they understand: he lectures them. Being a first generation Mexican American he has lived the experience that his students are living. He is one with his students of Mexican descent and has the expertise to know what ELs of other backgrounds need to be validated. He has taken time to learn about his students from Malaysia, Pakistan, Nepal, and other countries. When Andy shares the tale of what he did to build a future as a professional, he makes it clear to all his students that they too can be college graduates.

Andy prepares students to interact appropriately in mainstream culture. After a couple of weeks in his classroom I am no longer surprised at how he intertwines math and sermons. One day I hear him talk with the eighth graders about the next academic year. District administrators have asked him to move to a different school. He shares his concerns. He tells them, "I am planning to move to Harrison School but it's hard because I like the staff here. I am going because I want the seventh graders to fit in and I don't know if the teachers there will accept them. Do you remember how immature you were last year? You have grown a lot. The seventh graders need more time to learn how to act at school." A few weeks later as I walk into the same classroom I hear Andy admonishing the students as is typical in the Mexican culture (Delgado-Gaitan, 1993). He tells them "You have to assume responsibility. We only have a third of a year left. Everything is on you once you get to high school. Marta was not doing well in math but now she is doing awesome. When I asked her why she told me that now she is studying the journals I make you guys keep and she pays attention in class. I can only control what happens in this class. Sometimes you guys' parents don't make you do anything. You guys don't even take out the garbage!" At this point Luli offered, "Last night I tried to make tamales but I burnt them." The teacher immediately validated her efforts with "But you learned."

Comments from Andy's students support the premise that he succeeds because he is invested in them as people who form his extended family. When I asked the students what they think of the sermons, their comments show that they are okay with these. They agree that before taking this teacher's math class they "never got math." They seem fine with the paternal role that Andy exhibits. Jaime said, "He tells us that we live in two worlds and that we need to know how to act in both." Lucie said, "He reminds us to lower our voices because we are not in Mexico." Ana told me, "I like hearing his stories. He talks about what he did when he was our age and how he got to where he is now. He had a teacher who cared about him. He learned to act right." Mohammed said, "He knows about my family and how we escaped." (All names are pseudonyms.)

Andy models discursive patterns that result in empowering classroom conversations. He does not ask the ELs to set aside their cultural norms or communication patterns. He is a trapeze artist in the way he models how a person can straddle different norms. In his class students learn that they are more than a person familiar with only one culture, one language, and one set of norms. Instead, they have the opportunity to bring all their experiences into the learning community. He knows that academic success for the ELs will come through his pep talks and from comprehensible math instruction.

On the day of a school wide assembly Natalie and Andy's commitment to the students is visible once again. With Andy and Natalie's help the ELs have built a paper maché *mojigangas* of a bird representing the school mascot. This consists of a giant torso that is placed on a person's shoulder so the individual walks around with the *mojiigangas* balanced on the head and shoulders. Students of all backgrounds are following a Mexican tradition that contributes to the school spirit and validates who they are. They are an integral part of the assembly as they proudly share a cultural practice of celebration.

IMPLICATIONS FROM THE MATH WORKSHOP

The ELs' test scores improve in the math workshop because Andy and Natalie position the students to succeed. Everyone works hard! The coach warms up the team with the help of the catcher and no players are allowed to sit on the bench. First, the workshop becomes a familiar and predictable set of routines that focus on math and language. Second, the students' responsibilities for learning are clear to them. The team engages in simultaneous whole and small group work as they work through examples that are relevant to their lives. Third, concepts are introduced by the teacher, and then examined with ongoing comprehension checks by all members of the team. During the workshop the ELs do not hesitate to offer answers and feel safe to admit that they do not understand.

An important factor in the improved test scores is reflected in the students' acclaim for their teacher as a person who cares. They tell me "It is okay to get the answer wrong." They share that Andy teaches math like no other teacher they ever had. Over and over I hear references to the way he relates to them. Nena says, "He tells us stories. He talks to us." Ana adds, "He compares our lives to his." Luisa comments, "He explains math different." Angel shares, "We like it when he gives his talks." Antonio and his buddies agree that, "In classes before we didn't understand the questions." Elena tells me "I don't know why but I understand more in this class. He just explains it right." (All names are pseudonyms.)

RECOMMENDATIONS FOR ACTION

In your work, keep in mind how Andy and Natalie consider the sociocultural context of learning and who the students are as people. Teach math terms after you model ways to come to understand the underlying concepts using everyday words. Implement classroom routines that require students to complete tasks using the forms and meaning of words as used in math to analyze, prepare, and justify procedural descriptions and solutions (Donovan & Bransford, 2005; Khisty, 2009). Teach students to look for the organizational signals that are typically used in presenting math problems. This will become the process your ELs follow as they read and analyze questions. Feeling secure about how they think and learn will help the ELs develop the arguments they need to succeed at thinking abstractly in math.

The following suggestions framed from my observations of Andy's classroom will be useful to you as you work to provide an equitable and appropriate instructional paradigm that assures academic success for your ELs:

1. Investigate students' funds of knowledge and identify their cultural capital so that you can provide appropriate examples within your instruction that make sense to them.
2. Seek to understand students' thought processes and how they are interpreting your words. Ask yourself: How is culture shaping their notions? Make certain your students feel free to examine and critique what they are learning, and to tell you when anything in a question or an explanation is not comprehensible.
3. Uncover what students know and provide bridges to understanding. Always look to find out what they know and may not be revealing to you.
4. Make your classroom a welcoming environment for all students. Enroll students and their families in your vision of the ELs' academic success. Help your students look to the future and to what education can gain for them.
5. Teach prereading strategies for a mathematical context. Keep in mind what NCTM tells us is required to complete a mathematical task. Always remember that with ELs you are both a content area teacher and a language broker.
6. Plan lessons that consider the ELs are learning new concepts and address the language needed to understand these. Use everyday language to introduce academic language. Scaffold concepts in lessons and activities after identifying the language the ELs will need to understand what you are teaching.
7. Encourage and accept use of the ELs' home language when needed for clarifying the concepts of lessons. Examine what your ELs are doing to learn math and English.

8. Teach students to deconstruct and construct the language of the math problems until they understand the question being asked. Help them take on the challenge!

9. Supplement and modify written text for the ELs by using culturally sensitive sheltered English, charts, pictures, glosses, and word banks. Once you prepare these, ask your ELs to examine them to be sure everything is accessible to them with their level of English.

10. Prepare and share summaries of the key points in the day's lesson. Consider doing this as Andy does in the anticipatory set. Remember that the ELs must understand the language to grasp the math concepts.

11. Decorate your classroom with illustrated math word walls prepared by the students. Remind them to refer to what is on the walls such as formulas for calculating the area and the slope.

12. Engage ELs in tasks they will understand and that have a purpose that is visible to them beyond the classroom context. Talk with students about the possibility of future careers in math and science.

13. Make sure formative math exams are not tests of English.

14. Prepare the ELs for summative evaluations such as achievement tests. Let them know the evaluations will test their English and math competencies. Enroll students in the task of turning the school house into an equitable environment. Teach them to advocate for themselves.

15. Address all language domains in the classroom; ask the ELs to listen, read, write, and speak. Engage students in conversations that will help them build connections and thus internalize concepts.

16. Require the ELs use the language you are using to teach to explain and justify their answers. Once you are sure they understand both the language and the content, hold the same expectations of success for them that you hold for all students.

17. Share with students their responsibilities in the learning and establish routines that will help them develop metacognitive skills. If they walk away from your class ready to guide their learning, you will have given them a great gift.

RESOURCES

- The website of the National Council of Teachers of Mathematics offers valuable information to guide teachers to plan instruction aligned to twenty-first-century skills: http://nctm.org.
- To find information on how students are expected to show their knowledge, consult PAARC at http://www.parcconline.org.

- To jump start your lesson planning, go to **PBS** at http://www.pbs.org/teachers/math/.
- If you want to invite your students' families to join you in their children's math experiences, look up www.nctm.org/resources/families.
- Just as the name suggests, investigate this great website: http://www.math-isfun.org/great-math-websites-for-teachers.
- Make sure your ELs are able to integrate technology to their advantage. Refer to_http://www.educatorstechnology.com/2014/01/20-great-math-websites-for-teachers-and.htm.

NOTE

1. In our conversation I will use the term ELs to encompass students who are working to learn math in a language that is not their native language in the United States and in other countries. I am doing so because the acronym ELs is short and not because second learners throughout the world are all learning in English. I believe my observations related to how Andy creates a positive classroom climate, and the ways his pedagogy addresses the language needed to understand math concepts is useful information for all teachers, regardless of the geographic location where they work.

Chapter 4

Using Art and Literature to Enhance Critical Thinking and Vocabulary Development for English Learners

Chris Carger

In this chapter, I share a success story involving the use of Reaching Out through Art and Reading (ROAR), aimed at advancing university students' instructional practices, and improving English language students' language and literacy achievement outcomes.

To the background sounds of voices whispering, "They're here!, están aquí!" and the sounds of papers and books being hastily shoved into desks, half a dozen college students enter a second grade classroom full of excited bilingual children. A little girl runs up to one college student and hugs her so hard she almost loses her balance; a little boy proudly shows his Spiderman drawing to one of the male college students. This is a typical scene in Brookside Elementary School's bilingual program on Wednesday afternoons when project ROAR arrives. ROAR is a service learning outreach program initiated by the Literacy Department of Northern Illinois University (NIU). The premise of a service learning course is to provide interaction and support for the community while earning college credits in a course that integrates theory and hands-on experiences.

In over thirty years of working with Latino English Learners (ELs), I have observed many classroom teachers look to phonics as the solution to improving the literacy skills of the growing numbers of elementary school children in the United States whose home language is not English. I have witnessed an over reliance in phonics to produce ELs who are "word callers" that laboriously decode with little meaning or sense of enjoyment attached to the texts with which they struggle. Children's literature, multicultural or mainstream, is rarely included in the ELs' curricula unless they are fortunate enough to have a reading basal series that integrates it. Emphasis on phonics in reading instruction for ELs often consumes teacher time and book discussions are typically cut out of their curriculum (Triplett & Buchanan, 2005).

Comprehension questions take the form of literal understandings, the who, what, where, when and how of things. It is often assumed that ELs cannot handle higher-level thinking because of their language limitations (Lau, 2012) so inferential and critical levels of thinking are not addressed. Latinos' historic lack of power and voice within the United States also contributes to a lack of confidence that Latino children can handle critical thinking in academic contexts (Mendoza & Garcia, 2010). These same attitudes also restrict ELs of other minority cultural backgrounds as language proficiency becomes equated with cognitive ability. The words of art educator Elliot Eisner (2000), "The limits of our language do not define the limits of our cognition," are especially applicable to ELs.

When I decided to initiate a service learning course that would center on helping young ELs develop their English vocabulary and reading comprehension at the university where I teach, I knew that I wanted to use interactive read-alouds of children's literature as the centerpiece of the program ROAR. Over the past thirty-five years, several researchers have suggested that the way read-alouds are conducted affects the many benefits they can yield. When done in an interactive manner and children are asked open-ended questions linked to the book, read-alouds can have a greater impact on vocabulary growth and expressive language (Beck & McKeown, 2001; Heath, 1983; Whitehurst et al., 1988). I envisioned teaching preservice teachers in my college classes how to encourage such interaction with ELs as they read aloud to them.

I also knew that I wanted to use art as another form of communication for ELs rather than emphasizing only verbal and print systems of language. Through using art and literature, I hoped to reach higher levels of thinking skills with the ELs rather than emphasizing basic skills. In addition, as technology developed over the years, I wanted to integrate visual literacy using the classroom computers and projectors. And finally, I wanted to teach the preservice early childhood and elementary program college students who delivered the ROAR project not to ignore or negate their young students' native-language abilities and cultural connections while they endeavored to teach them English.

RESEARCH AND THEORY

I had once overheard an entire cohort of preservice teachers at my university lamenting the fact that they had been placed in a school with a high Latino EL population. "Those kids are just lazy," I heard a young woman proclaim and her peers agreed. "They just lay their heads down on their desks in the afternoon," this student continued. When I had that group for a workshop

I supervised, I knew I had my work cut out for me. We talked about the model used by the district for their ELs which was a "sink or swim" English as a second language emersion approach. We talked about how tiring trying to listen and learn for hours in your non-native language each day could be. We viewed videos of dual language classes and read a research article about the efficacy of using the first language as the new language is acquired. But I realized that this was a Band-Aid remedy at best for the linguistic bias I had discovered. This led to my design of a service learning style course in which preservice teachers would actually experience working closely with a small group of ELs in an elementary school setting. Most of the preservice teachers in our early childhood and elementary education programs do not include diversity but follow the common trend in the United States of having mainstream teachers instruct diverse students. Less than one-sixth of college preservice teacher education programs include working with ELs (Ballantyne, Sanderman, & Levy, 2008). As a preservice teacher in the early seventies, I had the advantage of having witnessed a lively history of 1960s activism which birthed the service learning movement in higher education. Dedicated high school teachers of mine initiated service learning programs which I participated in, tutoring after school hours in urban community centers in northern New Jersey, a stone's throw from New York City. Service learning, when linked to multicultural education, allowed me to engage my students in community activities and place curricular concepts in the context of real life (O'Grady, 2012). For example, multicultural education classes often cover the concept of the differences between social language and academic language for ELs. For years, referred to as Basic Interpersonal Communication Skills (BICS) and Cognitive Academic Language Proficiency (CALP) (Cummins, 2000), this is a fundamental linguistic distinction that teachers of bilingual students need to understand. Through ROAR, that concept comes to life for preservice teachers who experience firsthand the ability of their young students to converse with them about hot topics in their classroom from Angry Birds games to soccer matches and what they're having for lunch. But when faced with understanding the vocabulary in a grade level nonfiction book on life cycles of a frog, they stumble over the content-specific words and even sight words they need for good comprehension of basic science concepts linked to their curriculum. The abstract idea of BICS and CALP become palpable to the preservice teachers. College students come to more subtle realizations as well. In their journals I have been touched by reflections they have made about the concern they have heard when a child confides in them that their parent is losing a job or that their father has to work two jobs and they miss him. There were times I felt I saw prejudice being deconstructed right before my eyes. A female student with long blond hair wrote that her third grade African American/Latina student asked if she could touch her hair because she had never seen blond hair "up close" before. She responded that she could and that she had never touched hair like hers either. In another instance, the college tutors had to walk through the cafeteria to get to a small room where they could eat their own bag lunches and the class they had just read stories to, spontaneously stood up as they passed and applauded. These are powerful experiences that I am convinced lead to authentic educational growth. Many ROAR tutors decide to apply for teaching positions in districts where they can work with ELs after participating in the ROAR project.

The ROAR project grew planted in a constructivist philosophy in the fertile soil of children's literature, with the tools that art and technology provide using the valuable resources afforded by the university, namely preservice teachers and literacy materials. I looked to Elliot Eisner and Maxine Greene, two preeminent educational researchers who wholeheartedly recommended the inclusion of the arts in a students' curricula, as I designed the project. The work of Karen Ernst (1994), Karen Gallas (1994, 2003), Barbara Kiefer (1995), and Short, Kauffman, and Kahn (2000) affirmed the integration of the visual arts and language arts as complementary partners in meaning-making and understanding the world. For Gallas (1994), linking art to literacy activities offered more than disembodied lessons on technique, media, or art history. Like Ernst, she saw art as "a creative process to offer children broad avenues for expression and understanding," in the language arts as well as in other content areas (Gallas, 1994, p. 112). Using not only the visual arts, but also multiple sign systems, Short et al. (2000) found that art, music, math, drama, and movement provided "multiple perspectives and points of connection that enriched students' talk about literature" (p. 160).

Why then, I wondered, don't teachers use art to support ELs as they acquire their new language? Greene and Eisner wrote about the importance of "aesthetics" in making meaning. Albers and Harste (2007) believed that "we are likely to read, feel, understand and discuss more each time we read art" (p. 11). Why not apply these ideas to ELs as well as mainstream language arts instruction? Though the research is sparse, I had conducted a study of my own on using art with second through fifth grade urban ELs (Carger, 2004). Results indicated that art could offer ELs alternative routes of self-expression and often provided a springboard into book discussions. Cloud, Genesee, and Hamayan (2009) highly recommend art and visual literacy development for use with ELs because they afford them additional avenues into communication and literacy. Hadaway, Vardell, and Young (2002) briefly discuss the value of including the visual arts in ELs' curricula in their book which concentrated on the use of children's literature with ELs. It seemed to make sense to me given the importance of visual images in the twenty-first century and the motivational benefits I had observed firsthand when art was integrated into a language lesson.

PRACTICAL APPLICATIONS

ROAR places preservice teachers in bilingual first through fourth grade class-rooms that desire to participate in the project. ROAR has serviced inner city and very economically challenged schools in Chicago as well as suburban and semirural schools in Midwestern towns where farming and food packing dominate the employment opportunities of many bilingual families. In each school setting the classroom teachers work with the project in deciding which themes they would like to integrate with the children's literature that is selected, in grouping the bilingual students, and giving feedback to the pre-service teachers on their lessons. In many of the districts ROAR has included, there is a transitional bilingual program that terminates after fifth grade. ROAR's cooperating teachers have all expressed their support for the project to develop vocabulary in English for the bilingual students in their care who they know will be contending with all English classes at some point in the near future. The cooperating teachers also feel that reading aloud is often overlooked because of time constraints and core curricula demands. Because art time has been cut back or nonexistent in the districts ROAR has served, the teachers enjoy the opportunities afforded their students in that area of the curriculum as well.

ROAR's emphasis on vocabulary development for ELs is well supported by many researchers (August, Carlo, Dressler & Snow, 2005; Graves, 2006; Wallace, 2007). Vocabulary knowledge is strongly related to reading com-prehension and school achievement in general (Beck, McKeown, & Kucan, 2002, p. 1). Storybook reading has been cited as "the most powerful source of new vocabulary, including those academic words that are valued in school discourse. Books are literally where the words are" (Stahl & Stahl, 2004, p. 67). Therefore, I decided, ROAR would find its target words from the children's literature that the college students would read aloud to elementary school-aged ELs. Several target words would be selected for each children's book using the Beck, McKeown, and Kucan (2003) tier method which categorizes words as known, somewhat familiar, and completely unknown, novel words. For example, *flower* might be considered a tier one, commonly known word; *blossom* might be a tier two word that is somewhat familiar but a bit more precise; and *germinate*, a less common word that is more specific and technical would fall into the third tier. It is also important to consider the frequency and utility of vocabulary words to emphasize. For example, *between*, a sight word frequently encountered in reading, might be a useful target word to include. Cognates, words that are very similar in spelling and meaning across two languages, are included in target word lists. Native-language skills should always be welcomed when teaching literacy skills in English. By relating instruction for ELs to what is familiar it allows them to make sense of it and to acquire new skills and knowledge more quickly (Cloud, Genesse, & Hamayan, 2009).

In order to acquire a new vocabulary word, research has informed teachers for many years that students need to hear and use it approximately seven to twelve times (Stahl, 1986). In ROAR sessions, college tutors present the target words through direct instruction with flashcards that have a visual image of the word on one side and the printed word on the other side. They then discuss a comprehensible meaning for the word. The tutors work on generating easily understood explanations for words, avoiding the terse, often confusing dictionary-type definitions. Tutors also facilitate a vocabulary game using the target words. Bingo cards are created, concentration matching games, simple game boards featuring spaces with new vocabulary words printed or pictured, or Smart Board games are used to provide vocabulary practice. Words are recycled through these games from week to week. The target words are heard again in the context of the literature being read aloud. ELs are asked to raise a quiet hand to indicate when they've heard one of their target words in the read-aloud. Before, during, and after the read aloud activity, ELs are encouraged to interact with the text through questions prepared by the tutors who, once again, integrate new vocabulary into the book discussion. Finally, during the art project or visual thinking strategies portion of the lesson tutors are taught to slip in the use of target vocabulary as much as possible. These activities expose ELs to definitional and contextual practice for a manageable amount of new vocabulary words that are recycled.

After vocabulary is presented and practiced, the children's literature is read aloud and discussed, and the art portion of the lesson is facilitated in ROAR sessions. Art may take the form of a culturally relevant, hands-on art project, the introduction of art techniques or media inspired by book illustrations, or a methodology called Visual Thinking Strategies (VTS) which uses questions to lead children to note and comment on art in detail. For example, after hearing the book *Diego Rivera: His World and Ours* (Tonatiuh, 2011), which described the early life of Mexican painter Diego Rivera, ROAR's second graders designed and created a mural for their classroom. They used craypas as the medium, an art material that was new to them. In third grade, ELs responded to questions about prints of two of Rivera's murals using the VTS method. With open-ended questions such as, "What's going on in this picture?" a teacher can encourage a conversation about a book illustration. By repeating and confirming comments back to the class, a teacher can allow students to control the discussion with their genuine responses to the art work.

Using the book, *Biblioburro* (Winter, 2010). ROAR tutors selected the target words: jungles, crates, reins, bandit, borrowed. Within that list, reins (*reindas*) and bandit (*bandido*) are cognates whose similarities in English and Spanish were explicitly pointed out. Burro was not selected as a target word because it is exactly the same in English and Spanish and easy to visualize in the book. *Biblioburro* tells the true story of Luis Soriano, a Columbian man who brings books to remote jungle villages in his country to lend to children who have no library access. He straps the books to two burros named Alfa and Beto. This book allowed us to integrate visual images through technology because there is a YouTube clip showing the real Luis and his moving library that is narrated in Spanish. The second graders were mesmerized by this YouTube which was shown before the book was read-aloud to them. It served several purposes. It demonstrated the value that tutors gave the ELs' native language. It also gave the students the support of hearing about the subject matter of the story in their native language before hearing it in English and it helped them to see that a book can tell a nonfiction, real life story. New Common Core State Standards (CCSS) emphasize the use of nonfiction in primary grades. Nonfiction is considered especially helpful for building content-specific vocabulary, expanding background knowledge, and increasing students' familiarity with expository text styles (Hickman & Pollard-Durodola, 2009).

The vocabulary game for *Biblioburro* was designed for the Smart Board which each ROAR class has in their rooms. Smart Board software contains templates for vocabulary games. Tutors can choose a template and input the vocabulary and meaning information in print or with pictures very easily, hand-tailoring the game to their students' developmental levels and their target words.

After *Biblioburro* was read aloud, ELs were guided with oral questions that moved them from literal to inferential and critical levels of thinking. Literal level questions like, "What did Luis decide to do with his many books?" and" Where did he bring his books?" start our discussion. They are followed with inferential questions such as, "Why do you think Luis named his burros Alfa and Beto?" and "Which story do you think Luis read to the children as they wore pig masks?" Answers to inferential questions cannot be found word-for-word in the text but need students to combine what they've heard or seen in the book with some of their own background knowledge in order to respond. Finally, ELs were asked if they would risk being stopped by bandits to deliver books to children and if they thought it was a town's responsibility to provide a library for its children. These questions engaged children in critical thinking which involved reflection, judgment, opinion, and/or connections between text and real life experiences. It is extremely important to give ELs the opportunity to go beyond parroting facts from text to thinking about their responses more deeply. Students tend to answer based upon the kinds of questions they expect from the teacher. Their English language limitations should not infer a lack of intellectual ability and relegate them only to basic, literal questioning. In ROAR, we have found that the more our tutors follow this progression of literal to inferential to critical levels of questioning, the better our ELs are able to express critical, complex thought.

A worksheet I use in our ROAR seminars (see table 4.1) is very helpful to tutors who themselves did not receive much practice in answering anything but literal questions about literature shared with or read by them.

For the last part of the ROAR session, the college tutors moved into the facilitation of the art portion of the session. Because most of our ELs are of Mexican origin, we decided to try a particularly culturally relevant craft called tin art seen commonly in ornaments, mirrors, and frames from that country. Many jungle animals were depicted in *Biblioburro* which gave our young students the perfect subject for their tin art. Reasonably priced, thin aluminum sheets were purchased from an art supply catalog. Impressions can be made on these sheets with the blunted point of a pencil and they can be easily cut with scissors. Permanent markers can be used to color in features on the sheets. Again, the computer was used to show students examples of tin art ornaments in shapes of animals. Our ROAR students rate the books and art projects they experience on a Likert Scale which uses smile faces in the fashion of the Garfield Scale that uses Garfield the Cat faces. *Biblioburro* and tin art were unanimously ranked in the highest categories on the scales by the ELs.

Another very successful ROAR session was based on the book, *The Pot That Juan Built* (Andrews-Goebel, 2002). This book mixes genres and tells the true story of Juan Quezada in a cumulative poem that mirrors the structure of the old English rhyme, "The House That Jack Built," on one side of the

Table 4.1   Examples of Lower and Higher Levels of Questioning

Lower-Level Thinking Skills Required	*Higher-Level Thinking Skills Required*
What are laws?	Can you imagine what life would be like with no laws?
Can you name a type of saltwater fish we saw in the book?	What do you think would happen if we put a saltwater fish in a tank of fresh water?
How many people are there worldwide?	If our population keeps growing, what do you suppose life will be like in the twenty-second century?
After reading *The Empty Pot*, what kind of plants did the children bring to show the emperor?	Do you think the children were justified in putting plants in the pots the emperor gave them?
After reading *DIRT*, what is found in dirt that is necessary for plants?	What do you think people can do to grow food plants in places that have no dirt?
After reading *Smoky Night*, list what happened to stores during the riots.	Do you think it is okay to take things from a store that was broken into? Do you think people have the right to riot?

page with the nonfiction, expository account of Juan's accomplishments on the opposite side. It is available in English and Spanish and a bilingual edition. Juan Quezada revived the failing economy of his rural Mexican town by starting a pottery business that used natural, traditional materials to create paints and vessels. He employed local artisans to etch distinctive decorations into the pots. The college tutors found beautiful images of Juan's pots on the Internet and shared them with their third grade students to build background knowledge before the art portion of the session took place. This book provided the perfect introduction to sculpting clay for our ELs who had not experienced using this art medium. Air-dry clay was purchased because it is easy to handle and can be colored or painted on the same day it is sculpted. College students learned how to direct their groups in making pinch pots and coil pots. This project and book also received unanimously high ratings on the Likert-type scales the students completed with written comments like, "I love clay!!! I love it, I love it, I love it!"

In the posttests administered by the college tutors, simple matching exercises using print and pictures, vocabulary scores improved by a higher percentage for the books we supplemented with computer images, either pictures or videos. Multimodalities appeared to have provided varied representations that assisted ELs in comprehending novel vocabulary. We have also noted in our assessment data that books with culturally relevant topics typically yield higher vocabulary scores from our ELs.

In fact, the selection of the children's literature is of key importance in the success of ROAR sessions. As mentioned earlier, we strive to use both narrative and nonfiction, genres of books. For many ELs, the traditional read-aloud event is something that takes place only at school or in a library setting, if at all. Lack of books, fears about immigration status and the use of a public library, the financial necessity of working double shifts and jobs, and language and literacy barriers are just some of the real issues with which bilingual parents struggle when it comes to sharing books with their children at home. I have also noticed the use of oral storytelling and poetry sharing in some bilingual families, which provides a rich alternative to the read-aloud for some children.

RECOMMENDATIONS FOR ACTION AND RESOURCES

I search for culturally relevant books because I want our ELs to make text-to-self and text-to-world connections growing out of their background experiences. I also look for traditional tales and rhymes for our Latino population. Three anthologies of poetry for young children collected by Alma Flor Ada and F. Isabel Campoy that are very popular with Latino bilingual children are *Mamá Goose: A Latino Nursery Treasury* (2005), *Pío Peep: Traditional Spanish Nursery Rhymes* (2003), and *¡Muu,Moo! Rimas de Animales/Animal Nursery Rhymes* (2010). We have found that our young students are frequently familiar with the rhymes, lullabies, and riddles which are colorfully illustrated in these collections and chant them while playing games on the playground. They provide nice ice breakers or transitional activities during ROAR sessions for our youngest ELs. The text is written in Spanish with a thoughtful English translation that captures the playful sense of the poetry rather than trying to translate it word for word. *Pío Peep* has a CD version available as well (2006).

A traditional tale we have found very engaging in ROAR is *Prietita and the Ghost Woman/Prietita y la Llorona* (Bilingual edition, 2014). Many Latino ELs are familiar with the legend of the "crying woman," la Llorona, who provides a cautionary tale to deter children from straying away from their families. In Anzaldua's version, however, the Llorona is depicted as being helpful to a young girl who is searching for an herbal remedy for her sick mother. Wonderful critical levels of discussion have emerged debating whether or not the Llorona, who in many versions of the tale murders children, would ever be helpful.

Two children's book award lists are particularly helpful in finding books that are of distinctive literary quality and culturally relevant for Latino bilingual students, the Pura Belpré Award (www.ala.org/alsc/awardsgrants/book-media/Belpremedal/) and the Américas Book Award for Children and Young Adults (www4.uwm.edu/clacs/aa/). Both awards were initiated in 1996 and are given to authors and illustrators who authentically and engagingly portray Latino and Latino American experiences in works of literature for children and young adults. Authors must be of Latino heritage to receive the Pura Belpré Award; books also must be considered to have exceptional potential for classroom use to win the Américas Award.

Another two book awards used to select ROAR materials are the Jane Addams Children's Book Award (www.janeaddamspeace.org/jacba/) and the Notable Social Studies Trade Books for Young People list (www.social-studies.org/resource/notable). Jane Addams' award books actively promote peace, social justice, world community, and equality of the sexes. They are frequently wonderful books to engage students in higher-level thinking about substantive yet comprehensible issues. One of the Jane Addams winners that engendered good critical thought in a ROAR session was *Nasreen's Secret School: A True Story from Afghanistan* (Winter, 2010), which told the story of girls' struggles to be educated despite the Taliban's taboo on female schooling. Boys in the village helped to hide the girls' forbidden activity and ROAR students pondered how they would have handled the situation and what risks they would have been willing to take. This year's Jane Addams

Awards noted another book on this topic, *Razia's Ray of Hope: One Girl's Dream of an Education* (Suneby, 2013). Notable Social Studies Trade Books for Young People are categorized into several areas that range from racial and cultural to environmental issues. The Notable choice, *¡Sí, Se Puede!/Yes. We Can!: Janitor Strike in L.A.* (Cohn, 2005), demonstrated that our ELs had background experiences that helped them to fully understand the necessity for laborers to stand together and strike for fair living wages. Many of our third and fourth graders spoke of their own parents' need to work multiple jobs as seen in this story, just to be able to provide basic food and shelter for their families. Expressing opinions about such injustices gave our ELs authentic purposes for wanting to communicate meaningfully about a topic they genuinely cared about despite language limitations. As an art project, the third and fourth graders designed picket signs that could have been carried by the janitors.

The CCSS speak specifically to vocabulary expectations in content areas (Fisher & Frey, 2014). The bilingual cooperating teachers working with ROAR are concerned with their students' performance in this area as it affects so many subjects. The Notable list is also helpful as we connect to content area topics across primary grade levels we serve in ROAR. It leads us to high-quality nonfiction books that exemplify themes submitted by the cooperating teachers such as community, cooperation, and environmental adaptation. We have also found many engaging biographies, a genre always covered in our third and fourth grade ELs' curricula. Instead of formulaic, outdated biographical series books found in so many school and public libraries, the notable list provides fresh and original biographies in creative formats with stunning art work. We find a better representation of women and cultural diversity in the subjects of notable biography awards such as the books *Me . . . Jane* (McDonnell, 2011), which relates the story of scientist Jane Goodall and *Pablo Neruda: A Poet of the People* (Brown, 2011), which relates the early life of the Chilean Nobel Award winner.

CHILDREN'S BOOKS CITED

Ada, A. F., & Campoy, F. I. (2003). *¡Pío Peep! Book and CD.* New York: Rayo. Traditional Spanish language poems and songs for young children with sensible English translations.

Ada, A. F., & Campoy, F. I. (2005). *Mamá Goose: A Latino nursery treasure.* Bilingual edition. New York: Hyperion Books. Lullabies, rhymes, riddles and more from Spanish-speaking sources for young children.

Ada, A. F., & Campoy, F. I. (2010). *¡Muu,Moo! Rimas de animals/Animal nursery thymes.* Bilingual edition. New York: Rayo. This book presents a collection of animal rhymes from the Spanish-speaking world.

Andrews-Goebel, N. (2011). *The pot that Juan built.* New York: Lee & Low Books. A cumulative poem describes the process of pottery making in a small Mexican village on one side of the page and gives nonfiction facts about the home grown industry on the opposite page.

Anzaldúa, G. (2014). *Prietita and the ghost woman/ Prietita y la llorona.* Bilingual edition. San Francisco, CA: Children's Book Press.

Brown, M. (2011). *Pablo Neruda: Poet of the people.* New York: Henry Holt. A lyrical biography of the famous Chilean poet.

Bunting, E. (1999). *Smokey Night.* New York: HMH Books for Young Readers. After the L.A. riots, a young boy, his mother, and their pet attempt to reestablish their lives and live in harmony with their neighbors.

Cohn, D. C. (2005). ¡Sí, *se puede!/ Yes, we can!: Janitor strike in LA.* El Paso, TX: Cinco Puntos Press. A young boy tries to understand what his single mother is going through as she joins a protest for better pay from her employers.

Demi. (1996). *The empty pot.* New York: Square fish. The emperor devises a test to find a worthy heir to the throne and succeeds in finding one honest child.

McDonnell, P. (2011). *Me . . . Jane.* New York: Little, Brown Books for Young Readers. A beginning biography of scientist-activist Jane Goodall explains some of her life's work with animals and the environment.

Suneby, E. (2013). *Razia's ray of hope: One girl's dream of an education.* Toronto: Kids Can Press. The story of a girl in Afghanistan who hopes to convince her family to allow her to attend a girl's school.

Tomecek, S. (2007). *DIRT (Jump into Science Series).* Des Moines, IA: National Geographic Children's Books. An informational book about soil and dirt which encourages conservation awareness.

Tonatiuh, D. (2011). *Diego Rivera: His world and ours.* New York: Harry N. Abrams. An introduction to the art work of muralist Diego Rivera that poses questions for modern day children to think about regarding art.

Winter, J. (2009). *Nasreen's secret school: A true story from Afghanistan.* New York: Beach Lane Books. A young girl copes with the loss of her parents and is encouraged to continue her education despite the Taliban's opposition to female school attendance.

Winter, J. (2010). *Biblioburro.* New York: Beach Lane Books. Based on a true story, this book relates the story of Luis Soriano who supplies children in remote Columbian villages with books he delivers by mule.

Chapter 5

The Case for Young Adult Literature

Using Narratives in the English Learner Classroom

Melanie D. Koss

In this chapter, I address the contribution of young adult (YA) literature to adolescent English learners' (ELs') reading experience and then provide useful resources for teachers and students.

> Because [works of young adult literature] are about adolescents and for adolescents they put students at the center of the learning experiences we devise. (Salvner, 2000, pp. 96–97)

Reading can be an enjoyable pastime, and reading increases literacy skills, so encouraging teens to read and finding appropriate reading materials for them is of key importance. Reading for pleasure is one of the best ways to increase literacy (e.g., Brown, 2007; Guthrie & Wigfield, 2000), as reading promotes increased language skills including vocabulary (e.g., Brown, Waring, & Donkaewbua, 2008; Frantzen, 2002), grammar (e.g., Hall, 2005; Tayebipour, 2009), fluency (e.g., Allington, 2007), comprehension (e.g., Guthrie et al., 2004; Herz & Gallo, 2005), critical thinking (e.g., Stover, 2001), and writing (e.g., Parkinson & Reid Thomas, 2000). It also helps teens figure out their wider world and their place in it, as developmentally they are exploring their identities and in the midst of rapid and significant physical, intellectual, and emotional change (Caskey & Anfara, 2007). So, the more teens read the more they learn. The question is, what engaging and interesting texts do teens enjoy reading?

Educators play a crucial role in developing students' attitudes toward reading and of influencing their levels of motivation to read (Ryan & Patrick, 2001; Taylor, Pearson, Peterson, & Rodriguez, 2003). Students who are positively motivated to read are more likely to engage in reading activities because they believe in their abilities to succeed with the skills they possess

(Guthrie et al., 2004). The engaged reader is confident, metacognitive, and understands how reading impacts learning. They are motivated to read by personal goals and interests, knowledgeable regarding what they read, and strategic when comprehending (Guthrie, McGough, Bennett, & Rice, 1996).

Fostering reading motivation is critical for ELs (Cummins, 2003) who are not only reading for enjoyment, but also to learn the English language. One way to get EL teens to read more is to expose them to books that interest them and connect to their lives and needs. Cultural and background knowledge play an important role in an ELs' understanding of reading selections (Peregoy & Boyle, 2015). One challenge for ELs is that in school they may deal with literary texts that have unfamiliar topics and do not value or capitalize on their cultural norms (Peregoy & Boyle, 2015). Also, the reading materials often found in EL classrooms are explanatory articles that do not capture ELs attention and are not emotionally and topically relevant (Lillie, Markos, Arias, & Wiley, 2012; Miller, 2001). This dichotomy may negatively impact adolescent ELs ability to make meaning of a text. YA literature offers a vastly different reading experience.

"There has been an increasing awareness of the significance of integrating literature in EFL/ESL curriculum" (Amer, 2003, p. 63), as ELs thrive in classrooms containing language-rich literacy instruction (Herrera, Perez, & Escamilla, 2010; Ogle & Correa-Kovtun, 2010; Peregoy & Boyle, 2013; Reiss, 2012; Shanahan & Beck, 2006). Students need a wide range of reading materials available at their instructional or independent reading level (Allington, 2007), as well as literature that is interesting and engaging to them. YA literature encompasses a wide variety of high-interest topics and genres, and can be found at a range of reading levels, making it a rich venue of text to explore.

WHY YA LITERATURE?

In the broadest sense, YA literature is literature published and marketed to readers between the approximate ages of twelve and eighteen. They often have adolescent protagonists and tackle issues on the experiences and explorations typical of that age level, making them relatable to adolescent students. According to Langer (1997), literature is inviting for ELs "because it taps into what they know and who they are" (p. 607). This aligns with Rosenblatt's (1995) seminal transactional theory of reading that states that the transaction between a reader and a text capitalizes on one's personal background experiences and allows one to relate to characters and themes in an engaging, relevant, and meaningful way. Readers create meaning by reflecting on their own experiences. Using literature in the classroom offers a range of teaching opportunities to strengthen EL adolescents' learning. It encourages interaction and discussion, which can value each student's culture and lead to many language learning opportunities.

YA literature is approachable, accessible, and relatable. Because YA books are for young adults, students can identify with them more easily than they can identify with other literary genres. Teens prefer to read about other teens (Kelley, Wilson, & Koss, 2012), and YA literature often puts real-life situations in simple contexts and covers a wide variety of topics relevant to ELs' lives (Stover, 2001). YA literature also has engaging content. It has the potential to attract and hold the interest of adolescent ELs as they are developing their identities in relation to self and community (Watts, 1999).

Of particular significance for ELs, YA literature uses authentic adolescent language, which is often straightforward and easier to read than textbooks or older, more classic texts. It is often written using simple, modern English (Monseau, 2000), using a first-person point of view, with linear plots, and at an appropriate level for intermediate to low-advanced students while still being high-quality writing. It also often uses American colloquialisms, expressions, and slang, which affords an opportunity for ELs to learn American English as teens speak it.

YA literature provides cultural insight. For ELs who have recently moved to the United States and are learning about this country's culture, YA books provide insights to events and daily life occurrences familiar to teens, giving ELs a glimpse into their new country's behaviors. YA literature can show how a typical American teenager understands and acts with regard to certain life events, such as dating, participating in sports, or dealing with the gritty realities of life such as urban environments, drugs, gangs, and so on.

Importantly, YA literature, specifically multicultural literature, allows adolescents to see themselves in the books they read, which lets them feel valued. In her research, Rudine Sims Bishop (1992, 1990) posited that children and adolescents need to see themselves reflected in literature (i.e., look into a mirror), to see the lives of others (i.e., look into a window), and also see themselves being able to transverse between groups and worlds (i.e., passing through a sliding glass door). Bishop, in her research with Cai (1994), also stated the need for children's and YA books to reflect parallel cultures; different cultures need to be depicted and shown as equal, both in representation and portrayal. Multicultural YA literature values the lives of adolescents who read them (Meminger, 2011). Books that depict diverse characters from a variety of cultures and backgrounds allow students to begin to connect to all people, and to connect their personal sense of self to others they connect with. Seeing self is critical, but not seeing self is even more critical as adolescents may feel marginalized and not think of themselves as valued members of society (Landt, 2006; Susag, 1998).

It is imperative that teachers provide students with a broad array of literature that includes diverse perspectives as a way to offer all students visions of self in what they read, give students windows in to the world, and help break down barriers. When students encounter images and stories of characters similar to themselves they experience a sense of belonging and are able to connect to what they read. By including an abundance of literature depicting diverse perspectives, teachers open doors to awareness and understanding. (Landt, 2011, p. 1)

TWO ADDITIONAL YA FORMATS OF NOTE

In addition to YA trade literature, two additional novel formats are relevant for ELs: hi-lo books, and graphic novels.

Hi-Lo Books

Hi-lo books are high-interest, low-vocabulary texts. They come in a range of genres and levels and offer typically contemporary, interesting, and fast paced books that use sheltered language suitable for ELs. Quality hi-lo books feature strong, often culturally diverse protagonists that tend to be highly relatable to adolescent readers. They have linear, straightforward plots on topics relevant to early adolescents and older teens alike. Hi-lo books are published for different age levels and at different reading levels, and they are intentionally targeted for ELs and struggling readers with age-appropriate content.

Strengths of hi-lo books for ELs are that they have accessible vocabulary and sentence structure written at age level. They are also written with linear plots, without literary devices such as flashbacks, have minimal characters, and have clear contexts—elements that bring down the reading difficulty level without sacrificing high-interest content. They include authentic dialogue that mimics both contemporary YA novels and contemporary speech. And, they are often shorter texts with short chapters.

They are also intentionally designed to foster English and reading learning by utilizing larger white-space borders and less text on a page, larger spaces between lines of text, and larger text size. They are published with covers that appear similar to those of other YA literature mainstream titles, allowing ELs to read books that look age-appropriate and not like typical lower-level reader. Lastly, they are often published in series to allow students the ability to get invested in a world and set of characters' lives.

Graphic Novels

Graphic novels incorporate picture support with text, providing an extra layer of meaning utilizing additional comprehension strategies and encouraging

[handwritten in left margin: resources for next year]

visual literacy. Students who read graphic novels have been shown to better read and interpret gestures, facial expressions, cultural expressions and dress, and language patterns (Cary, 2004; Rudiger, 2006), in addition to other picture cues related to "visual grammar" (Cohn, 2014). Evidence suggests that readers exposed to graphic novels become better readers overall, and that graphic novels can serve as a "conduit to harder reading" (Krashen, 2005, p. 2) for struggling readers and ELs.

> The new popularity of Graphic Novels lends itself perfectly to becoming the new frontrunner for reading motivation. . . . Their eye-catching illustrations give contextual connections to the written text, making them perfect for remedial readers. They give confidence to frustrated readers with non-threatening, much needed practice and experience. This also leads to the reader's progress to more challenging text. (Heckman, 2004, pp. 3–4)

In addition, graphic novels often address critical issues in society such as racism, war, poverty, justice, inequality, and gender rights, topics of high interest to many adolescent readers, making them an essential component within YA literature.

RESOURCES FOR TEACHERS

Websites

Association of Library Service to Children (ALSC): http://ala.org/ala/mgrps/divs/alsc/compubs/booklists/growingupwrld/americas.pdf. A list of children's and young adult books about "Growing Up in the Americas." It provides a list of titles organized by country.

Children's Book Council Diversity Committee: www.cbcdiversity.com. Strives to increase the diversity of voices and experiences contributing to children's and YA literature. The website includes new items of note on diverse literature, opportunities to bring authors into the classroom, and book finding resources.

Children's Literature Web Guide: http://people.ucalgary.ca/~dkbrown/index.html. Offers links to children's and YA literature titles and descriptions, including award-winning titles, discussion boards, links to author websites, teacher resources, and children's literature organizations, publishers, and book sellers.

¡Colorín Colorado!: www.colorincolorado.org. A website focusing on the importance of reading for ELs with a focus on Latino children. It provides booklists, resources, family literacy tips, and video clips of Latino authors to share with students.

Cooperative Children's Book Center: http://ccbc.education.wisc.edu/ books/multicultural.asp; and http://ccbc.education.wisc.edu/books/graph-icnovelsasp. A noncirculating children's and YA literature collection based at the University of Wisconsin-Madison. Each year they publish booklists of titles of note, multicultural titles, and statistics on the number of multicultural books published for and by culturally diverse authors. They also provides information on graphic novels, including book lists and related websites.

Cynthia Leitich Smith's Children's and Young Adult Literature Resources: www.cynthialeitichsmith.com. Smith is a celebrated Native American author and advocate for the use of diverse books. This website is a wonderful resource for updated book lists, interviews with authors, and up-to-date discussions on current issues in diversity in children's and YA literature.

Diamond Bookshelf: www.diamondbookshelf.com. A graphic novel resource for educators and librarians. This site promotes the inclusion of graphic novels into a curriculum and provides information on the newest releases, interviews with authors and illustrators, book reviews, and lesson plans. It also provides core lists of graphic novels for a range of age groups, including kids, young adults, and older teens.

Diversity in YA: www.diversityinya.com and http://diversityinya.tumblr.com/. A blog focused on recent issues being discussed on the inclusion of diversity in YA literature publishing. A quality site for discovering multicultural book titles, as well as current news articles and publications relating to diverse children's and YA books.

Get Graphic: The World in Words and Pictures: www.getgraphic.org. A website focused on graphic novels for teachers and librarians. It provides lists of books, explanations on using graphic novels in classrooms, resource pages for teachers and librarians, and a blog on newly released titles and items of note within the graphic novel world.

¡Imagínense Libros!: Celebrating Latino Children's Literature, Literacy, and Libraries: http://imaginenselibros.blogspot.com/. This website provides a collection of Latino children's and YA literature that includes title information and teaching resources.

Print Resources

Book Bridges for ESL Students: Using Young Adult and Children's Literature to Teach ESL. **Suzanne Reid. 2002. Scarecrow Press.** A handbook accessible and easy to use by teachers. Includes book titles, teaching activities, suggested materials, lesson plans, and tips for selecting a variety of literature for use with ELs. Literature suggestions range from picture books for older readers through YA literature.

***Building Literacy Connections with Graphic Novels: Page by Page, Panel by Panel.* James Bucky Carter. 2007. National Council of Teachers of English.** Each chapter pairs a graphic novel with a traditional/classic text and examines the connections between them through a variety of practical activities. Using words and images, themes, language, and literary craft can be taught to readers of all levels. This book also provides an extensive appendix of additional graphic novel titles appropriate for use in middle and high school classrooms.

***Ethnic Book Awards: A Directory of Multicultural Literature for Young Readers.* Sherry York. 2005. Linworth Books.** This book is a solid resource for identifying book awards focused on diverse populations, as well as a straightforward annotated bibliography of award winners. Culturally specific populations targeted include African American, Caribbean, Latino, Jewish, and Asian American. This resource helps teachers find titles for diverse student populations.

Light 'N Lively Reads for ESL, Adult, and Teen Readers: A Thematic Bibliography. La Vergne Rosow. 2009. Libraries Unlimited. A unique annotated bibliography of high-interest/low-readability titles perfect for use with ELs. Of note is that this book includes fiction and nonfiction texts, including books, magazines, and letters, and is organized according to reading level. Also included are teaching activities focused on using literature with ELs.

***Teaching Graphic Novels: Practical Strategies for the Secondary ELA Classroom.* Katie Monnin. 2013. Maupin House.** A resource on how to effectively incorporate graphic novels into the classroom. Her focus is on capitalizing on the unique skills required for reading graphic novels and applying these to standards-based lesson plans on topics such as media literacy, comprehension, response to text (oral and written), and critical thinking. Numerous graphic novel titles are suggested and used as examples. Also provided are graphic organizer reproducibles and concrete lesson ideas for use with all graphic novels.

***Teaching YA Lit through Differentiated Instruction.* Susan L. Groenke & Lisa Scherff. 2010. National Council of Teachers of English.** Which YA titles are beneficial to bring into the classroom? Which are better for whole-group, small-group, or independent instruction? How can YA literature authentically be brought into the classroom to address the needs of diverse readers? These focal questions are concretely addressed and discussed in this text. Each chapter focuses on a specific genre of YA literature, and discusses ways to teach that genre through whole-group, small-group, and independent activities targeted to a range of learning levels. They include a list of titles, organized by genre, that are of high interest to teen readers.

Hi-Lo Series (High-Interest/Lower-Reading Level)

Bluford Series: http://bluford.org/. This series from Townsend Press centers on a group of high school students, their families, and the high school they attend. These high-interest/low-readability novels cross a range of genres and have a mix of male and female protagonists of different ethnic backgrounds. They're set in contemporary United States and contain edgy topics such as peer pressure, bullying, violence, family, trust, and friendship.

Darby Creek, an imprint of Lerner Books: www.lernerbooks.com. Contains a number of series for second grade through high school which cover a range of literary genres by popular authors, including fantasy, horror, humor, and realistic fiction, on topics of high interest to adolescent readers. The imprint also has a presence on Facebook, Twitter, Pinterest, and YouTube, encouraging readers to create social networking opportunities related to the books.

HIP (High Interest Publishing): www.hip-books.com. Publishes six hi-lo series targeted for students across different ages and interest levels. The website provides information about each series and contains teacher and parent resources. Series include: HIP Junior, novels for middle school students with contemporary problems and action-filled plots without romance or violence; BATS Mystery, a mystery series suitable for middle school readers; HIP Fantasy, two middle and high school appropriate fantasy series; HIP Xtreme, high-action survival stories appropriate for middle and high school readers; HIP Senior, contemporary stories for high school students; and HIP Edge, a gritty series that contains romance and violence following a group of high school students through their teen years.

Lorimer Children's and Teens Books for Reluctant Readers: www. lorimer.ca/childrens. Books for reluctant readers that are high-interest, action-driven, contemporary novels at a variety of accessible reading levels. They have different series, including SideStreets, Sports Stories, Amazing Stories Nonfiction, and Read Justice Nonfiction. The website has a searchable book finder according to age, grade, subject, gender, diversity, series, and format as well as free downloadable teacher resources that include whole-class, small-group, and independent reading activities incorporating response activities, language activities, and assessment materials.

Orca Books: www.orcabook.com. Numerous hi-lo series including Orca Currents (middle school fiction titles with contemporary themes) and Orca Soundings (targets teen readers).

Oxford Bookworms Library: www.oup.com/bookworms. EL leveled readers of classic titles adapted to six different English proficiency levels that consider vocabulary, grammar, and sentence structure.

Publishers of Multicultural and Bilingual Books

Arte Público Press: Piñata Books: https://artepublicopress.com. Piñata Books is the children's and YA imprint of Arte Público Press, a publisher that focuses on contemporary literature by U.S. Hispanic authors. Their mission is to publish books that authentically and realistically portray themes, characters, and customs unique to U.S. Hispanic culture.

Asia for Kids: www.afk.com. Publishes bilingual books and language learning materials with a primary focus on Chinese and other Asian/Asian Pacific cultures and languages.

Cinco Puntos Press: www.cincopuntos.com. An independent publisher focused on publishing books by and about the Southwestern United States and Hispanic populations. They publish fiction and nonfiction books for children and teens across texts types including picture books, chapter books, folktales, poetry, and graphic novels. Many of their books are bilingual in English and Spanish.

Lee and Low Books, Children's Book Press: www.leeandlow.com. An independent publisher that focuses on publishing children's and YA literature by and about underrepresented populations, specifically people of color.

Part II

USING ASSESSMENT DATA TO DOCUMENT STUDENT PERFORMANCE AND INFORM INSTRUCTION

Chapter 6

Using Metacognitive Assessments to Identify Students' Reading Comprehension Strengths and Needs

Kouider Mokhtari

This chapter describes a metacognitive assessment survey that teachers of English learners (ELs) can use to help identify students' reading comprehension strengths and needs. Teachers have an opportunity to learn how to administer the metacognitive assessment survey, how to interpret the results obtained, and how to use the assessment data obtained to inform reading instruction for ELs in middle school, high school, and college classrooms.

RATIONALE FOR ASSESSING STUDENTS' METACOGNITIVE AWARENESS AND USE OF READING STRATEGIES

When adolescent readers reach upper elementary and middle school grades, they are expected to have sufficiently adequate levels of reading proficiency that permit them to read to learn across the disciplines. However, the reality is that significant numbers of these students who are deemed literate simply do not read sufficiently well to meet the increasingly complex literacy demands of middle school, high school and college. In other words, many can read (i.e., decode words and sentences fluently), but have difficulties understanding what they read.

There are at least three main reasons why students (native and non-native speakers of English) encounter reading comprehension difficulties when they reach upper elementary and middle school grades.

First, when students make the transition to upper elementary and middle school grades, they are expected to *read different types of texts* ranging from narrative texts such as those found in language arts and literature classes to informational texts such as those found across different disciplines such as science, social studies, and mathematics. Oftentimes, students may lack background or world knowledge about the various topics, issues, and questions explored in informational texts found across the disciplines. In addition, they may not be aware of the ways in which information is organized in these two types of texts, and as a result they may have difficulties understanding and learning from these texts.

Second, in upper elementary grades including middle, high school, and college classes, students are expected to *read greater amounts or volumes of information* across the various disciplines. In these classes, they are often asked to *read more complex texts and engage on more complex tasks*. These tasks range from locating information about specific topics, issues, or questions using multiple text sources; summarizing information obtained from one or more texts; critically evaluating the credibility of information gathered, and communicating that information to others verbally, and in writing using various media.

Third, in upper and middle school grades, students' *levels of motivation and interest in reading and learning dramatically decrease*, in part because of the volumes of texts they are expected to read, the complexity of information they are expected to process, and the degree to which they have the skills and strategies to read and learn from these texts.

Finally, some of the students in these grades may have low levels of English language proficiency, which may prevent them from accessing and making sense of what they read. National report cards indicate that ELs have historically achieved lower levels of success on key academic achievement tests than their native-speaker peers, in part due to difficulties associated with reading, writing, and learning academic content in a new language. The 2007 NAEP report indicates that ELs in fourth and eighth grade scored thirty-six and forty-two standard-scale points, respectively, below the performance of their native speakers of English peers (Grigg, Donahue, & Dion, 2007; Lee, Grigg, & Donahue, 2007). Academic achievement gaps indicate that many ELs may not have attained the English language proficiency or subject matter content needed to participate fully in mainstream classrooms.

Clearly, the sources of difficulty become even more important in light of the implementation of the Common Core State Standards (www.corestandards.org) (CCSS, 2014), which place greater emphasis on (a) using higher-level thinking skills during reading and writing instruction, and (b) acquiring skills in the new digital literacies of online research and comprehension. These two key elements present opportunities and challenges for ELs and their teachers. The integration of these two key elements give students an opportunity to gain equal and greater access to rigorous instruction along with higher expectations for academic success, regardless of English proficiency. The new CCSS expectations will also nudge teachers to rethink in new and different ways about how to identify students' reading comprehension strengths and needs and how to use that information to address the needs of

ELs in the mainstream classrooms (Brown & Kappes, 2012; Schleppegrell & O'Hallaron, 2011).

USING METACOGNITIVE ASSESSMENTS TO IDENTIFY STUDENTS' READING COMPREHENSION STRENGTHS AND NEEDS

Reading comprehension research has shown that most struggling upper elementary and middle grade readers are often unskilled and unaware that they are unskilled (Kruger & Dunning, 1999). Some of this research, which addresses metacognitive awareness and use of reading strategies across languages, indicates that there are various validated tools and strategies for assessing students' awareness and use of reading strategies when reading. Examples of these tools and strategies include, but are not limited to:

a. Informal interview protocols (e.g., Goodman, Watson, & Burke, 1987), which are designed to determine readers' judgments of their own reading abilities, their perceptions of themselves as readers, and the metacognitive strategies they use when reading.
b. Think-aloud procedures (e.g., Wilhelm, 2012), which are designed to uncover the actual thinking processes that readers engage in before, during, and after reading.
c. Self-report instruments (e.g., Mokhtari & Reichard, 2002), which assess the type and frequency of reading strategies students report using when reading academic reading materials.

For purposes of this chapter, I focus exclusively on one self-report metacognitive assessment instrument: The Survey of Reading Strategies (SORS),which assesses students' metacognitive awareness and use of reading strategies across languages. In consideration of space limitations, I will briefly describe the instrument, and explain how teachers can administer to their students, how to interpret the results obtained, and how to use the insights gained to inform instruction. More detailed information about the development of the SORS instrument development, its psychometric properties, and its limitations can be found in Mokhtari and Sheorey (2002).

DESCRIPTION OF THE SORS INSTRUMENT

The SORS instrument is designed to assess students' metacognitive awareness and use of specific reading strategies when reading print materials (e.g., book chapters, journal articles, reports) that are typically used in academic settings. The SORS instrument is adapted from another instrument, the Metacognitive Awareness of Reading Strategies Inventory (MARSI) (Mokhtari & Reichard, 2002), which was originally designed to assess native English speakers' metacognitive awareness and use of reading strategies.

Although the MARSI and SORS instruments are fairly similar in terms of design and implementation features, the SORS instrument included here differs in three important ways. First, it includes certain reading strategies (e.g., used of cognates, code-mixing or code-switching, and translation across two or more languages) that are characteristically used by biliterate or multi-literate readers when reading academic texts in English. Second, the instructions for administration as well as interpretation of the results have been slightly revised for clarity and readability purposes. Finally, the score ranges used to guide the interpretation of the results obtained have been slightly adjusted to reflect the pattern of scores obtained by students across various grades through ongoing refinement of the instrument. A copy of this version of the SORS instrument is found in this chapter's appendix.

METACOGNITIVE READING STRATEGIES
ASSESSED BY SORS

The SORS instrument consists of a total of thirty individual reading strategies, which are operationally defined as plans selected intentionally by the reader to accomplish specific goals or to complete particular tasks (Paris, Wasik, & Turner, 1991). These individual strategies are grouped in three broad categories: global reading strategies (GRS), problem-solving strategies (PSS), and support reading strategies (SRS). These strategy categories (or subscales) are based on factor analyses and other theoretical considerations addressed in the development of the instrument. Brief descriptions of each strategy SORS category along with the number of strategy statements within each category are as follows:

- GRS are intentional, carefully planned actions skilled readers initiate by way of monitoring or managing their reading. Examples of such strategies include setting a purpose for reading, previewing text for length, organization and other aspects, or using visual or typographical aids such as tables and figures (thirteen strategy statements).
- PSS are actions and procedures skilled readers deploy while working directly with the text. These are localized, focused actions used when problems develop in understanding textual information. Examples include adjusting one's speed of reading when the material becomes difficult or

(SORS) Survey of reading strategies

easy, guessing the meaning of unknown words, and rereading the text to improve comprehension (nine strategy statements).
- SRS are tools intended to aid or provide support for readers to facilitate text comprehension. Examples include using dictionaries, taking notes, or underlining or highlighting textual information (eight strategy statements).

ADMINISTERING THE SORS SURVEY INSTRUMENT

The SORS instrument can be administered to individual ELs in clinical settings or to groups of students in classroom settings. It should be administered to students who have sufficient language proficiency (e.g., a Level 3, "developing" English proficiency) that enables them to read and understand the survey instructions and the strategy statements. Students with lower levels of English proficiency should be given translated versions of the SORS instrument, which are available from the author.

The SORS instrument uses a five-point Likert scale ranging from 1 ("I have never heard of this strategy before") to 5 ("I know this strategy well and I always use it when I read"). After explaining the purpose of the SORS instrument, teachers should direct students to read each strategy statement and to circle the number that applies to them, indicating the degree to which they use the reading strategy specified in the statement when they read. In general, higher strategy ratings indicate higher levels of awareness and potential use of the strategy in question.

Prior to completing the survey, it is important for teachers to remind students that (a) SORS is a survey (not a test) that asks them to estimate how often you use specific strategies when you read school-related materials in English such as chapter books, journal articles, and reports, as there are no time limits for completing the survey; (b) there are no time limits to complete the survey, even though it takes most students about ten to fifteen minutes to complete it; (c) responses are to refer primarily to the strategies they use when reading school-related materials such as chapter books, journal articles, and reports rather materials they read freely and voluntarily outside of school time; and (c) they can ask for assistance or pose questions about any aspect of the survey they do not understand at any time.

Scoring the SORS Instrument

Scoring either SORS survey is easy and can be done by the students themselves. Students simply transfer the scores obtained for each strategy to the scoring sheet, which accompanies the survey instrument. After the individual scores are recorded, they should be added up for each column (or strategy category) to obtain a total score for the entire instrument. The scores obtained can then be interpreted using the score key guide provided.

Interpreting the SORS Results

The suggested score key guidelines are informed by the scores obtained by students in the "norming groups" used when developing the instrument. These guidelines were then slightly adjusted based on the performance patterns of students across various middle, high school, and college grades who have completed the SORS survey instrument in the years following its original development. Three levels of reading strategy awareness and usage are identified: high (4.0–5.0), medium (3.0–3.9), and low (1.0–2.9). These awareness or usage levels provide a recommended benchmark that teachers can use for interpreting individual student scores obtained from each of the strategies, strategy categories, or the whole survey instrument.

As a general rule of thumb, the overall or total survey score averages indicate the degree of awareness or potential use of reading strategies when reading academic or school-related materials. The averages for each subscale or category show which group of strategies (i.e., GRS, PSS, or SRS) students report using when reading academic materials. Individual strategy scores refer to levels of awareness and use of particular reading strategies.

Using SORS Data to Inform Instruction

When interpreting the data obtained from the SORS survey instrument, it is helpful to look for broad patterns of performance across strategy categories as well as across the whole survey instrument for individual students (e.g., average scores obtained by one student for each category of strategies and for the whole instrument) or for groups of students (e.g., average scores obtained by all thirty students in a sixth grade language arts classroom). In each of these circumstances, a low score associated with a given category of strategies (e.g., problem-solving strategies) may indicate a need for supplemental instruction in problem-solving strategies such as "adjusting reading rate," "rereading for better understanding," or "using visuals" or graphic organizers devices to help synthesize and remember information read.

However, it is most helpful to also review individual student performance on individual reading strategies. For instance, a student who assigns a rating score on 1 "I have never heard of this strategy before" to GRS "I have a purpose in mind when I read" or "I think about what I know to help me understand what I read" may need instruction in setting purpose for reading and using prior knowledge when reading: Both of these strategies are critically important in skilled reading.

RESEARCH TO PRACTICE RECOMMENDATIONS

During the past five or six decades, significant advances have been made in the area of reading comprehension, its assessment, and teaching to all students, including ELs. While space does not permit a review of all of this research, the following four research findings are directly relevant to the metacognitive assessments and instruction issues addressed in this chapter and have practical applications for assessing and teaching ELs.

1. Reading comprehension researchers have found that most struggling middle grade readers are often unskilled and unaware that they are unskilled (Kruger & Dunning, 1999). As EL teachers, *consider using metacognitive assessments to help identify students' awareness and use of reading strategies when reading. Using a combination of metacognitive assessment tools and strategies such as interview protocols, think-alouds, and self-report measures such as the SORS survey instrument would yield the best results. You can then use the information obtained from these metacognitive assessments to differentiate reading strategy instruction based on their students' strengths and needs.*

2. Reading comprehension is an active process that entails an intentional and thoughtful interaction between the reader, the text, and the context in which the act of reading takes place. This type of *constructively responsive reading* requires the active use of reading comprehension strategies (Kamil et al., 2008; Pressley, 2000; Pressley & Afflerbach, 1995). Consistent with these and other established research findings, *consider providing your ELs with direct, explicit instruction in reading comprehension strategies such as the ones outlined below, which will help them better understand and eventually learn from what they read.* The rationale for the explicit teaching of comprehension skills is that comprehension can be improved by teaching students to use specific reading strategies or to reason strategically when they encounter barriers to understanding what they are reading.

3. In carrying out its meta-analysis of 205 studies of reading comprehension, members of the National Reading Panel found that (a) text comprehension improves when readers actively relate the ideas in print to their own knowledge, (b) successful reading comprehension strategies include using prior knowledge, asking pertinent questions while reading, summarizing information read, monitoring one's reading comprehension processes, and evaluating what one reads, and that (c) teaching a combination of reading comprehension strategies together rather than individually is most effective in improving students' reading comprehension performance. As teachers with EL teachers, *consider devoting five to ten minutes a day to the teaching of reading comprehension strategies and how they are used*

when reading materials pertaining to your respective disciplines. Be a model for your students. Show them how you, as a skilled reader, use reading strategies when you read text in your discipline.

4. There are various well-validated ways to help increase students' reading comprehension skills through metacognitive reading strategy instruction. Although there are several instructional frameworks that have been shown to work quite well in helping teachers organize instruction when teaching reading comprehension strategies, literacy experts recommend using the Gradual Release of Responsibility framework (Pearson & Gallagher, 1983), which helps teachers organize instruction and document progress with regard to student learning and engagement. In this instructional approach, teachers hold the majority of responsibility in teaching at the beginning of the lesson, but then slowly release that responsibility over to the students until learning is fully controlled by students. The approach consists of the following four interrelated components:

   a. *Verbal explanation.* The teacher begins the lesson with a brief explanation of selected reading strategies and how they work.

   b. *Modeling.* The teacher models or demonstrates how to use one or more strategies individually or in groups to construct meaning from text. He or she "talks-aloud" the strategic processes skilled readers use before, during, and after reading.

   c. *Guided Practice.* The teacher puts students in the driver's seat, so to speak, giving them an opportunity to apply reading strategies while reading self-selected texts. Students can then work with other students to gain additional practice and the process continues until they are fairly comfortable in using reading strategies.

   d. *Independent practice.* Students work independently or in small groups, giving them the opportunity to apply reading strategies in text selections of their choosing. The teacher monitors progress and assists students who need extra help.

Other highly effective instructional frameworks for raising students' metacognitive awareness and use of reading strategies when reading is *reciprocal teaching*, a framework developed by Palinscar and Brown (1984). The main goal of reciprocal teaching is to improve student's reading comprehension using four comprehension strategies: predicting, questioning, clarifying, and summarizing. These strategies are scaffolded through modeling, guided practice, and application of the strategies while reading. Palincsar and Brown (1986) found that when reciprocal teaching was used with a group of students for just fifteen to twenty days, the students' reading on a comprehension assessment increased from 30 to 80 percent. Teachers interested in learning more about metacognitive assessments and instructional approaches such as reciprocal teaching and may find the references cited in this chapter quite helpful.

A CAUTIONARY NOTE

There is no doubt that metacognitive assessment tools such as SORS and others are very helpful in identifying the reading comprehension strengths and needs of their students. However, these assessments have limitations. When interpreting the assessment data obtained from self-report instruments such as SORS, teachers need to keep in mind the following two limitations.

One limitation is that self-report instruments such as SORS are designed to tap generalized student perceptions of strategy use—not actual strategy use. When students complete the instrument, they're thinking about a broad range of reading materials and tasks and they report strategy use in a generalized sense, without referring to any specific use of any particular reading task. Prior research on metacognition and reading has shown that generalized knowledge about reading processes and strategies may be necessary, but it is not sufficient for skilled reading. For instance, Forrest-Pressley and Waller (1984) found that skilled readers not only know that there are different ways of reading, but they also know how to monitor the efficiency and how to regulate them.

A second limitation of self-report instruments such as SORS is that often students have a tendency to overestimate their metacognitive awareness and use of strategies judgments. A possible explanation for this phenomenon might be related to the fact that students see instruments such as SORS as tests, which they have to "pass." When administering SORS instrument, it is important that students realize that their responses to the strategy statements are not considered "right" or "wrong" and that their scores will not be used to evaluate their performance as readers.

APPENDIX

SURVEY OF READING STRATEGIES-Revised (2014), (SORS-R)

Instructions: This is not a test. It is a survey that will ask you to estimate how often you use specific strategies when reading school materials in English such as chapter books, journal articles, and reports.

Five numbers (1, 2, 3, 4, & 5) follow each statement, and each number means the following:

1. I have **never heard** of this strategy before.
2. I have **heard** of this strategy, but I **don't know** what it means.
3. I have **heard** of this strategy, and I **think I know** what it means.
4. I **know** this strategy, and I **can explain** how and when to use it.
5. I **know** this strategy **well**, and I **always use** it when I read.

Handwritten margin notes: *Survey then use # 1-30 for the month's*; *repeat*; *have exit tickets verbally to each strategy.*

Kouider Mokhtari

After reading each statement, ***circle the number*** (1, 2, 3, 4, or 5) which applies to you. There are **no right or wrong responses** to any of the survey statements. There is **no time limit,** either.

Survey of Reading Strategies

Category	Strategy	Rating Scale				
GRS	1. I have a purpose in mind when I read.	1	2	3	4	5
SRS	2. I take notes while reading to help me understand what I read.	1	2	3	4	5
GRS	3. I think about what I know to help me understand what I read.	1	2	3	4	5
GRS	4. I take an overall view of the text to see what it is about before reading it.	1	2	3	4	5
SRS	5. When text becomes difficult, I read aloud to help me understand what I read.	1	2	3	4	5
GRS	6. I think about whether the content of the texts fits my reading purpose.	1	2	3	4	5
PRS	7. I read slowly and carefully to make sure I understand what I am reading.	1	2	3	4	5
GRS	8. I review the text first by noting its characteristics like length and organization.	1	2	3	4	5
PRS	9. I try to get back on track when I lose concentration.	1	2	3	4	5
SRS	10. I underline or circle information in the text to help me remember it.	1	2	3	4	5
PRS	11. I adjust my reading speed according to what I am reading.	1	2	3	4	5
GRS	12. When reading, I decide what to read closely and what to ignore.	1	2	3	4	5
SRS	13. I use reference materials (e.g. a dictionary) to help me understand what I read.	1	2	3	4	5
PRS	14. When text becomes difficult, I pay closer attention to what I am reading.	1	2	3	4	5
GRS	15. I use tables, figures, and pictures in text to increase my understanding.	1	2	3	4	5
PRS	16. I stop from time to time and think about what I am reading.	1	2	3	4	5
GRS	17. I use context clues to help me better understand what I am reading.	1	2	3	4	5
SRS	18. I paraphrase (restate in my own words) to better understand what I read.	1	2	3	4	5
PRS	19. I try to picture or visualize information to help remember what I read.	1	2	3	4	5
GRS	20. I use typographical features like **bold face** and *italics* to identify key information	1	2	3	4	5
GRS	21. I critically analyze and evaluate the information presented in the text.	1	2	3	4	5
SRS	22. I go back and forth in the text to find relationships among ideas in it.	1	2	3	4	5
GRS	23. I check my information when I come across new information.	1	2	3	4	5
GRS	24. I try to guess what the content of the text is about when I read.	1	2	3	4	5
PRS	25. When text becomes difficult, I re-read it to increase my understanding.	1	2	3	4	5
SRS	26. I ask myself questions I like to have answered in the text.	1	2	3	4	5
GRS	27. I check to see if my guesses about the text are right or wrong.	1	2	3	4	5

Survey of Reading Strategies

Category	Strategy	Rating Scale
PRS	28. When I read, I guess the meaning of unknown words or phrases.	1 2 3 4 5
SRS	29. When reading, I translate from English into my native language.	1 2 3 4 5
SRS	30. When reading, I think about information in both English and my mother tongue.	1 2 3 4 5

SCORING S GUIDELINES FOR THE *SURVEY OF READING STRATEGIES-REVISED*

Student Name:_____Date: _____

1. Write the number you circled for each statement (i.e., 1, 2, 3, 4, or 5) in the appropriate blanks below
2. Add up the scores under each column and place the result on the line under each column.
3. Divide the subscale score by the number of statements in each column to get the mean for each subscale.
4. Calculate the mean score for the total scale by adding up the subscale scores and dividing by 30.
5. Use the interpretation guidelines below to understand your averages.

Global Reading Strategies (GRS Subscale)	**Problem-Solving Strategies** (PRS Subscale)	**Support Reading Strategies** (SRS Subscale)	**Total Reading Strategies**
1. _____	7. _____	2. _____	**GRS:** _____
3. _____	9. _____	5. _____	**PRS:** _____
4. _____	11. _____	10. _____	**SRS:** _____
6. _____	14. _____	13. _____	
8. _____	16. _____	18. _____	
12. _____	19. _____	22. _____	
15. _____	25. _____	26. _____	
17. _____	28. _____	29. _____	
20. _____		30. _____	
21. _____			
23. _____			
24. _____			
27. _____			

_____ GRS Score	_____ PRS Score	_____ SRS Score	_____ Total Score
_____ GRS Mean	_____ PRS Mean	_____ SRS Mean	_____ Total Mean

SCORE KEY   4.0 – 5.0 = High   3.0 – 3.9 = Medium   1.0 – 2.9 = Low

INTERPRETING YOUR SCORES

The combined or total reading strategies mean score indicates how often you report using reading strategies when reading academic materials. The average score for each subscale shows which group of strategies (i.e., Global, Problem-Solving, or Support reading strategies) you report using most often when reading. Your individual score can vary depending on your reading ability in English, the type of material read, and your knowledge of yourself as a reader. A low score on any of the strategies (or subscales) of the inventory indicates that you may not be aware of these strategies, and that you may want to learn more about and consider using when reading.

Chapter 7

Classroom Assessment of Language Levels to Address Common Core Standards–Based Instruction with English Learners, K–8

Paul Boyd-Batstone

In this chapter, I describe a new assessment tool, Classroom Assessment for Language Levels (CALL), which helps teachers to rapidly assess the language level of an English learner (EL) and use the information gained to plan and deliver instruction aimed at enhancing students' language and literacy achievement outcomes.

In a resource brief on the *Application of Common Core State Standards for English Language Learners*, the National Governors Association Center for Best Practices and the Council of Chief State School Officers state that they "strongly believe that all students should be held to the same high expectations outlined in the Common Core State Standards. This includes students who are English learners (ELs). However, these students may require additional time, appropriate instructional support, and aligned assessments as they acquire both English language proficiency and content area knowledge" (http://www.corestandards.org/other-resources).

These expectations do not specify where schools will find additional time, what is appropriate instruction, or what assessments will support English language proficiency. Time is not on the teacher's side; nor is it on the ELs' side. The moment an EL student arrives in a classroom, the teacher is expected to provide appropriate instruction even though they may have little to no information about the student's level of English language proficiency.

The purpose of this chapter is to provide the classroom teacher a way to quickly assess the language level of an EL the moment the student arrives so that appropriate instruction that is aligned with Common Core State Standards (CCSS) can begin. The tool described in this chapter is the CALL (Boyd-Batstone, 2013). This chapter includes a discussion of the background for language level assessment, a description of the CALL, implementation and instruction, followed by a selection of CCSS for Listening and Speaking that have been expanded according to language level to address instructional support for ELs.

BACKGROUND FOR LANGUAGE LEVEL ASSESSMENT

With the advent of the standards-based instructional movement spurred on by federal legislation (No Child Left Behind Act, 2001), an intense focus on assessment and differentiated instruction for ELs emerged. Sato et al. (2005) documented how linguists began to explore how language development and academic achievement were linked. Rather than designing assessments based on conventions of grammar and punctuation, language performance and usage became the object of assessment (Butler et al., 2004/2005).

Overtime, the professional organization, Teachers of English to Speakers of Other Languages (TESOL), developed and refined standards to gage language performance that were ranked according five levels of proficiency (TESOL, 1997/2004/2006). The five proficiency levels were as follows: 1 = Starting, 2 = Emerging, 3 = Developing, 4 = Expanding, and 5 = Bridging (see table 7.1).

According to the framers of the TESOL Standards,

> The use of five levels reflects the complexity of language development and allows the tracking of student progress across grade levels within the same scale. The five levels of language proficiency reflect characteristics of language performance at each developmental stage. The language proficiency levels are intended to highlight and provide a model of the process of language acquisition that can be adapted by individual districts and states. (http://www.tesol.org/docs/books/bk_prek-12elpstandards_framework_318.pdf?sfvrsn=2)

Subsequently, the California State Department of Education developed English Language Development Content Standards (California Department of Education, 1999) patterned from the TESOL standards that also used

Table 7.1 The Development of Standards or Descriptors for Language Proficiency Levels

Standards or Descriptors By Level	TESOL (1997/ 2004/2006)	CELDT (1999)	WIDA (2004)	California ELD Standards (2012)
Level 1	Starting	Beginning	Entering	Emerging
Level 2	Emerging	Early Intermediate	Beginning	****
Level 3	Developing	Intermediate	Developing	Expanding
Level 4	Expanding	Early Advanced	Expanding	****
Level 5	Bridging	Advanced	Bridging	Reaching

five levels of proficiency. This led to the development of summative measures such as the California English Language Development Test (CELDT, 1999), which produced a five-point rating scale (1 = Beginning, 2 = Early Intermediate, 3 = Intermediate, 4 = Early Advanced, and 5 = Advanced).

In 2004, the Center for Applied Linguistics (CAL) collaborated with the Wisconsin Center for Educational Research (WCER) to develop the World-class Instructional Design and Assessment (WIDA) language level (http://www.wida.us/standards/). Similar to the TESOL standards, the WIDA descriptors used a five-point rating scale (1 = Entering, 2 = Beginning, 3 = Developing, 4 = Expanding, 5 = Bridging).

More recently in California, the State Department of Education revised its English Language Development Standards (California Department of Education, 2012) to incorporate the work of the above groups in an effort to align ELD with CCSS for English language arts. A significant change in the revision was to reduce the number of levels of proficiency from five to three. The levels are more broadly defined to encompass the same range from beginning to advanced language proficiency, but borrowed the descriptor titles from TESOL and WIDA (Emerging/Expanding/Reaching). The rationale for reducing the number of levels was apparently for pragmatic instructional purposes—instructional adaptations were deemed to fit more easily in three levels than in five levels (see table 7.1).

Several key points can be drawn from this brief background review. First, language proficiency became the object of measurement. In other words, language proficiency was designed as performance-based assessment. Second, leveled descriptors of language usage, rather than conventional categories such as parts of speech were being measured. This is important for the classroom teacher to be able to readily use a set of descriptors of language performance to identify an ELs' level of proficiency to differentiate instruction. Third, the documents mentioned are not uniform. They reflect different descriptions of language performance, which can be confusing to use for instructional purposes. Finally, the classroom teacher still needs a tool for formative assessment of an EL's language level. The assessment tool needs to be administered in a short period of time; it should also tie the language level descriptors to appropriate instructional strategies to support differentiated instruction. This brings us to the CALL (Boyd-Batstone, 2013).

THE CALL

[handwritten annotation: Classroom Assessment for Language Levels]

As a classroom teacher and teacher-educator, I saw the need to develop a quick assessment tool that tied language levels to appropriate instructional strategies, and that could fit on a single page. The CALL is a single-page formative assessment tool that in a matter of moments helps teachers identify the language level an EL and what strategies would be appropriate at that level (see figure 7.1, The Classroom Assessment of Language Levels).

The components of the CALL:

Level/Stage Descriptors/Duration

- **Level:** A five-point rating scale for quick reference. The numbered scale allows for quantifying language levels to facilitate data collection and reporting purposes.
- **Stage:** Five descriptors of the stage of language proficiency (1 = Beginning, 2 = Early Intermediate, 3 = Intermediate, 4 = Early Advanced, and 5 = Advanced). I distinguish the difference between a level and a stage in two ways. The level is a numbered, quantifiable measure. The stage is a more fluid descriptor of language usage. I chose CELDT (Revised 2014) descriptors because they provided graded language (beginning through advanced) that corresponded to each level. Also, it is easier to communicate to parents that the student is at an "advanced stage of language proficiency" than trying to explain that a student is "bridging" (TESOL, 2006) or "reaching" (WIDA, 2003).
- **Duration:** Expected duration that the EL should be at a given level, which is drawn from the work of Collier and Thomas (1987). It may be useful to indicate if a student is lingering too long at a level and not progressing in their language development.

Implementation

The CALL can be implemented two ways. It suggests questions to facilitate a one-to-one interview between the classroom teacher and an ELL. However, recognizing that teachers, especially at the secondary level do not have the time to conduct single interviews, the CALL suggests small group interactive tasks or techniques to involve the ELL so that specific language performance behaviors can be observed.

- **Questions for Direct Interview:** If the teacher has the opportunity to sit down for a few moments to engage the EL in a brief interview, the CALL suggests a series of questions that are designed to require progressively more involved language usage. For example at the Beginning Stage the EL can answer with simply "Yes/No" or a single word response. As the questioning progresses the EL must provide longer answers, more details, explanations and justifications, and then synthesize themes, as well as posing questions of their own.

- **Interactive Techniques for Small Group Observation:** If the teacher would rather observe the EL's language usage while interacting with a small group of other students, the CALL suggests tasks or interactive techniques that require little language proficiency at the beginning, but increasingly demand more language complexity at each level. For example at the Beginning Stage, the teacher observes if the student is able to list items in a picture, and categorize or sequence pictures. This requires very little language usage, which is appropriate at the Beginning Stage. However, to demonstrate greater language proficiency, the techniques become increasingly demanding such as asking for details, retelling of events at level 2; then at level 3, looking for writing explanations and justifications of reasoning; then at level 4, looking to what extent the EL uses problem-solving language; and finally at level 5, observing if the EL can synthesize what others have been saying in a group discussion or seeing if the EL takes on a leadership role in a small group discussion.

Observation

- **Student Behaviors:** This section describes twenty-two language specific behaviors that are arranged in order of complexity in alignment with their respective level of proficiency. The classroom teacher can utilize this section in several ways. First, the teacher can utilize the behavioral descriptors to focus observations. In other words, the teacher can target behaviors to identify a language level. For example, if the EL speaks in simple sentences, but does not provided expanded vocabulary, the teacher can reliably identify that that the student is at level 2 Early Intermediate Stage. Second, the teacher can appropriate the descriptors to record observations without the need to compose new language for a report. Another advantage of appropriating the descriptors is it increases the accuracy and consistency of reporting the language level to other members of the schooling community—the language is already aligned with the respective language level.

Appropriate Instruction

Differentiated Strategies: This section includes twenty-four differentiated instructional strategies that are aligned with the respective language level. Once the teacher identifies the level of the EL, he or she can reference three to four readily applicable strategies that match the EL's proficiency level. As with the other items in the CALL, the strategies are arranged progressively so that at each level there is an increasing demand in language usage and proficiency (refer to figure 7.1).

Level	Stages	Duration	Questions for Direct Interview	Interactive Techniques for Small Group Observations	Student Behaviors	Differentiated Strategies
1	Beginning	6 mos	•Yes/No questions: "Is this an apple?" •Fill in the blank (cloze): "This fruit is an ___?"	•List items •Categorize and sequence pictures	•Can be silent •Yes/No responses •Can name objects •Offers 1-2 word responses •Shows comprehension by following directions	•Simple speech, caretaker speech •Use realia, visuals, meaningful gestures (TPR) •Do not force speech •Read to student
2	Early Intermediate	3 mos-1 yr	•Who, when, what, where questions: "Who is that?" "When di this happen?" •Open ended questions: "What were you thinking?"	•Name attributes and identify essential details in a picture or simple text •Invite retelling of events	•Speaks simple sentences •Retells story events •Reads basic vocabulary, simple sentences •Makes frequent grammatical errors in speech	Use all of the above •Use predictable books •Use books with vivid illustrations •Develop storyboard frames •Interactive journals •Create chart stories •Direct instruction of vocabulary
3	Intermediate	2-3 yrs	•Descriptive details •How, why questions: "How did she do that?" "Why did she do that?"	•Encourage inquiry •Request explanations and justifications in writing	•Retells using expanded vocabulary •Identifies main ideas/details •Summarizes texts •Makes comparisons •Defines new vocabulary •Justifies reasoning	Use all of the above •Tap experiences •Teach study skills •Use cognates •Explore word origins •Teach writing for a purpose •Use/create media
4	Early Advanced	3-4 yrs	•Analysis and synthesis questions: "What is the difference…?" "How are they the same…?" "What is the theme?"	•Use problem solving approaches	•Appears to be orally fluent •Uses limited academic vocabulary and language •Needs to attain grade level reading/writing in academic areas •Analyzes, compares, contrasts	•Shift focus from oral to written language development •Expand study/learning skills •Provide formal grammar instruction •Use SDAIE strategies
5	Advanced	>3 yrs	•Pose all questions •Encourage student to pose questions	•Invite leadership roles in collaborative groups •Synthesize what others are saying	•Comprehends content material •Generates discussions •Is socially comfortable •Reads/Writes at grade level	•Expand academic vocabulary •Refine writing skills •Refine research/study skills •Complete complex projects

Figure 7.1   Classroom Assessment of Language Levels

ADDRESSING CCSS FOR LISTENING AND SPEAKING WITH ELs

Now that the CALL has been introduced, we turn from assessment to differentiated instruction. More specifically, we will apply the language levels of the CALL to performance tasked selected from Common Core English Language Arts, appendix B. Each task will then be differentiated according to language level to meet the needs of the EL.

The following selection of standards and performance tasks are designed to be illustrative, rather than a comprehensive treatment of CCSS. (For a comprehensive treatment of CCSS Listening and Speaking, K–12, see Boyd-Batstone, 2013.) The selected standards address Comprehension and Collaboration. I've selected standards from across five grade levels (kindergarten, fourth grade, and eighth grade—which are combined as the same set of standards). I selected clusters of standards to show that there is actually a common theme across grade levels with CCSS. Additionally, clustering standards allows me to demonstrate that a quality activity can address multiple standards and facilitate differentiation at the same time.

In CCSS parlance, "comprehension" refers to demonstrating text-based understanding, and "collaboration" refers to listening, asking, and responding

Textbox 7.1   Kindergarten: Common Core Listen and Speaking Standards

CCSS.ELA-LITERACY.SL.K.1
Participate in collaborative conversations with diverse partners about kindergarten topics and texts with peers and adults in small and larger groups.

CCSS.ELA-LITERACY.SL.K.1.A
Follow agreed-upon rules for discussions (e.g., listening to others and taking turns speaking about the topics and texts under discussion).

CCSS.ELA-LITERACY.SL.K.1.B
Continue a conversation through multiple exchanges.

CCSS.ELA-LITERACY.SL.K.2
Confirm understanding of a text read aloud or information presented orally or through other media by asking and answering questions about key details and requesting clarification if something is not understood.

to questions, and justifying one's thinking through a range of media. Listening and speaking refer to receptive language and expressive language. The standards are labeled accordingly: CCSS.ELA-Literacy.SL.K1

- CCSS = Common Core State Standard
- ELA = English language arts
- SL = Speaking and Listening
- K = Kindergarten
- 1 = Initial standard for that set
- 1.A = Secondary standard for that set

A "Performance Task," which is taken from the Common Core State Standards English Language Arts, appendix B, follows the selected grade level standards. The performance tasks are instructional activities, which are aligned with CCSS grade level standards.

Each selected performance task is followed by differentiated instructional strategies that are appropriate for three stages of language proficiency: Beginning, Intermediate, and Advanced (see textbox 7.1).

Comprehension and Collaboration (http://www.corestandards.org/ELA-Literacy/SL/K/)

Performance Task: Students (with prompting and support from the teacher) compare and contrast the adventures and experiences of the owl in Arnold

Lobel's (1975) *Owl at Home* to those of the owl in Edward Lears' (YEAR) poem "The Owl and the Pussycat." (http://www.corestandards.org/assets/ Appendix_B.pdf, p. 28)

Differentiation according to language proficiency:

- **Materials needed:** Supply the following pictures and real objects to give meaning and context to the texts including pictures of owls, cats, toads, turkeys, and pigs with a ring in the nose; also home gardens and seascapes and islands. Provide the following objects: peapod seeds and sprouted peas, a pea-green boat model, a five-pound play money note, a jar of honey, a ring, a runcible spoon (a spoon/fork combined into one implement, in school cafeterias they are commonly referred to as a "spork"). Use the following media to assist with the read-aloud: https://www.youtube.com/ watch?v=7Kf04ktysQM.
- **Beginning:** Have students sort the pictures and objects into two groups according to each text. Ask either/or questions such as, "Do these seeds belong with *Owl at Home* or *The Owl and the Pussycat*?" Follow with, "Point to the place in the text where it describes seeds."
- **Intermediate:** Continue to utilize the pictures and objects. Have students collaborate in small groups to create two storyboards, one for each text. Ask the students to include as much detail in each storyboard panel as possible based on the text they are illustrating. Ask students to explain and justify to each other why they inserted various pictures. Have students point out from where in the text each illustration came. Ask them to explain why they depicted a character or object in a particular way. In addition, ask them cut out and paste a selected words and phrases that correspond to the illustrations at the bottom of each illustrated panel. Within the small groups, ask students to compare and contrast the different storyboards.
- **Advanced:** At the kindergarten level, if the EL is at the advanced level, they are probably are functioning at native-like fluency. I would recommend asking advanced staged ELs participate in all of the activities. The next level of language complexity would be to ask the kindergartener to present the completed storyboard to the rest of the group. Ask the students to explain how their group represented the similarities and differences between the two texts.

Differentiating Common Core Performance Task
(http://www.corestandards.org/ELA-Literacy/SL/4/)

Performance Task: Students make connections between the visual presenta- tion of John Tenniel's illustrations in Lewis Carroll's (1992/1865) *Alice's*

Textbox 7.2   Grade 4: Comprehension and Collaboration

CCSS.ELA-LITERACY.SL.4.1
Engage effectively in a range of collaborative discussions (one-on-one, in groups, and teacher-led) with diverse partners on grade 4 topics and texts, building on others' ideas and expressing their own clearly.

CCSS.ELA-LITERACY.SL.4.1.A
Come to discussions prepared, having read or studied required material; explicitly draw on that preparation and other information known about the topic to explore ideas under discussion.

CCSS.ELA-LITERACY.SL.4.1.B
Follow agreed-upon rules for discussions and carry out assigned roles.

CCSS.ELA-LITERACY.SL.4.1.C
Pose and respond to specific questions to clarify or follow up on information, and make comments that contribute to the discussion and link to the remarks of others.

CCSS.ELA-LITERACY.SL.4.1.D
Review the key ideas expressed and explain their own ideas and understanding in light of the discussion.

Adventures in Wonderland and the text of the story to identify how the pictures of Alice reflect specific descriptions of her in the text (http://www.corestandards.org/assets/Appendix_B.pdf, p. 70).

Differentiation according to language proficiency:

- **Materials Needed:** Provide individual dry-erase response boards, dry-erase pens, and erasers. Conduct an Internet search and print out various images of John Tenniel's illustrations. Copy and cut out corresponding passages of Lewis Carroll's writing. Mount the pictures and passages on heavy stock paper that is cut to the same size.
- **Beginning:** (1) Model the performance task for all the students with particular focus on the need of ELs to see an image first before understanding the text. Show a selected illustration by John Tenniel. Identify and name the various significant details; then read aloud the corresponding passage from Lewis Carroll's book. Highlight the descriptive vocabulary in the text. Using the dry-erase response boards, ask students to pick a word or phrase

from the text that describes something from the illustration. (2) Additionally, play a matching game. Mix up the mounted pictures and corresponding passages. Ask students to match the illustration to the appropriate text. (3) Continue by having students draw their own illustration based on a selected text from Carroll's book; then have students label each component of their drawing using words from the selected text.

Cinquain Poem

1. _____(Title or subject)
2. _____ _____ _____(3 nouns)
3. _____ _____ _____(3 adjectives)
4. _____ _____ _____(3 adverbs)
5. _____(A word related to the title or subject)

Textbox 7.3 Grade 8: Comprehension and Collaboration (http://www.corestandards. org/ELA-Literacy/SL/8/)

CCSS.ELA-LITERACY.SL.8.1
Engage effectively in a range of collaborative discussions (one-on-one, in groups, and teacher-led) with diverse partners on grade 8 topics, texts, and issues, building on others' ideas and expressing their own clearly.

CCSS.ELA-LITERACY.SL.8.1.A
Come to discussions prepared, having read or researched material under study; explicitly draw on that preparation by referring to evidence on the topic, text, or issue to probe and reflect on ideas under discussion.

CCSS.ELA-LITERACY.SL.8.1.B
Follow rules for collegial discussions and decision-making, track progress toward specific goals and deadlines, and define individual roles as needed.

CCSS.ELA-LITERACY.SL.8.1.C
Pose questions that connect the ideas of several speakers and respond to others' questions and comments with relevant evidence, observations, and ideas.

CCSS.ELA-LITERACY.SL.8.1.D
Acknowledge new information expressed by others, and, when warranted, qualify or justify their own views in light of the evidence presented.

• **Advanced:** Students at this level can freely participate in the above activities. To extend the language usage, by doing the following. Utilizing the word bank as a reference, select an illustration by John Tenniel and write a one to two paragraph descriptive narrative in the style of Lewis Carroll's writing.

Performance Task: Students summarize the development of the morality of Tom Sawyer in Mark Twain's (1876) novel of the same name and analyze its connection to themes of accountability and authenticity by noting how it is conveyed through characters, setting, and plot (http://www.corestandards. org/assets/Appendix_B.pdf, p. 89).

Differentiation according to language proficiency:

• **Materials Needed:** (1) Provide access to an online dictionary such as http://www.merriam-webster.com. (2) Provide audio book versions of Mark Twain's Tom Sawyer. (There are several free services including YouTube: https://www.youtube.com/watch?v=SF7lSyjmZwQ; and Audio-Book Treasury: http://www.audiobooktreasury.com/tom-sawyer-mark-twain/.) (3) Provide large sheets of chart paper divided into four columns (see sample in figure 7.2). Label the columns and rows as follows:

Accountability	Examples and Page #s in text	Authenticity	Examples and Page #s in text
What does it mean? (Define)		What does it mean?	
What does it look like? (Illustrate)		What does it look like? (Illustrate)	
When was Tom not showing accountability? (Illustrate)		When was Tom not showing authenticity? (Illustrate)	
When did Tom achieve accountability? (Illustrate)		When did Tom achieve accountability? (Illustrate)	

Figure 7.2 Accountability

- **Beginning:** Ask students to look up the words "Accountability" and "Authenticity." Discuss what the words mean and cite examples in life that illustrate those concepts. Read aloud from chapter 2 of *Tom Sawyer* "The Glorious Whitewasher." Model ways to identify examples from the text of "accountability" and "authenticity." Give the students the opportunity to read selected passages of Tom Sawyer using audio book versions from YouTube or the AudioBookTreasury.com. Ask the students to identify one more example throughout the book of "accountability" and "authenticity." In small groups, invite the students to illustrate and cite where Tom displayed "accountability" and "authenticity."
- **Intermediate:** Include all students in these activities. To extend the use of language to the Intermediate stage of proficiency, ask students to identify, cite and illustrate counter examples of "accountability" and "authenticity." With each cited example, they must include a paragraph explanation of why they selected a particular text in the book as a counter example.
- **Advanced:** Include all students in the above activities. In order to extend the use of language to the Advanced stage of proficiency, ask students to organize a presentation of their illustrated chart. The presentation should involve all the students who contributed to the illustrated chart including Beginning Stage ELs. To do this, the group needs to establish rules for presentation and discussion. They also must generate questions for their classmates based upon the information presented in the chart.

In summary, addressing CCSS for ELs requires that the classroom teacher be able to assess in the moment the language level of the student. The assessment is only the first part of the solution. The assessment needs to be tied to language usage so that appropriate instructional accommodations can be made. At each stage of language proficiency, the complexity and rigor increased in accordance with the expected language performance. Additionally, CCSS can be clustered around a language-rich activity or set of activities that can be accommodated to engage ELs across language levels. In this chapter, I provided selected standards and performance tasks at three grade levels (kindergarten, fourth, and eighth grade) in order to illustrate how instruction can be differentiated by stage of language proficiency using virtually the same grade level activity to engage all learners.

Part III

SUPPORTING STUDENTS LITERACY DEVELOPMENT IN DIGITAL SPACES

Chapter 8

Digital Literacies for English Learners

Theory and Practice

Ian O'Byrne and Martha Castañeda

In this chapter, we explore the how digital literacies can be used to support the language and literacy needs of English learners (ELs) in the mainstream classrooms.

Today's mainstream classrooms increasingly include students for whom English is a second language. Current digital literacy practices provide novel and effective opportunities for educators to support ELs in the classroom. This chapter will explore the use of digital literacies to inform the teaching of ELs in the mainstream classroom. First, the chapter will make a case for the use of new digital texts and tools when working with ELs. Next, the chapter will identify opportunities for teaching and research in line with best practices of teaching ELs with new technologies. Given the burgeoning use of digital literacies when working with ELs, it seems important to synthesize the research, practices, and beliefs of these technologies as they apply to the mainstream classroom.

The nature of literacy, multicultural education, and inclusion of the Internet and other communication technologies demand an expanded view of "text" to include visual, digital, and other multimodal formats (Alvermann, 2002; New London Group, 2000; Rose & Meyer, 2002). A richer and more complex definition of literacy thus requires a richer and more complex theoretical framing of literacy research (Leu, O'Byrne, Zawilinski, McVerry, & Everett-Cacopardo, 2009). To frame the work we discuss in this chapter, we used a multiple theoretical perspective approach (Labbo & Reinking, 1999) that incorporated several accepted and tested perspectives, including those from EL instruction and new literacies research and practice. These two perspectives were the foundation upon which we modified an instructional model for providing direct instruction and experience for educators as they work with ELs.

ENGAGING STUDENTS IN ENGLISH
LANGUAGE INSTRUCTION

As the EL student population grows much faster than the overall student population (OELA, 2010) and just as ELs' academic performance continues to lag behind their native-speaker peers (NAEP, 2009), educators seek ways to engage ELs in the classroom. Before we venture into a discussion of the use of new digital texts and tools for reaching and teaching ELs, it is important to discuss the optimal conditions for learning a second language. With its roots well established in linguistics, sociolinguistics, child language acquisition, and education, the field of second language acquisition (SLA) has flourished.

Fostering Second Language Acquisition

In this chapter, we will focus our efforts on language learning that occurs in an academic setting otherwise known as instructed SLA. SLA refers to the theory and pedagogy associated with the learning of another language in addition to an individual's first language (Ellis, 2005; Krashen, 1982). Reviews and research on best practices to facilitate language learning have reached conflicting conclusions. Still, according to Erben, Ban, and Castaneda (2009), SLA research provides teachers with guidance through a set of five principles that foster language development. In the following section we will list each principle and discuss the foundational theory and research behind each assumption.

Principle 1: Give ELs many opportunities to read, to write, to listen to, and to discuss oral and written English expressed in a variety of meaningful ways. For the receptive skills of listening and reading, it is imperative that language learners access target language input. Krashen (1985, 1994) concludes that the key to success in acquiring a new language is dependent on the amount of input received. Learners need exposure to abundant comprehensible and meaning-based input (Krashen, 1985, 1994). Similarly, for the productive skills of writing and speaking, learners need to be pushed to produce output. Swain (1995) hypothesized that language learning is facilitated when learners are encouraged to produce comprehensible input. Moreover, both the input and output learners receive need focus on meaning. To develop English fluency, learners must actively decode and encode messages in real communication (DeKeyser, 1998). Thus giving ELs ample opportunities to listen and read authentic texts coupled with writing and discussing real-world tasks fosters language development.

Principle 2: Draw attention to patterns of English language structure.
There are three ways that language instruction can aid language acquisition.

The first is through formulaic expressions. When educators teach and draw attention to widely used formulaic expressions, learners can internalize the material, use the terms, and break down the language components at a later time (Ellis, 1984; Myles, Mitchell, & Hooper, 1999). Formulaic expressions maximize learners' participation in conversations. The second approach to drawing attention involves using the ELs' existing built in language syllabus (Ellis, 1993; Littlewood, 1984). Within this syllabus, grammatical structures emerge in a relatively systematic fashion. Educators provide ELs with a language-rich environment that highlights the structures in the built in syllabus. Finally, educators can actively engage ELs in language learning by drawing attention to language forms. According to Schmidt (2001), language acquisition requires conscious noticing and therefore instruction should direct learners' conscious attention to the form in the input. When used in meaning-based tasks, drawing attention to the patters of the English language structure can have an effect on language development.

Principle 3: Give ELs classroom time to use their English productively. As mentioned previously, ELs need ample opportunities to get actively involved in classroom activities that require language output production. The benefits of language output include: testing out a language hypothesis, confirming one's language premises, noticing the structure of language, better internalizing language knowledge, and finding one's linguistic style and voice (Skehan, 1998). Classroom activities can also foster fruitful interactions. The interaction hypothesis proposed by Long (1996, 2006) hypothesizes that acquisition is facilitated through interaction. It is within the window of interaction that learners can engage in negotiation of meaning and make communicative modifications as needed to make their message understood. The importance of activities that engage ELs in language production and interaction cannot be underestimated in language development.

Principle 4: Give ELs opportunities to notice their errors and to correct their English. Lyster and Ranta (1997) analyzed copious amounts of teacher and student classroom interaction data and focused on the types of feedback teachers provide and analyzed which types of feedback lead to repair on the part of the learner. Teachers tend to most often provide recast type of feedback, an implicit reformulation of the error with teacher production of the correction (e.g., Student: "Yesterday I eat banana"; Teacher: "Oh, yesterday you ate a banana"). Lyster and Ranta (1997) found that instances where the teacher elicits, rather than provides the correction, leads to more student-generated repairs. Teachers are encouraged to follow student errors with elicitation (e.g., "say that again"), metalinguistic feedback (e.g., "is that past tense?"), and clarification requests (e.g., "I did not understand").

Principle 5: Construct activities that maximize opportunities for ELs to interact with others in English. The relevance of classroom activities that maximize the opportunities for ELs to interact with others cannot be underscored. Activities that focus on meaning (DeKeyser, 1998) draw attention to language patterns (Ellis, 1984; Myles, Mitchell, & Hooper, 1999), expose students to large amounts of input (Krashen, 1985, 1994), give opportunities for learners to notice their errors (Lyster & Ranta, 1997), and require learners to produce language (Swain, 1985) all have been shown to assist learners in developing language proficiency.

Engaging Students in New and Digital Literacies

As the Internet and online informational texts become more prevalent in schools and society, it is important to build the knowledge, skills, and dispositions students will need as they read online from diverse cultures to form a global classroom. This is challenging since teaching and learning in the Internet era can be totally different from the way most teachers were educated. Put simply, the Internet and other information communication technologies (ICTs) require that we continue to define and redefine what literacy is and how individuals learn. We're well aware that outside of school, students regularly read, write, and collaborate with others online. However in our classrooms we sometimes view this as a distraction rather than an opportunity to educate children using online texts that they are accustomed to using. Through the careful use of online informational text in the classroom, instructors can help students recognize text structure and features and use them to effectively communicate to multiple audiences in school and in personal communications. Guided by the intentional instructional use of ICTs, teachers can guide ELs as they search and sift through online informational text.

As we study and embed digital literacies in our classrooms, it is important to consider that the nature of literacy is rapidly evolving as ICTs emerge (Coiro, Knobel, Lankshear, & Leu, 2008). To make these changes happen in the classroom, an expanded view of "text" to include visual, digital, and other multimodal formats is needed (Alvermann, 2002; New London Group, 2000; Rose & Meyer, 2002). Important in this expanded view of "text" as it relates to EL instruction is an opportunity to create "a vehicle through which individuals communicate with one another using the codes and conventions of society" (Robinson & Robinson, 2003). In essence, the SLA classroom is able to consider the cultural and societal elements involved in literacy-based practices (Black, 2009).

It is important to consider that comprehension of online informational text may provide challenges for some students. Young children are provided with far too few formal experiences with learning how to read informational texts in school classrooms (Duke, 2000; Duke, Bennett-Armistead, & Roberts, 2003).

This is problematic in classrooms where ELs may struggle with not only academic achievement, but also literacy and language acquisition (Proctor, Dalton, & Grisham, 2007). There is an understanding that elementary students need to be provided with more instructional opportunities to engage with informational text (e.g., Chall, Jacobs, & Baldwin, 1990; Duke, 2000; Gregg & Sekeres, 2006; Smolkin & Donovan, 2001). There are also research-based instructional strategies available to guide instruction (e.g., Biancarosa & Snow, 2004; Davis, Spraker, & Kushman, 2005). Even with this focus, many students are unable to comprehend the informational texts that have become so prevalent on the Internet (Biancarosa & Snow, 2004; Duke, 2000, 2004; Leach, Scarborough, & Rescorla, 2003). Despite these challenges, it is clear that ELs need to be provided with multiple opportunities to work with online informational text (Proctor, Dalton, & Grisham, 2007; Proctor et al., 2011).

Critical Readers of Online Information

We know that reading comprehension is an active, constructive, meaning-making process in which the reader, the text, and the activity play a central role (RAND Reading Study Group, 2002). Reading of informational text often proves to be a bit more challenging for students (Duke & Pearson, 2002) as they serve the purpose of communicating information about the natural or social world (Duke & Purcell-Gates, 2003; Weaver & Kintsch, 1991). This is increasingly more complex for students that might be learning the primary language of the text (Anderson, 2003). Informational texts may include complex concepts, specialized vocabulary, and unfamiliar text structures that significantly impact a reader's ability to locate, understand, and use the information contained therein (Cox, Shanahan, & Tinzman, 1991; Kintsch, 1992; Weaver & Kintsch, 1991). The intersection of these two areas proves problematic for teachers and ELs using online text in the classroom.

Critical literacy provides new opportunities when incorporated into a classroom that uses various digital texts and tools for instructional purposes. Because these texts and ICTs are constantly changing (Leu, 2000), we must reflect these changes in our classrooms (Cuban, 2001; Reinking, 1997; Zhao, Pugh, Sheldon, & Byers, 2002). It is the duty of educators to authentically and effectively integrate these online informational texts into the classroom (Torres & Mercado, 2006). This use of the Internet as a text in the classroom allows the teacher and students to build language acquisition skills while engaging in literacy practices.

Critical Writers of Online Information

Second language instruction is increasingly viewed as including multiple modes of information (Kern & Schultz, 2005). In SLA instruction this

Ian O'Byrne and Martha Castañeda

involves writing using different modes of communication including language, image, audio, video, gesture, and other semiotic resources to make signs in explicit social contexts (Brock, Case, Pennington, Li, & Salas, 2008; Kress & Van Leeuwen, 2001). In this process we have the opportunity to understand and discuss aspects of truth, knowledge, understanding, and identity situated within a culture (Buckingham, 2013; Kress, 2003). Additionally, the use of ICTs in writing of text with ELs empowers individuals to reconfigure or remix the mode or message into an entirely different mode or message (Kress, 2009; Shiga, 2007). Students as producers of multimodal content, may chose to recreate, or remix an online text. In this process a student can recreate or rewrite the text, change the mode (e.g., transform from text to image or video), or change the message entirely using a critical literacy lens. This in turn sets the stage for elements of critical multiliteracies when working with ELs.

Based on elements of critical literacy and new literacies, a multiliteracies perspective is built on a pedagogical agenda of social change and empowered students as "active designers of social futures" (Cope & Kalantzis, 2000). Multiliteracies include critical literacy tenets of having students "reading the word and reading the world" (Friere & Macedo, 1987) while integrating the teaching of writing (Cope & Kalantzis, 2000) and ICTs. Pedagogy defined by multiliteracies theory and influenced by elements of multimodal design build aspects of critical engagement between students and text to promote social justice through process and product. This use of multiliteracies as a tool to assist students in thinking critically about online information was also consistent with work in multimodal design (Cope & Kalantzis, 2000).

PRACTICAL APPLICATIONS

As has been detailed in this chapter, ELs frequently have a difficult time learning and accessing the English language. The intentional use of digital texts and tools in instruction provides opportunities for students to practice English skills and discourse practices without worrying about the response of peers or the instructor (Dukes, 2005). Additionally, the inclusion of the ICTs into instruction provides opportunities for students to build skills in new and digital literacies (Proctor, Dalton, & Grisham, 2007), critical multiliteracies (Black, 2005; Genesee, 2006; Shetzer & Warschauer, 2000), and generally improve students' motivation to learn (Butler-Pascoe, 1997).

ICTs provide challenges and opportunities for providing ELs with the visual and aural stimulation necessary to render new concepts more accessible (Cummins, 2009b, 2011). This draws on Vygotsky's (1978) sociocultural theory that indicates that learning is facilitated through interaction with the social environment (e.g., interpersonal learning) as opposed to intrapersonal learning. Strengths of the inclusion of ICTs in instruction include the ability to scaffold students as they construct meaning in a digital environment (Healey & Klinghammer, 2002). Digital texts and tools can also be used to support learners as they engage in vocabulary and verbal language development (Green, 2005).

Challenges associated with the inclusion of ICTs into instruction mostly focus on the access and training associated with use of digital texts and tools. With the use of technology in any setting, especially the classroom there is the likelihood that computers will crash, hardware fails, or software is nonexistent (Kuroneko, 2008). Frequently, in schools that need access to technology for use with ELs, it is underutilized, or misappropriated and collects dust, or sits in a storage closet (Ware, 2008). Finally, the key component in the successful use of educational technologies in a classroom setting involves the proper training and support of the individual teachers and ELs that need to use the digital texts and tools (Smith, Higgins, Wall, & Miller, 2005). For the most part, all of these challenges may be averted through the strategic training and empowerment of educators and the logical distribution of educational technologies (Brown & Warschauer, 2006; Hefzallah, 2004). Much of the work that focuses on the use of educational technologies in second language and bilingual education environments is included under the umbrella of Computer Assisted Language Learning (CALL).

Computer Assisted Language Learning

CALL is an instructional approach that integrates technology use into literacy instruction to create learning opportunities for ELs. Through various implementations, CALL provides opportunities for differentiation of instruction through manipulation of instruction and materials to focus on student pacing, content, interest, and medium (Hubbard & Levy, 2006). CALL provides authentic and effective learning opportunities to allow ELs to negotiate language learning and comprehension while acting as a "springboard" for literacy learning activities (Meskill, 1999). As detailed earlier in the section on critical multiliteracies, CALL also enables students to learn and interact in challenging, task-based activities that include "different perspectives and opinions" (Meskill, 1999, p. 3) to allow for development of argumentation and consensus building in use of complicated literacy skills (Bley-Vroman, 1989; Donato, 1994).

Second language instruction that includes CALL represents a shift in the way that literacy is defined through a series of constantly evolving and interconnected cultural and global semiotic systems (Borsheim, Merritt, & Reed, 2008; Richardson, 2006). This shift in the intersection of literacy and technology embeds theory and perspectives included in new and digital literacies, multiliteracies, and are the pillars of the framing of the ORMS model (McVerry, 2013; O'Byrne & McVerry, 2015) that was used to guide this chapter and the investigation of opportunities to scaffold digital literacies for ELs. Effectively applied, a pedagogical model like the ORMS model or CALL provides opportunities in "meaning-rich contexts" which can engage students in real-world authentic learning tasks without merely focusing on language acquisition or technology skill use (Warschauer & Meskill, 2000).

Web Literate ELs in Digital Spaces

It is necessary to identify opportunities to empower students using digital literacies (Henry, Castek, O'Byrne, & Zawilinski, 2012). The ability to read and write using digital tools has been shown in EL contexts to construct "spaces" for learning and sharing of interests (Lam, 2000). Digital literacies for ELs have also been used to construct "virtual ethnographies" to document identity using multimodal information (Carel, 1999). This has also identified possibilities to develop a rich, "transcultural identity" constructed across cultural perspectives using ICTs (Black, 2006). As evidenced by some of the research presented earlier, the use of digital literacies in classrooms provides opportunities for ELs to acquire a target language and possibly use it as a lever for purposes of empowerment (Abraham, 2008; Liu, Moore, Graham, & Lee, 2002).

To address these concerns and support educators and students as they authentically and effectively use online informational text in the classroom, the Online Research and Media Skills (ORMS) model was developed and tested. The purpose of the ORMS model is to prepare students for a digital and global economy while also reinforcing reading, writing, speaking, listening, and viewing of subject area content. This instructional model uses a multiple theoretical perspective approach (Labbo & Reinking, 1999), incorporating several theoretical perspectives, including those from reading research, critical literacy, and new literacies to frame the cornerstones.

There are three cornerstones in the ORMS model which support lifelong reflective learning which empowers students through online inquiry, composition, and comprehension with the use of learning environments that utilize authentic, productive, and ethical use of applications required in today's global economy:

- **Online Collaborative Inquiry:** A group of local or global learners who arrive at a common outcome via multiple pathways of knowledge
- **Online Reading Comprehension:** The skills, strategies, practices, and dispositions students need to locate, evaluate, and synthesize information during problem-based inquiry tasks

• **Online Content Construction:** A process by which students construct and redesign knowledge by actively encoding and decoding meaning through the use of ever shifting multimodal tools

To better understand the three cornerstones of the ORMS model, an open online educational resource was developed to help explicate the intricacies of each cornerstone (https://sites.google.com/site/ormsmodel/). Online reading comprehension (Leu et al., 2009) is framed as reading of online information as a process of problem-based inquiry that takes place as students use the Internet to search and sift for answers to problems. This cornerstone is viewed as reading of online information. Online collaborative inquiry is framed as collaboration and co-construction of a body of information by a group of local, or global connected learners. This cornerstone is viewed as collaboration by learners as they search, sift, and synthesize online informational text. Online content construction (O'Byrne, 2013) is framed as the skills, strategies, and dispositions necessary as students construct, redesign, or re-invent online texts by actively encoding and decoding meaning through the use of digital texts and tools. This cornerstone is viewed as including the process and product of writing using digital texts and tools. As these skills are propelled by technological advances, these literacies will be paramount for success in a global, networked community.

Readers and Writers of Online Information

Given the changes and shifts that are occurring to literacy as a result of technology, it can be a challenge to thoughtfully and routinely embed digital texts and tools. As detailed throughout this chapter, this integration of ICTs should be viewed as a literacy, and as a result is a social imperative for all classrooms. This is an even more pressing concern for classrooms as teachers and ELs identify possibilities to acquire target languages while considering the sociocultural factors that affect discourse systems. With these challenges, and the dire need for this instruction in all classrooms, not only second language acquisition environments, we believe there is a rich opportunity and a need for innovative instructional and research uses that explore the intersections of language acquisition and digital literacies.

To provide an overview of the complexities and opportunities for scholarship in this area we would like to highlight a couple case studies that reflect possibilities for current and future digital literacy instruction for ELs. The following three case studies presented are not an exhaustive list, they are merely a representative example of the possibilities available when instruction is imbued with digital literacies. We urge researchers and educators to continue on with this focus and continue to examine ways to include digital literacies with ELs.

Case Study 1: Online Content Construction

Javier Figueroa is a seventh grade teacher of ELs in a small neighborhood in New York City. Most of the students in his class that are designated as ELs come from four to six different languages. Additionally, many of the students could be considered to be illiterate in their primary language. To combat this, helps his students engage with ICTs while learning the target language by having them construct online content as they discuss identity in relation to class readings. Computer supported collaborative tools like Google Apps and Google Drive are used to support his students as they collaboratively research and synthesize online information with their peers. These online documents are always available for his students as they plan, revise, and edit their work. These online documents also allow Javier to spend more time asynchronously supporting students. Finally, Javier provides opportunities to engage students in multimodal authoring, or writing of online texts using tools like Glogster EDU, the CAST UDL Book Builder, or Mozilla Popcorn. In each of these scenarios, students are encouraged to examine their identity and culture, while utilizing digital literacies for SLA.

Elements of work involved in online content construction are of high importance as they begin to identify not only some of the challenges and opportunities that exist in the use of digital literacies in SLA instruction. They indicate the responsibilities that exist for the teacher, and we would also suggest the students when engaging in this instruction. Teachers not only bear a responsibility for including digital texts and tools in instruction, but they also need a certain amount of appreciation for the uncertainty that exists when using the ICTs as a text and tool (O'Byrne, 2012). Teachers must consider and plan for the complexities, challenges, and opportunities that exist in the online informational space. Researchers must consider these complexities as they investigate the use of the Internet as a communication tool in processing, sharing, and connecting information in a global ecosystem and the effects of this on language. Finally, ELs bear a certain amount of responsibility in the classroom as they must engage as an active participant in an ICT infused classroom (Greenhow, Robelia, & Hughes, 2009).

Case Study 2: Online Collaborative Inquiry

Shu Heng Chen teaches adult ELs in Shenzhen, China. To keep his students focused on studying English in context and to better understand English discourse in online spaces he creates "Internet scavenger hunts" in which students must search online for clues and answers to his queries. As students research online, they are to collaborate and share responses to the questions that he provides. Most of these queries are high-interest, inquiry-based items that were provided by previous students. These questions involve current music, old television shows, food, and fashion. The primary focus is on the critical and interpretative lenses that students use as they individually and collaboratively engage with online and offline texts in SLA instruction. This work identifies challenges that exist in the ways that teachers and their students conceptualize and approach the business of "school." In turn, the language learning preferences of the ELs help educators calibrate their pedagogy and expectations in the classroom.

The online collaborative inquiry presented in this case study identifies the nuanced changes in literacy and technology that teachers must account for in SLA instruction. This is not meant to suggest that younger students, or millennials are "hard-wired" to handle this form of multimodal information because they're younger. There is a misguided belief that "digital natives" are fundamentally different than their predecessors because they are surrounded by these new technologies and literacies (Prensky, 2001). The research shows that this assumption is unfounded and students are not privileged or presupposed to be more facile with ICTs thanks to their digital native moniker (Bennett, Maton, & Kervin, 2008; Kennedy, Judd, Churchward, Gray, & Krause, 2008). The inclusion of digital literacies into the classroom, especially an English as a second language classroom, requires educators and students to account for not only the content knowledge and text or tool knowledge, but also the pedagogical implications of this form of instruction (Koehler & Mishra, 2009).

Case Study 3: Online Reading Comprehension

Jose Mora Santos teaches fifth grade in an elementary school outside of San Antonio, Texas. The school is in an economically challenged school district in which most of the community includes non-native English speakers. Jose tries to utilize elements of online reading comprehension to create a third hybrid space between school and home that he can use to support students and their parents. Jose understands that many of the students in his class are the primary translators for their families. He asks students to bring in websites and online information that parents and families routinely visit to help in translating these materials in class. Additionally, Jose uses a classroom website to curate and share websites from local health organizations and public outreach groups that connect to curricular goals. Students translate and discuss these texts in class, and then are able to bring them home to share more information with their families. These varied texts and tools provide opportunities for ELs and teachers to engage with nontraditional forms of the nontraditional texts that proliferate on the Internet. These digital tools engage students with digital texts in the real world to allow for student engagement and collaboration. This example of online reading comprehension provides students with multiple opportunities to engage with online information in a highly engaging interface.

This case study identifies highly engaging uses of online informational text to allow teachers and students to work together to search and sift through informational and instructional texts. This work is exciting because it not only identifies possibilities for the use of digital literacies in the classroom, but it also identifies opportunities for global uses of technology. In many classrooms technology access is a challenge. If utilized effectively, mobile uses of technology, including mobile phones, tablets, and handheld devices can be valued in the classroom. These devices provide opportunities to support learners and classrooms where technology access is problematic. More importantly, mobile devices allow for breaking down the barriers of the classroom and allowing students to experience language learning in real-world contexts. Students and educators are able to record digital media of target language use in the "real world" and bring this back to the classroom for examination and debriefing. Students and teachers also can use mobile devices to socialize, communicate, and video conference with individuals using communication tools like Google Hangouts. This type of learning using mobile apps, mobile devices, and platforms like augmented reality has the potential to engage ELs in thoughtful, practical study and use of a target language.

RECOMMENDATIONS FOR ACTION

In this chapter, we summarized the theories and perspectives used across the work conducted while utilizing digital literacies in EL instruction. During this examination we shared specific insights gained from working with teachers and students during training, implementation, and assessment of this work. Within this framing and discussion, we suggested the changing roles and responsibilities needed by teachers and students when using ICTs as a tool for socializing and communicating in the modern English as a second language classroom. Specifically, we addressed the opportunities and challenges associated with teaching and assessment of work process and product included in use of these digital texts and tools in the EL classroom. We are excited by not only the challenges and opportunities that exist in this area, but were motivated to write this chapter, and push for a special themed issue to further explore the complexities of this work. Viewing digital literacies as an essential, fundamental right, this work is even more important as we examine the complexities and freedoms that exist in SLA.

As learners engage in SLA, there is a certain amount of power and potential for empowerment that exists in the integration of a new discourse system (Gee, 2000; McHoul & Grace, 1993, 1993; Scollon, Scollon, & Jones, 2011). There is inherent power in literacy (Bennett, 1983; Cope & Kalantzis, 1993), and technology is increasingly being embedded in all literate practices (Livingstone, 2004; Selfe, 1999). Technology not only provides opportunities to break down classroom walls, it also allows individuals to engage in a global marketplace. Acquisition, and in some cases mastery, of literate practices is paramount to success or failure when working and interacting across global and cultural systems. As these global networks increasingly connect individuals globally, it is important to consider that for the most part, English has been the primary language used on the Internet (Crystal, 2003). Paradoxically, we need to consider that the next wave of citizens to join the Internet will primarily be non-native English speakers from global areas where the Internet hasn't taken root yet. The Internet has become this generation's defining technology for literacy and is almost always connected to online and digital media (Horrigan, 2010; Lenhart, Purcell, Smith, & Zickuhr, 2010). As educators and scholars we need to investigate and develop best practices associated with digital literacy use for ELs in varied global and cultural contexts.

Chapter 9

Supporting English Learners' Academic Literacy Development Through Social Media

Dong-shin Shin

In this chapter, I describe how a second grade teacher uses Web 2.0–based social media to support her English learner (EL) students' language and literacy development. I also share challenges teachers and students encounter when using social media in K–12 classrooms, and offer examples to show how these media can be used to promote and support students' academic literacy development.

Web 2.0–based social media have become a common form of communication that students use with peers in affinity groups (collaborative groups within and across schools) or with family members outside of school. Increasingly, students are coming to school with the ability to use social networking technologies such as instant messengers, multiplayer online games, Facebook, wikis, tweets, and blogs. Even primary school-aged children often come to school, knowing how to use Internet resources, log on to social networks, and explore sites designed for their particular age group (Dodge, Husain, & Duke, 2011; Shanahan, 2013). Research on students' uses of social media in nonschool settings has shown that social media involve changes in modes, authorship, styles, genres, social relationships, and time and space of writing practices (Gee & Hayes, 2011; Knobel & Lankshear, 2009; Lam & Warriner, 2012; Yi, 2007). This kind of language practice has been shown to support language and literacy development, giving expression to a wider variety of authorial goals for expanded audiences and providing powerful avenues for active engagement, which leads to robust learning (Atkinson & Swaggerty, 2011; Beach, Hull, & O'Brien, 2011; Gebhard, Shin, & Seger, 2011; Kist, Doyle, Hayes, Horwitz, & Kuzior, 2010).

Although an increasing number of research studies have provided strong evidence for the affordances of Web 2.0–based social media in academic language and literacy development of ELs, most studies have focused on second language (L2) learners' out-of-school literacy practices, and little is known about the use of social media in school by L2 students (Bloch, 2007; Egbert, Huff, McNeil, Preuss, & Sellen, 2009; Shin, 2014; Warschauer, 2006). There is a need for more support for teachers to use social media in K–12 settings and for more studies that report teachers' uses of those technologies.

ACADEMIC LITERACY AND THE ENGLISH LANGUAGE ARTS CURRICULUM

In conceptualizing academic literacy development, I draw on Systemic Functional Linguistics (SFL) and socioculturally oriented educational linguistics (Eggins, 2004; Halliday, 1985; Martin & Rose, 2008; Schleppegrell, 2004). From these theoretical perspectives, language is not a set of decontextualized rules that students can master through drill and practice for "accurate" use or as an innate capacity that will be acquired in a natural developmental sequence through exposure and interaction with academic texts. Rather, these perspectives help educators to view language as a dynamic system of choices that students learn to use to accomplish a wide variety of social, academic, and political goals in and out of school (Gebhard, Harman, & Seger, 2007; New London Group, 1996). Accordingly, the job of the teacher is to heighten students' awareness of linguistic variations depending on contexts (e.g., different closing statements or modal verbs depending on recipients and purposes of a letter), and to broaden students' ability to use language across a variety of social and academic contexts to accomplish specific kinds of work (e.g., writing a science lab report, an argumentative essay, an e-mail to a teacher, text messages to friends).

To support students in making more informed and appropriate linguistic choices for the communicative contexts in which they are engaged, teachers and students can explore the ways in which language functions serve to convey ideas in specific mediums of communication, while enacting relationships among participants. These functions operate simultaneously in any given speech act or text, which Halliday (1985) calls ideational (representing experience), textual (organizing experience), and interpersonal (enacting relationship) functions. To give an example of the three functions, a short written essay delivers experiential meanings that describe "who does what to whom" in a specific condition, and the essay thus creates textual meanings that show specific arrangements of meanings relevant to the medium of composition. In addition, the essay creates interpersonal meanings between a reader and an author, since the author accommodates and positions readers in a certain way when she or he writes the essay.

School-valued academic English differs significantly from everyday practices (e.g., Christie, 2002; Dyson & Genishi, 2007; Heath, 1983; Michaels, 1981) and takes years of learning to develop expertise in its discourses. As Cummins (1984) observed, developing the cognitive academic language proficiency can take from five to seven years, but a relatively short time of two years for the basic interpersonal communication skills. For ELs, these differences are greater and take on even more significance as students are required to read and write about unfamiliar topics, using technical language and drawing upon meaning-making resources that differ from the language practices they use at home or that are valued by their peers (e.g., Dyson, 2003; Ibrahim, 1999). Therefore, successful academic literacy development entails developing an understanding of how language functions and varies according to different discourses. To this end, teachers and students can analyze how texts vary in relation to who is communicating with whom, what they are communicating about, and the modes through which they are interacting, while examining how lexical and grammatical choices of texts operate at the word, sentence, and discourse levels.

The teacher that I introduce in this chapter taught a second grade class in an urban elementary school in Massachusetts. According to the school district English language arts (ELA) curriculum framework, second grade students were expected to develop competency in various genres of writing, including letters, recounts, expository texts, reports, and argumentative essays. Adopting SFL perspectives on academic writing, the teacher intended to make learning the school-mandated academic writing genres more meaningful to her students. She provided them with reading and writing activities in which they could express their various interests and concerns to personally important audiences. She incorporated blogging into her ELA writing center activity and utilized the affordances (contributions) of social media in teaching academic genres. In other words, informed by a notion of affordances that means "the possibilities for action which people identify in relation to specific recourses" (Barton & Potts, 2013, pp. 186–87), the teacher configured the pedagogical possibilities that blogging as social media offers for teaching academic writing genres. A primary goal for her blog-mediated writing curriculum was to support ELs who are emergent readers and writers in developing a critical understanding of how structural, grammatical, and lexical patterns associated with writing genres are selected functionally for the purposes of texts, instead of fixed rules that work in any contexts. As such, her ELA curriculum aimed to support students developing expertise in making grammatical and lexical choices appropriate to the context of the text they were being asked to read and write.

Given the degree to which second graders are routinely asked to produce narratives both orally and in writing, the teacher made the genre of recounts a centerpiece of the blog-mediated writing center activities. When the genre was introduced to the students, they were invited to write about memorable life experiences. For the purposes of this chapter, I focus on a recounts unit, even though I drew on relevant data from curricular units for other genres to obtain grounded data.

The genre of recounts is a high frequency genre, as it is an entry point genre for school-based writing. A recount is a simple narrative retelling of a sequence of events in chronological order (Derewianka, 1990; Knapp & Watkins, 2005; Schleppegrell, 2004). Recounts differ from narratives in that they contain a less complicating plot and they do not necessarily have a fully developed resolution (Knapp & Watkins, 2005; Martin & Rose, 2008). The recounts include an orientation (e.g., the naming of the participants, time, and place) and a record of events. In addition to these structural features, recounts also have typically valued grammatical and lexical features. For example, recounts rely on material processes to construe concrete actions central to the plot (e.g., do, swim, go) in the past tense, and use temporal connectives such as "when," "next," "then," "in the end" to organize the sequences of events.

INSTRUCTIONAL SETTING

I conducted this blog-mediated writing project in collaboration with a second grade teacher, Mrs. Smith at Fuentes Elementary School (all names are pseudonyms). Located in a low-income urban area, Fuentes serves a predominantly Latino population. According to school demographic information, about 75 percent of the school population is Latino, and about 90 percent of the students receive free or reduced-price lunch. The students who speak English as a second language (ESL) make up about 35 percent of the school population. The school is designated "under-performing" due to low scores on the state-mandated standardized test, MCAS (Massachusetts Comprehensive Assessment System). In regard to technology, the school did not have a computer lab and the students did not have computer classes. Moreover, like many urban schools serving poor communities, much of what was available to students was outdated or in need of repair.

Reflecting the school's demographic features, the second grade class was composed predominantly of Latino students—twelve Puerto Ricans, three African Americans, and two others. Most used English only in school while relying on Spanish as a primary language; three were ESL students, and four were repeating second grade. All students received free lunch, and 30 percent of them had computers outside school, according to the survey the teacher conducted at the beginning of the school year. All had limited experience with computers and Internet-related activities. To compensate for accessibility issues, the class went to the local public library on Friday mornings and conducted English language arts classes there. The teacher planned library visits in the hope that it would lead the students and their families to use community resources regularly during the weekends. In addition, Mrs. Smith obtained eight laptops for the academic year through her participation in ACCELA Alliance (Access to Critical Content and English Language Acquisition), a federally funded partnership between the University of Massachusetts Amherst and local school districts (Gebhard & Willett, 2008; Shin, 2014). Beyond securing access to computer technologies, she provided students and parents guidance on how to use computers and Internet resources through workshops held in the classroom and the library.

The classroom teacher is a well-regarded veteran instructor who is interested in using instructional technologies in her teaching. When the blog-mediated writing project was initiated, she was working toward her master's degree with ACCELA and became invested in supporting ELs' academic literacy development and providing explicit instruction on academic genres using SFL. I supported her in designing, implementing, and reflecting on the blog-mediated writing curriculum throughout the school year.

Class Blog and Blog-Mediated Writing Curriculum

Class Blog

The current project utilized Web browser-based blogs (e.g., Blogspot, Kidblog, Typepad, Wordpress,) that provide free, easy-to-use templates and design choices. After reviewing several blogs, Mrs. Smith created a class blog site with Typepad, adding a password protection function to its login process to prevent issues related to identity theft. Using the ID and password that were shared among student, parents, and teachers, her second graders logged onto the class blog.

The blog contained student texts organized by the genres that they produced over the course of the school year, and related comments between students and their audiences along with illustrations and paintings made by the students.

Blog-Mediated Writing Framework

Mrs. Smith incorporated a blog into the writing center of her ELA lessons, and she managed her blog-mediated writing curriculum using a writer's workshop approach, which apprentices students into the recursive writing process of generating ideas, receiving explicit instruction, drafting, receiving

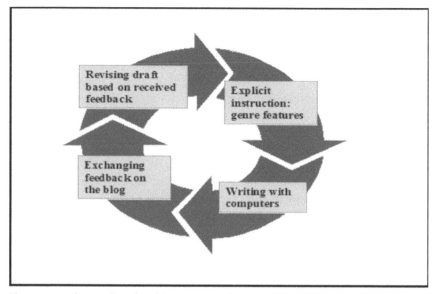

Figure 9.1   Blog-Mediated Writing Framework

feedback, and revising. She utilized blogging as part of everyday writing center activities rather than as an add-on activity in teaching academic genres. The students composed their texts through the step-by-step writing procedures illustrated in figure 9.1.

Explicit Instruction   First, Mrs. Smith supported the students in using their own life experiences to compose recounts, while modeling for the students how to brainstorm ideas and to move the ideas into written texts. She also invited parents to the class in order to provide more support for the students in using their funds of knowledge (Moll, Amanti, Neff, & Gonzales, 1992), along with stocking the class library with books about student languages, cultures, and communities from a belief that curricular materials relevant to the student population could be a key factor for engaging the ELs. She then offered explicit instruction on genre and register features of recounts, by sharing her own writing sample with the students, presenting several completed recounts from her previous class, and jointly writing a recount with the whole class. Her explicit instruction utilized metaphors and graphic organizers for complicated genre features, to accommodate second grade students' pedagogical needs. For example, the teacher introduced the organizational structure of recounts with analogical terms for air flight such as "big picture," "zoom in," and "back to the big picture." After her explicit instruction, the students had opportunities to write their recounts by using a graphic organizer that included an orientation (e.g., introduction of participants, time, and place), and an organizational structure to describe activities within a series of events. While learning these genre features, the students received explicit instruction on lexical and grammatical choices that could be varied according to the purposes and audiences of their texts.

Composing with Computers   After Mrs. Smith's provided explicit instruction on recounts, the students either composed recounts on the computer or they wrote them in longhand on paper before typing them, depending on their preferences. While the students were composing their texts on the computer, they received mini-lessons about features of written language such as avoiding chained sentences with the word "and," conventions, and spelling. At this stage, the teacher showed them how to use the spell-check function of Microsoft Word.

Exchanging Feedback on the Blog   When the students finished their first drafts of recounts, the drafts were posted on the class blog for feedback. Mrs. Smith instructed students how to comment on each other's texts in the blog, by attending to contents first and then to the linguistic features of texts. To make school writing more meaningful to the students, she invited students' parents, teachers, family members, and librarians to the class blog and encouraged them to comment on the students' recounts.

Revising Drafts Based on Feedback Received   After exchanging feedback on each other's texts, the students revised their first drafts by drawing on the feedback comments. In this revision process, Mrs. Smith guided the students to examine whether the recommended linguistic or grammatical choices were appropriate to the purpose and audience of their texts. When the students revised their first drafts, the teacher posted the revised texts to the class blog for publication.

INFLUENCE OF BLOG-MEDIATED WRITING ON STUDENTS' ACADEMIC LITERACY DEVELOPMENT

To examine the impact of the blog-mediated writing curriculum on ELs' academic literacy development, I employed an ethnographic approach to collecting and analyzing data. As an active participant, I collected multiple domains of data including written texts, blog postings, video recorded classroom interactions, informal conversations, interviews, and instructional materials. The unit of analysis that I drew on in this study was the blog-mediated writing texts, within the contexts of curricular units such as recounts. For data analysis, first, I analyzed themes across multiple domains of the collected data, identifying emerging themes such as types and goals of blogging, constructed relationships with audiences, and emerging identities. I then did a linguistic analysis of blog posts and genre texts, looking at textual organization, lexical and grammatical choices, and conventions regarding experiential, interpersonal, and textual meanings. This combination of ethnography and textual analysis highlights linguistic features in language use for ELs' blogging practices and their learning experiences. In the following section, I will introduce the impacts of blog-mediated ELA writing curriculum in the areas of learning academic writing genres, constructed identities in and out of school, and transformation of the ELA curriculum.

Mrs. Smith's blog-mediated writing allowed her ELs to learn a school-mandated writing genre while being engaged in socially meaningful activities. In other words, the student authors appropriated writing for the blog as opportunities not only for learning writing genres but also for proving their growing academic literacy. While learning academic genres, ELs actively provided each other feedback on the linguistic choices for their genre texts on the blog. The asynchronous environments for exchanging feedback on the blog allowed the students to become competent peers to their classmates. As seen in the blog comment excerpts in textbox 9.1, the students helped their peers to become attentive to the linguistic features of their texts, appropriating what Mrs. Smith taught about the genre and register features of recounts (e.g., teaching word choices or organizational structure with beginning, middle, and end). Through this practice, the expanded audiences of the blog-mediated writing led the ELs to expand their purposes and meaning resources for writing activities. As such, the blogging practice provided the ELs with opportunities to present themselves as confident and capable students to their peers.

The ELs endeavored to present themselves with academic confidence to their teachers and to become proud daughters or sons to their parents. With regard to their roles as capable students, for example, the ELs often posted their completed work for the following day's reading response assignment from home the previous night. The students also proudly shared what they had discovered about computer knowledge and online learning sites (e.g., Funbrain) with friends and teachers. At home, the students became "technology brokers" for their family members and helped them use computers and Internet resources. Through these digital practices, they were developing confident and capable student identities among their classmates, teachers, and family members in and out of the class. To this end, the comments in textbox 9.2. are representative of the students' growing confidence. The first two examples are the comments that Marianna received from her mother on a recount about her first birthday. She was repeating the second grade due to low test scores,

Textbox 9.1   Blog Comments for Academic Purposes

Dear Diana,
You need more details and you need back to the big picture.
Your friend Lianne

Dear Lianne,
I will show some more stuff.
From Diana

DEAR DIANA
YOU NEED TO SAY MOM AND I.
Kate

Dear Maria,
I think it's a nice story. You have a good memory. You forgot to tell when was your birthday?
Your friend,
Angie

Dear Julie
I like your story because you used deatls.
Jose

Dear Ray
I like your story because you us upercace and spases and capitos.
Jose

which made her parents concerned about her academic performance. However, the recount and blog comments allowed Maria to show her growing confidence in academic writing to her mother. The remaining examples are the comments that an academically struggling EL, Jose, who belonged to the lowest level reading group in the class, received from his family members on his text and exchanged comments.

The students also used blogging to maintain their friendships by providing emotional support for classmates who wrote about difficult life experiences, endorsing or opposing certain behaviors, or complimenting good characteristics of the recounts as seen in textbox 9.3. It is also worthwhile to note that to make friends, the ELs used their funds of knowledge, including cultural and linguistic backgrounds; for instance, the students exchanged their experiences and information related to Puerto Rico and learning Spanish. Building social relationships through blogging was extended to become a regular part of school writing, in a way that made social goals a driving force for achieving academic goals.

Textbox 9.2 Blog Comments from Family Members

Hi Maria it is mom. . . . Keep up the good work. Mommoy loves you a
lot. . . . I enjoyed going to your classroom and reading about your first
birthday. . . . Once again I am very proud of you, keep up the good work.

Love your mom

I am very proud of your work with your 1st Birthday story. I have
printed it out and hung it up on the wall at work. Everybody in my job
has read it and say it is very nice and interesting. I hope you keep up the
good work and keep making mommy happy.

I love you very much.

Talk to you soon.

mom

HI JOSE IT WAS NICE OF YOU TO RESPOND BACK TO ME JOSE
I LOVE THE STORY YOU SHOW US AT HOME ABOUT YOUR
ANIMAL I THINK IT WAS COOL.KEEP THE GOOD WORK LOVE
MOM

hi jose keep the good work. love your big sister jane.

hi jose i like your story very much

sam

Textbox 9.3 Blog Comments for Social Purposes

Dear keyla
I feel bad for you because
you bork your back. So I
wonder how did you learn how
to walk again?
your friend Diana

dear Juliana,
I think I would knock somebody out if they call me a swear.
Jeremy

Dear Juliana,
I understand your feeling. But punching is not good.
You can tell your mom. Does your mom know this?
Your best friend,
Angie

Textbox 9.3   **Blog Comments for Social Purposes** (*cont.*)

Dear Diana,
It is really hot in puerto rico. Did you get to go in the candy store. I did
not no there was a candy store in puerto rico. Did you go to the beach it
is fun in the beach. I never went to the lake in puerto rico but I did go to
puerto rico.
your friend Alicia

Dear Diana,
I want to learn spanish with you.
Your Friend,
Keyla

Dear jose,
I really really like your story it re minds me of when i went to six flags
new england.
your friend, JAMSE

Dear Maria,
That was a nice letter for your birthday
Your Friend,
Nalie

Mrs. Smith's use of blogging in teaching academic genres generated a
transformative literacy practice. For example, the ELs achieved both academic and social goals such as learning academic writing genres while
maintaining friendships, which is a daunting task to achieve in the current
climate of standardized testing and accountability. In addition, within these
blog-mediated writing environments, the ELs' academic literacy development was achieved in a way that blurred traditional categories of technology
use, such as formal and informal and in- and out-of-school literacies. Students
learned the standard ways of writing that are valued in school, while simultaneously engaging in new forms of digital literacy practice through which
they built personal relationships with diverse audiences, and used diverse
semiotic resources for various communicative goals. Moreover, this kind of
literacy practice provided effective and yet meaningful academic learning
experiences to ELs, bridging the digital disconnects in and out of school, old
and new literacies. As the comment in textbox 9.4 written by Maria's mother
at the end of the school year shows, Mrs. Smith indeed transformed her ELA
curriculum with effective blogging.

Textbox 9.4   **Blog Comment from Maria's Mother**

Maria,
The is a great letter and I hope that you get the computers that you guys want.
I think it is a great idea how the Mrs. Smith is educating the students.
We need more teachers like her. Love your mom.

RECOMMENDATIONS FOR ACTION

This blog-mediated project has implications for K–12 educators who wish to provide transformative educational experiences for ELs' academic literacy development in culturally, linguistically, and economically diverse urban schools settings. Lessons learned from this project offer teachers new ideas for how they can more effectively reach and teach EL students using Web 2.0 media. First, teachers need to fully utilize what the current technologies afford as pedagogical tools. Transforming the ELA curriculum through social media means more than just replacing paper- and pencil-based literacy activities with digitally based ones. It requires shifts in pedagogy that teachers change from a traditional skill-oriented pedagogy to a multimodal real-life-oriented pedagogy for reading and writing. Such a change will allow students to use digital technologies, to find information, to solve real problems, to share ideas, and to connect with people. This approach goes beyond involving students in drilling and practicing discrete mechanical literacy skills.

Second, it is critical not to fall into the fallacy that technology transforms curriculum and instruction automatically. In this blog-mediated writing curriculum, the ELs' successful learning experiences were not possible without the teacher's efforts to maintain a curriculum that endorses students' academic and social goals and validates their funds of knowledge (Moll, Amanti, Neff, & Gonzales, 1992). In such a culturally responsive curriculum, the students could have more opportunities not only to read and write academic texts, interacting with multiple voices, other texts, and other writers and readers, but also to negotiate multiple identities beyond that of academically struggling ELs (Dyson, 2003; Shin, 2014). Thus, transformative education for ELs through Web 2.0 technologies entails an ethical curriculum that validates student interests and cultures from their peer worlds, their homes, and their communities in schooling.

Third, supporting successful academic literacy development of ELs through social media necessitates suggesting rich communication resources for meaningful interactions. In the case of teaching academic genres, the teacher could offer explicit instruction in academic genres and linguistic choices at the sentence and discourse levels of a text, beyond isolated academic vocabulary. At the same time, the explicit instruction needs to be designed based on a function-oriented and context-dependent view of language use that supports students not only in meeting academic demands across content areas, but also in achieving a variety of goals from official and unofficial domains of school life (e.g., peer worlds and mandated curricula) (Gebhard, Harman, & Seger, 2007). This kind of instruction involves flexible visions on the part of teachers of the powerful discourse of language, with a sophisticated understanding of the dynamic relationships between language and context.

Fourth, considering the material, logistical, and technical challenges that K–12 teachers face in using computer technologies for their instruction, collaborations among school, home, community, and university are crucial in achieving educational transformation through current technologies. This need is even clearer in economically struggling urban schools that cope with under-resourced facilities for access to new technologies (Reich, Murnane, & Willett, 2012). Through this kind of collaboration, teachers can solve digital divide issues for students from low-income communities. In particular, teachers need to secure material and cultural resources for ELs' effective and meaningful use of technologies.

Last, it is critical for teachers to have knowledge of, and to develop skills in, up-to-date technologies from virtual classroom management tools to authoring tools, as seen in textbox 9.5. Considering rapidly changing technologies, developing expertise in instructional technologies is not a simple task of mastering a certain set of skills. Rather, it is an ongoing learning process that entails a flexible mind-set of learning from others, regardless of one's role as a teacher or a student in completing a task.

Textbox 9.5   Resources

Web 2.0 tools that teachers can use with students in K–12 settings for social learning or multimodal writing:

CAST UDL Book Builder: http://www.bookbuilder.cast.org for creating e-books

Edmodo: http://www.edmodo.com for managing a social learning platform like Blackboard

Glogster EDU: http://edu.glogster.com for creating cards or texts with images, text, and videos

Kidblog: http://www.kidblog.org for creating kid-friendly educational blogs

Storybird: http://storybird.com for creating e-books

Wiki: http://www.wikipedia.org for creating class wikis

Voki: http://www.voki.com for creating speaking avatars

Part IV

USING KEY UNDERSTANDINGS ABOUT LANGUAGE AND LITERACY TO SUPPORT INSTRUCTION FOR ENGLISH LEARNERS

Chapter 10

Insights Gleaned from Research Syntheses about Teaching English Learners

John Evar Strid

In this chapter, I share insights gleaned from recent research, policy, and practice reports pertaining to various aspects of language and literacy development that have important implications for teaching English learners (ELs) in mainstream U.S. classrooms.

All teachers face the consequences of having large numbers of immigrant students in their classrooms who speak a language other than English. This linguistic diversity means that most teachers will at some point see students who have learned English since starting school and who most likely are still in the process of acquiring the language. Consequently, all teachers will need to know how to give these students extra support in both their acquisition of English and academic skills. ELs will need and instructional accommodations because their academic achievement may lag behind that of their peers who come to school already speaking English on all measures of academic achievement.

On the 2013 National Assessment of Educational Progress (NAEP), fourth grade ELs scored thirty-nine points below non-ELs in reading and twenty-five points below non-ELs in math. For eighth graders the gap was even larger between ELs and non-ELs: forty-five points in reading and forty-one points in math—suggesting that ELs fall further behind as they progress through school. In fact, the gaps between ELs and non-ELs are three to eighteen points greater than the gap between students who are and are not eligible for free or reduced-price lunch, implying that language status is more important than socioeconomic status (National Center for Educational Statistics, 2013b).

LANGUAGE OF INSTRUCTION

In the past few decades, a vigorous debate has taken place among researchers, policymakers, and practitioners about which language should be used for the instruction of ELs. This discussion has been strongly affected by ideological and political influences, with some individuals taking partisan positions based on preconceived notions. The controversial nature of language of instruction is seen in the fact that three states, namely California, Arizona, and Massachusetts, passed measures banning bilingual education and mandating the use of structured English immersion between 1998 and 2002. The results of these restrictive policies have not been good, with the achievement gap for ELs growing larger in these states. Rumberger and Tran's (2010) work suggests that restrictive language policies, with simply more English, have had a negative impact on the achievement gap for ELs. The gap is demonstrated by comparing NAEP fourth grade achievement in New Mexico and Arizona. New Mexico is a state that has maintained an emphasis on bilingualism with its large Latino population, while Arizona has similar characteristics with respect to population, but has implemented one of the more restrictive bans on bilingual education. It is significant that New Mexico's students' test scores are higher across NAEP reading, math, and science by a margin from thirteen to eighteen points.

RESEARCH AND THEORETICAL BACKGROUND
FROM TWO RESEARCH REPORTS ON
LANGUAGE AND LITERACY AMONG ELs

Despite the common belief that early exposure to English and increased immersion in the target language will lead to greater mastery, research shows the opposite. ELs' continued use and mastery of the home language helps support literacy development in English. In addition, knowing two languages confers obvious advantages—cultural, intellectual, cognitive, vocational, and economic. Some studies have found increased earnings for bilingual individuals (García, 2009). In light of this, California recently made its first move to rescind its ban on bilingual education, with a state Senate committee passing a measure to place a repeal of Proposition 227 on the ballot (McGreevy, 2014).

A great deal of research has been conducted about the language and literacy development of ELs in the United States. Much of this research has been synthesized in two reports, namely *Developing Literacy in Second-Language Learners: Report of the National Literacy Panel on Language-Minority Children and Youth* (August & Shanahan, 2006) and *Educating English*

Language Learners: A Synthesis of Research Evidence (Genesee, Lindholm-Leary, Saunders, & Christian, 2006). These reports provide a comprehensive synthesis of research conducted during the last two to three decades on the oral language, literacy, and academic development of ELs in kindergarten to twelfth grade in the United States. Insights from these research syntheses have, in turn, been summarized and interpreted for policymakers and practitioners by a few language and literacy experts. Claude Goldenberg (2008) provided one of the best discussion of insights from these reports in an article titled *Teaching English Language Learners: What the Research Does—and Does Not—Say*. In this article, Goldenberg discussed the following three conclusions gleaned from these two research reports, which have important implications for teaching ELs in all classrooms.

Key Idea 1: Contribution of the Home Language

As just noted, the syntheses found that teaching children to read in their home language promotes achievement in English. On this subject, August and Shanahan (2006) reported finding seventeen studies that met strict methodological criteria, leading them to conclude that teaching ELs to read in their home language and then in the additional language, or in the home and additional languages simultaneously (at different times during the day), when compared with teaching them to read in the additional language only, increases reading achievement in the additional language. The overall finding was that after two to three years of both home and additional language reading instruction, a student scores twelve to fifteen percentile points higher than a student who only receives reading instruction in the additional language. Home language literacy instruction is not a miracle worker, but nonetheless contributes significantly to reading achievement in English. In short, learning to read in both the home language and English helps students improve their literacy skills in the additional language. However, just learning to read in the additional language does not speed up mastering literacy in that language faster and, in reality, leads to lower levels of achievement. Research indicates that it takes between five and seven years for a child to be working on a level with native speakers as far as academic language is concerned (Cummins, 1981; Hakuta, Butler, & Witt, 2000).

A great proportion of the success of teaching literacy skills in the home language comes from its support of learners' cognitive development in a language that they can understand and then transfer of skills from the home language to the additional language. The advantage of continually fostering underlying cognitive development and developing higher-level language and literacy skills cannot be emphasized enough. Advanced cognitive information will sail right over the heads of learners if they do not have the language proficiency to understand. When teachers explain the more difficult concepts to ELs in their home language so they can understand these, they make it possible for ELs to keep up academically with students who come to school already speaking English.

While skill transfer between languages can be either positive or negative, positive transfer tends to tower over the negative (August, Calderón, & Carlo, 2002). Growth in underlying academic skills applies to any language. Some examples of positive transfer of literacy skills from the home language to English include phonological skills. Once learners understand the alphabetic principle—that words are made up of smaller constituent sounds represented by different letters—they most likely can apply the principle to any language that uses an alphabet. Decoding skills, as well as knowledge of many specific letters and sounds, are also very likely to transfer. The letter "m," for example, represents a similar or identical sound in many languages. Reading skills developed in one language transfer to additional languages even if the languages use different writing systems, although entirely different scripts may diminish the degree of transfer. For example, transfer of reading skills from a logographic system such as Mandarin might be less than from a language that also uses an alphabet similar to English. Studies of transfer between English and Spanish find relatively high correlations on measures of word reading, phonological awareness, and spelling. Reading comprehension strategies also transfer, with such skills even transferring readily between languages with very different scripts, such as English and Korean.

Many vocabulary words are similar across languages, especially for languages that are related to one another. Since English borrows very large numbers of words from Latin and Latin-based languages like French and Spanish, learners with these language backgrounds receive a large boost in acquiring word knowledge. For example, "receive" is a Latin-based word, meaning that Spanish speakers should recognize its relation to *recibir*, similar to the English word in both form and meaning. However, this is an area where learners do need to be careful since sometimes languages diverge in the meanings associated with words that were originally related. For example, *asistir* does not mean "assist" in Spanish but "attend." Perhaps the most infamous example of a false cognate pair between English and Spanish is "embarrassed" and *embarazada*, where the Spanish word means "pregnant."

Key Idea 2: Effective Instruction and Accommodations

The second important conclusion gleaned from the two research syntheses is that the basic components of effective instruction also apply to ELs. Great teaching works with everyone, although instructional accommodations are necessary to address the needs of language learners (including the language of instruction, discussed previously, and additional accommodations, discussed in the next section). Some examples of sound teaching practices that work with ELs include providing clear goals and learning objectives that are implemented using meaningful, challenging, and motivating learning contexts and a content rich curriculum. Additionally, instruction needs to be clearly structured and appropriately paced with opportunities for students to actively engage and participate. Once well-implemented initial instruction is complete, students need additional practice and application using the material through interactions with other students in motivating and appropriately structured contexts, permitting them to integrate and then generalize the new learning to additional contexts. Also during the practice and integration period, students need high quality and appropriate feedback from their teachers to help them perfect their understanding. Additionally, while the students are consolidating their knowledge, the teacher needs to make frequent formal and informal assessments to gauge the students' progress, and to establish if reteaching is necessary. Finally, for students to retain knowledge about a teaching point, it cannot be mentioned a few times and then dropped; instead it needs continuous consolidation over time, with periodic opportunities for review and practice. All of these are components of effective instruction that works with monolingual students and ELs alike.

Key Idea 3: Effective Teaching Approaches

The third major conclusion derived from the two syntheses concerns instructional accommodations for ELs' language and cultural differences. In contrast to the second conclusion that good teaching works for all, some teaching strategies proven effective with monolingual English speakers do not seem to work with ELs. For example, the National Reading Panel identified eight types of reading comprehension strategy instruction for ELs, including comprehension monitoring, question asking, and summarization. However, research summarized in the syntheses looking at these same strategies with ELs found no significant effects or increased academic achievement due to these strategies, suggesting that these strategies help learners acquire content, but that when learners also need to acquire language these are not as useful. Students who have mastered primary reading skills and are already fluent in the language are able to focus on academic content, while those who are not completely proficient in the language of instruction, need to focus on learning and understanding the language in which that content is taught before they can understand the content. I will now discuss specific accommodations to address ELs' language development needs as well as cultural differences.

A deficit in understanding of academic content becomes particularly acute as reading becomes an important vehicle for accessing academic content, a phenomena that has been commonly described as the *fourth grade slump*. In the earliest stages of learning to read, instruction tends to be somewhat simpler, with a focus on sounds, letters, and how they combine to form words. Reading materials at the initial stages can be very basic and not be a vehicle for delivering academic content. For this reason, with proper instruction ELs can make good progress and their reading development may not appear too different from that of students who came to school speaking English. However, when the initial instruction on sound spelling correspondences draws to a close and texts gradually become more challenging, increasing language demands means that English language proficiency limits academic progress. Usually around third grade vocabulary and content knowledge demands become crucial for continued reading (and general academic) success, but ELs are still working on basic language skills and do not have the necessary language skills and background information to make sense of the texts due to the increasingly complex vocabulary and syntax—in addition to the complex cognitive skills demanded by the material and the contextual background knowledge. In other words, they do not have the academic language needed to understand content area texts.

APPLICATIONS FOR PRACTICE

Many practical suggestions for educators follow from the three key research findings with additional recommendations arising from other research. The first and most important conclusion is that ELs receive home language support for as long as possible, preferably in a supportive program that teaches them literacy in both the home language and English. This program would last at least five to seven years and be structured to promote bilingualism and biliteracy as positive outcomes, letting students know that their home language is valued by the school culture and the larger society.

The home language needs to be viewed in a positive fashion by educators and as a resource to draw upon to help ELs master English. Teachers can find ways to explain key academic concepts in the students' home language. While some consider that students might become overly dependent on explanations in their home language and not exert themselves in English, this risk is worth taking until the learners have the ability to understand the content in English. Additionally, use of the native language can always be scaled back as the student becomes more proficient in their additional language and needs it less. Finally, a good strategy to integrate learning in the home language with English learning is preview-review, where new concepts are introduced in the primary language prior to the lesson in English, then afterward the new content is reviewed again in the home language.

A teacher does who does not speak a learner's home language can rely on the help of an interpreter, but this strategy requires great caution. The translator might make mistakes or mistranslate. In addition, it is wise to be aware of the translation abilities of any interpreter, being especially aware that peers might not be able to translate accurately since their understanding of the concepts that you are asking them to translate may still be developing and they may not be capable of expressing them clearly in their other language. They may never have heard such concepts before in that language or may have an incomplete understanding of a concept they are still learning themselves.

Most critically, even when the home language is not the primary language of instruction or used in an integrated fashion in content delivery, it should still be used as needed, thereby allowing the students immediate comprehension and speeding up their acquisition of the additional language. In all cases, the home language is a resource and a source of knowledge from which the student and the teacher may draw and build upon. In viewing ELs' prior knowledge of language in a positive fashion, teachers will be drawing on what they already know, and validating their culture and life experience, building a bridge between the language and culture of students' home and the school (Moll & González, 2003). For this reason, a school culture that accepts and nourishes the background knowledge children bring, permits teachers to make connections between what students already know and what they need to learn.

This is why instruction that offers connections between the languages of the home and school are valuable. These ensure transfer of knowledge from one language to the other. However, teachers need to avoid any assumption that students will automatically know how to transfer knowledge and skills between languages. In many cases, ELs do not know which areas transfer (or do not), so including this information in lessons is necessary. Students need to be explicitly taught to transfer knowledge from their home language to the additional language during classroom learning tasks. When building on the ELs' knowledge using the home language, educators need to guide ELs in what aspects are similar or different in both languages in terms of words, meanings, sounds, sound letter associations, and morpho-syntax. For example, for words and meanings, ELs need to be taught which cognates transfer and have the same meaning in both languages (and also the ones which do not). In general, teachers need to point out the similarities and differences between the home language and English in terms of language structures and literary practices that will help ELs build bridges between their home language and English. To do this successfully, teachers need to know how to explain these concepts. They will also need some knowledge about the home language, at a minimum having knowledge about cognates, word meanings, the sound system, morpho-syntax, and the writing system.

LEARNER LANGUAGE

As a classroom teacher you will want to acquire a basic understanding of ELs' language learning habits. By and large, immigrant children and their parents have the desire to learn English when they come to the United States. In reality, the only U.S. immigrants who do not learn to speak English fluently are generally in the first generation, and even many of them do, in fact, learn some English. The second generation children almost always learn to speak English sufficiently well, and by the third generation ability in the ancestral language is in many cases quite imperfect due to limited instruction offered in other languages in U.S. schools (Fought, 2003).

During the learning of and transition to English, language learners commonly mix their home language and the additional language at all levels of the grammar. This type of language mixing is commonly described as interlanguage (Selinker, 1972), a form of language that takes all of the language knowledge of a person into account. Language learners are combining their knowledge from all languages to create meaning in context—a system that has a structurally intermediate status between the language systems that are interacting within the language learner. According to this view, language is learned in context and the overgeneralization of grammar and adaptation of aspects of one language to another is normal and to be expected.

Additionally, in many cases, language learners and bilinguals choose to use both languages for purposeful reasons, appropriately code-switching with other bilinguals to communicate about realities in their bilingual world. Some words cannot be translated or in other cases, the language learner only has experience with communicating about a particular meaning or context in one of their languages. More recently, this sort of naturally occurring language mixing that is common in all language learners and bilinguals has been extended and described as translanguaging:

> For us, translanguagings are *multiple discursive practices* in which bilinguals engage in order *to make sense of their bilingual worlds*. Translanguaging therefore goes beyond what has been termed code-switching, although it includes it, as well as other kinds of bilingual language use and bilingual contact. (García, 2009, 45)

For many bilinguals, languages have different realms of use, and if asked to use a language in a setting where they normally use the other language, they would have problems doing so. Additionally, the mixing of the two languages is a perfectly acceptable strategy, depending on whom they are communicating with.

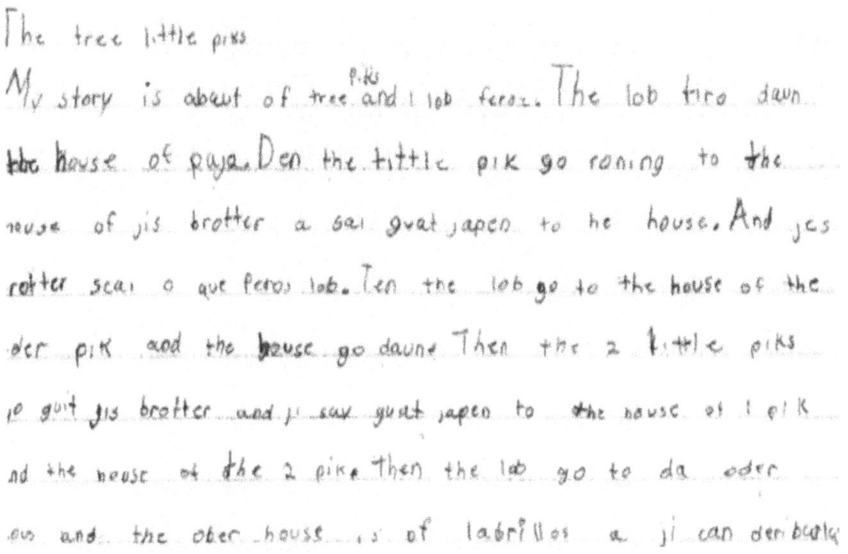

The tree little piks

My story is about of tree and 1 lob feroz. The lob firo daun the house of puja. Den the tittle pik go roning to the house of jis brother a sai gvat japen to he house. And jes rotter scai o que feros lob. Ten the lob go to the house of the oler pik and the house go daune Then the 2 little piks jo guit jis brotter and ji sau guat japen to the house of 1 pik nd the house of the 2 pike. Then the lob go to da oder ous and the ober house is of labrillos a ji can deribcatq

Figure 10.1   The tree little piks

We also see this sort of translanguaging practice in writing, where in the following essay, a developing writer strives to use skills from all of his languages to tell the tale of "The Tree Little Piks."

In this essay we see a child who is writing overall in English, but who also relies on knowledge of Spanish to communicate the story. For example, we find example of sound spelling correspondences from Spanish being used for English words: *piks* for "pigs," *jis* for "his," and *guat* for "what." We also find examples of Spanish syntax with *the house of paja* for "the straw house." In some cases, the child substitutes Spanish words for English words, such as *lob* (lobo) for "wolf," *paja* for "straw," and *feroz* for "ferocious." Teachers must be aware that this is in fact showing excellent ability to communicate and to build on this ability, understanding that translanguaging practices, such as code-switching and mixing is normal for bilinguals (Escamilla, 2012). The teacher's job is to build on these practices to further consolidate ELs' knowledge of language in general.

ENGLISH LANGUAGE DEVELOPMENT STRATEGIES

In general, teachers need to be aware of the level of English of the students they are teaching and make English language development (ELD) a part of all teaching. Clearly ELs need ELD since a major goal is for them to gain a mastery of English. In helping ELs master English, teachers need strive to meet the needs of their students through scaffolding or making the content more accessible for them when not using their home language (and strategically using the home language within the context of using or teaching English as previously discussed).

August and Shanahan (2006) conclude that ELs require "simultaneous efforts to increase the scope and sophistication of these students' oral language proficiency" (p. 448). Increasing vocabulary is important for all students, but particularly crucial for ELs learning to read in English. You will want to stress the development of their vocabulary base with the teaching of vocabulary in meaningful contexts. These students need explicit attention to vocabulary, including what seem like everyday words, as well as more specialized academic words. During early vocabulary learning, studies show that ELs acquire more vocabulary when the teacher explains words contained in a storybook being read to them. However, children who begin with lower English scores learn less than children with higher English scores, meaning that knowing less English makes it harder to learn additional English words. As ELs continue learning vocabulary, they need clear teaching of words, using words from texts likely to interest them, and repeated exposures to the words in numerous contexts (Institute of Education Sciences, 2014). In general, ELs are more likely to learn words when these are explicitly taught and when the words are from texts appropriate and interesting to the students. In addition, they need multiple exposures to the vocabulary and opportunities to use the words in numerous contexts (reading and hearing stories, discussions, posting target words, and writing words and definitions for homework). Taken together these approaches allow an increase in vocabulary that in turn leads to improvements in word learning and reading comprehension.

When the meaning of vocabulary is not known, teachers can use multiple strategies to clarify meaning, including identifying, highlighting, and clarifying difficult words and passages within texts and repeating as necessary. Illustrating the unknown words in the content using multiple cues to reinforce the meaning as much as possible can be done using pictures, objects, gestures, and body language. Additional visual representations that demonstrate how information is organized such as graphic organizers (tables, webs, Venn diagrams, graphic organizers) can also give a leg-up on understanding new information. Teachers can help students consolidate text knowledge by having the teacher, other students, and ELs themselves summarize and paraphrase the material. In your classroom, give ELs extra practice in reading to build automaticity and fluency. Additionally, be aware that students need the option of responding either nonverbally (by pointing or signaling) or in very simple utterances because of their language ability. Be prepared to accept and even encourage these sorts of responses and then attempt to build on them to foster further ELD.

The importance of making sure that all teaching in English, including content area teaching, has ELD as a major component cannot be overemphasized. Well-implemented ELD provides both clear and explicit teaching of the features of English (including syntax, morphology, vocabulary, pronunciation, and norms of social usage) and ample, meaningful opportunities to practice English in real, meaningful contexts. However, despite the reality that ELD is critical, it must be in addition to and not in the place of academic instruction designed to promote content knowledge.

The recommendations of the U.S Department of Education strongly support the integration of ELD into all content area instruction, along with supplying specific suggestions on how to do so (Institute of Education Sciences, 2014). This has become a major focus in many European countries and other parts of the world, successfully using a structured approach called Content and Language Integrated Learning (CLIL), where teachers plan all lessons keeping in mind both content and language objectives (Ruiz, 2014). Dual language immersion programs have the advantage of teaching both the home and additional language in a fashion that integrates learning with the content areas. Another promising approach for integrating ELD into content areas is the Sheltered Instruction Observation Protocol (SIOP) model, a framework for implementing such instruction (Echevarria, Vogt, & Short, 2008).

EFFECTIVE INSTRUCTION IN PRACTICE

In a fourth grade science class, we see a teacher put in place the second major recommendation gleaned from the research syntheses. She delivers quality instructions because she has set clear objectives that target the ELs and prepared her aide to support the student learning. The lesson, concerning environmental adaptation, starts with a reading about frogs in a freezing environment, includes preteaching of key concepts and vocabulary in the home language of ELs with an experienced aide that has been thoroughly trained in the subject matter, ensuring the correctness of the translation. The teacher has set clear, predictable, and consistent classroom management and learning routines to help ELs adjust to the class and the content. Due to preteaching activities, the teacher knows which vocabulary and concepts are most likely to give the ELs trouble, and has made sure that the aide will emphasize explanations of these. The teacher is aware of cognates and other linguistic aspects that transfer between languages in the reading and the lesson and call attention to these, as well as teaching about other linguistic structures important to understanding within the lesson. Key vocabulary words important to the lesson become a part of the class's word wall.

The lesson makes connections to the student's home culture. While teaching, the teacher maintains a slow rate of delivery, and gives the students plenty of chances to ask questions, nudging some ELs with questions to make sure that they are able to follow the lesson. The teacher has integrated many opportunities for the students to practice the material on their own into the lesson, with participation expected of all students. While going through the lesson student involvement is continuous on an individual level and in small group and whole class activities. The teacher gives feedback on student comprehension throughout all interactions, emphasizing not what is wrong but how to improve understanding in a positive manner building on the knowledge that the students have. Beyond the first day's lesson, the teacher builds many opportunities to revisit and practice the language and concepts covered in the lesson. Throughout the unit, the teacher uses different types of assessment to gage understanding and reteaches as necessary. Throughout the year, the teacher touches on the knowledge and concepts from the unit, consolidating the students' understanding through repeated mentions and practice.

ASSESSMENT AND INSTRUCTIONAL ACCOMMODATIONS

Following from the third major finding discussed from the syntheses, ELs need instructional modifications to make content accessible and comprehensible. Some of these are already apparent in the preceding discussion on language (learner language and ELD) but others do not directly relate to language but to culture. Intensive early intervention with at-risk students is very promising in furthering literacy skills in ELs, including Reading Recovery and tutoring (Institute of Education Sciences, 2014). Additionally, encouraging reading in both the home language and the additional language can also improve literacy skills. According to the Goldenberg (2008), ELs "benefit from explicit teaching of the components of literacy, such as phonemic awareness, phonics, vocabulary, comprehension, and writing. The NLP reviewed five studies that as a group showed the benefits of structured, direct instruction for the development of literacy skills among ELLs" (August & Shanahan, 2006, p. 17). These studies demonstrated gains from the explicit teaching of phonological and decoding skills to ELs in both the home and the additional language, especially when integrated into approaches to increase literacy among at-risk children.

An important modification necessary to reach ELs concerns cultural background. In teaching the content and ELD and all other areas of the curriculum, the students need to see their culture and themselves in the material. This means that teachers need to find and use culturally familiar items integrated with new information. Material with familiar content can help comprehension. Cultural or background knowledge is essential for comprehension for all learners, but is even more critical for ELs because of their need for additional support due to their language needs. For this reason, have students read material with content already familiar to them or make sure that they have sufficient exposure to the content in the text prior to asking them to read it. Another approach to ensuring familiarity is to teach a unit in which students read about a topic for several days or weeks. In doing this, start out with simpler and more familiar material, then make the curriculum progressively more challenging as students become more acquainted with the content. This approach has the advantage of easing comprehension challenges and building background knowledge simultaneously.

In their bid to make school material familiar to ELs, teachers need to focus on the home-school connection, bringing the home culture and sociocultural influences into the school. Parents can have very positive effects on literacy and learning outcomes if they are highly motivated to help children succeed in school and have at least rudimentary literacy skills and funds of knowledge that they can share with their children. In short, schools need to do more to encourage parents to support the school personnel's efforts to help children learn. All teachers can take advantage of what parents have to offer and can promote a culture that denies stereotypes and assumptions such as assuming that parents are part of a culture of poverty. In trying to involve parents, all stakeholders need to be aware that parents will not always spontaneously behave in the way educators anticipate due to the different roles and expectations from the home culture—making it the school's and teacher's task to find out about the home culture to identify ways to make the school more hospitable to families. Teachers need to become familiar with and to integrate their students' home culture into the school. As one teacher-educator put it, the most effective educators for ELs are those who are capable of crossing borders and understanding and appreciating the child's home culture (Bartolomé, 2002).

UNANSWERED QUESTIONS

The research in teaching ELs answers some questions, but others remain. Many areas need additional collaborative work between teachers and researchers to address questions about the appropriate curriculum to best help ELs and the best instructional techniques. Dual language immersion models that aim for bilingualism and biliteracy are promising, but educators have to explore their implementation on a broader scale. Additionally, more needs to be known about how to accelerate language acquisition in general, the appropriate use of the home language in English immersion, encouraging parental involvement to promote achievement, and better models to promote high levels of academic language and literacy development.

In the age of the Common Core State Standards (CCSS) (Common Core State Standards Initiative, 2014), a research agenda to better help ELs is critical due to their numbers and the high expectations set in the standards for English language use and literacy, including the ability to gather, comprehend, evaluate, synthesize, and report on information and ideas, using evidence from texts, engage with complex texts, and write to persuade, explain, and convey real or imagined experiences (García & Flores, 2014). The new standards reflect the way language is used in the present day, how students have to make sense and integrate information from a wide variety of texts at school, but they do not take into account the special language needs of ELs and developing bilinguals, instead expecting them to perform in a similar fashion to students who are entirely monolingual. The implementation of the CCSS will potentially be a huge barrier to ELs' success, unless their language needs are acknowledged and integrated into the teaching and the assessments driven by the new standards. In general, all teachers who work with ELs need to take into account the new standards and work to improve their students' literacy skills. A focus needs to be placed on developing writing skills, due to their importance in the standards and the tests, as well as being a difficult area for developing language learners (Institute of Education Sciences, 2014). In the implementation of the new standards, teachers have an important role to play as advocates for their students. Initial implementation of the two test consortiums associated with CCSS shows that Smarter Balanced has better accommodations for ELs than PARCC, integrating home language—both complete translations and computer-based glossaries—into the exam for use as necessary (Maxwell, 2014).

RESOURCES TO SUPPORT THE TEACHING OF ELs

The most important thing that you can do as a teacher to improve your preparation to teach ELs is learning the home language and culture of your students. Even if you do not ever become completely fluent in their language, developing your knowledge about the specific home language of your student population and language in general is crucial to being a successful teacher of ELs. Such knowledge will help you be able to teach English, in addition to giving you the crucial ability to create bridges between the home language and English. You will also gain much credibility in students' and families' eyes from your efforts to create connections between the home and school.

To develop a general understanding of how language works, studying applied linguistics is essential. This will give you a general knowledge of language development, allowing you the tools that you need to understand enough about any specific home language to make the necessary connections. Taking a class within a program that leads to licensure to teach English as an additional language would be ideal, as well as the other classes designed to help you understand methodology for teaching ELs. An excellent resource is the Center for Applied Linguistics (CAL) (http://www.cal.org/). For example, CAL had a role in developing some of the resources mentioned earlier such as the NLP report, *Developing Literacy in Second-Language Learners* (August & Shanahan, 2006), and the comprehensive resources on the SIOP, a framework for teaching ELs in all English settings.

In addition to learning about the language and culture of your students as well as a general understanding of how language works, you need to develop your knowledge of the best teaching practices for classrooms with ELs. Many different approaches have been suggested over the years, but you need the tools to understand them and why some are better than others. For example, SIOP is just one approach among many and needs independent validation from a source other than the developer. The Institute of Education Sciences (IES), a website sponsored by the U.S. Department of Education, offers independent analysis of SIOP as well as other approaches, giving access to many different general guides and strategies for teaching ELs and permitting you to develop your knowledge of the best teaching practices (http://ies.ed.gov/ncee/wwc/topic.aspx?sid=6).

Finally, all educators need quality standards and assessments to guide their work with ELs. For this reason, all teachers who work with ELs need to be aware of World-class Instructional Design and Assessment (WIDA), an organization housed at the University of Wisconsin and that works with thirty-five different states (WIDA, 2014). WIDA offers teaching standards for ELs, assessment tools, research, and professional development (http://www.wida.us/). The site is an excellent resource for all aspects of instruction involving ELs, as well as the specific tools of standards and assessment.

In conclusion, as you move forward to learning more about teaching ELs, remember that the most important component in all of your development as a teacher is to keep an open mind and to develop your knowledge base while respecting and striving to incorporate the language and culture of the students who you serve.

Chapter 11

Addressing the Reading Comprehension Challenges of English Learners in K–12 Classrooms Using Research-Based Practices

Fabiola P. Ehlers-Zavala

In this chapter, I discuss key components of reading instruction that are critical to the language and literacy development of English learners (ELs). I also offer recommendations for action and resources for supporting the reading comprehension challenges of these learners in the mainstream classrooms.

INTRODUCTION

The literacy development of all learners is a complex experience (Short & Fitzsimmons, 2007), not only for the learners themselves, but also for those who are critical mediators of this process, such as teachers, parents, and caretakers. In the U.S. K–12 context, this process becomes even more challenged because ELs need to develop high levels of academic literacy as they learn English for social and academic purposes. That is, they need to develop English to communicate with their teachers and peers, as well as to learn the academic language of each subject or content area for academic achievement (Brisk & Harrington, 2007; Cummins, 1979; Ehlers-Zavala, 2008; Ehlers-Zavala & Azcoitia, 2009). This EL challenge also becomes a teacher challenge because mainstream teachers are now expected to approach the process of English language teaching and learning from a vastly different perspective. Ensuring the academic success of ELs is no longer exclusive to teachers of English as a second language (ESL), it is a shared responsibility of all teachers. Therefore, all teachers need to be prepared to address and meet the cultural and linguistic needs of their ELs in a way that allows these learners to access the academic content encountered at school.

When thinking about the challenges ELs confront in the K–12 context, the development of reading skills for academic purposes across the subject areas is certainly at the top of teachers' list. In this setting, ELs are expected to develop their ability to "comprehend, analyze, and interpret various genres of academic discourse" (Kern & Schultz, 2005) in a relatively short period of time. Each content or subject area poses particular challenges for ELs, for they have to learn the unique linguistic features characteristic of each subject (i.e., social studies, math, science, language arts). Thus, within the larger context of language learning, for ELs the goal of becoming successful readers represents one of the key pillars to increase their academic success.

Nowadays, especially in K–12 contexts, it is a teachers' key responsibility to help their ELs employ their reading abilities to learn content and begin experiencing the benefits of being effective readers for personal and academic growth. In this process, ELs have several challenges to face and overcome. They are expected to develop advanced levels of language proficiency in English; they have to develop advanced literacy in English; and they are expected to learn academic content through English. Therefore, teachers of ELs are challenged with designing classroom instruction to address their ELs' language, literacy, and content needs. For teachers, effectively putting this knowledge into practice means that they need to successfully guide ELs in achieving the fundamental affective and cognitive goals of reading education, as articulated by Sadoski (2004, pp. 47–53) to include: Positive attitudes toward reading; personal interests and tastes in reading; the use of reading as a tool to solve problems; and the fundamental competencies of reading at successively higher levels of independence.

Very importantly, I do wish to acknowledge two very fundamental points to bear in mind, which mainstream teachers may wish to research further. First, the successful attainment of second language literacy development is facilitated when ELs have an opportunity to develop strong literacy skills in their dominant language. The benefits will be observed in time (anywhere between six to seven years in the best of educational contexts and personal circumstances), not immediately (see Baker, 2011, for developing a foundational understanding of bilingualism). Second, the attainment of academic literacy involves the four language skills (listening, speaking, writing, and reading). However, given the space limitations of this chapter, my primary goal is to highlight some of the key research-based findings that have been shown to matter in helping ELs become effective readers in the area of reading. In doing so, I will provide some practical recommendations teachers can implement in their classrooms to help learners become successful readers. After all, we can confidently predict that, when ELs are given a chance to experience reading success, they will be more inclined to develop the inner motivation necessary to immerse themselves in the world of reading and become lifelong learners. Thus, they will experience both personal and academic growth. Finally, I will conclude with three key recommendations for action and offer some suggestions for further reading on those topics.

ESSENTIALS FOR EFFECTIVELY ENGAGING ELs IN ACADEMIC READING

As "a literate process" (Hedgcock & Ferris, 2009, p. 3), academic reading represents a considerable challenge for ELs. The main reason for this challenge is that, more often than not, ELs must acquire or develop a substantial cultural and linguistic repertoire about both the target language and culture to make sense of the texts they read at school, especially those that are expository in nature (i.e., informative, persuasive, argumentative). In Bernhardt's words, learners must have a "substantial linguistic arsenal—an arsenal that seems to be contextually sensitive. In some contexts, grammar and vocabulary seem to be enough; in other contexts, grammar and vocabulary cannot adequately compensate for other forms of contextual knowledge" (2011, p. 84). Because reading requires that learners "engage with the written language" (Painter, Martin, & Unsworth, 2013), beyond vocabulary and syntax, learners must also develop the ability to understand how written discourse unfolds in a variety of contexts. Moreover, as if the verbal aspects of reading were not enough, learners must also develop the ability to understand how written texts interact with other elements that may accompany them (e.g., when reading illustrated or multimodal texts). Therefore, reading development needs to consider an EL's ability to comprehend both written and visual textual material that may accompany the texts they read. In this process, as one may anticipate, the EL's cognitive processes that are activated during textual processing will interact in many complex ways. Hence, in this next section, I will highlight some fundamentals of aspects of reading instruction that teachers need to attend to when supporting the reading development for ELs. In doing so, I will offer some practical research-based recommendations as I illustrate each point.

The Role of Vocabulary

For ELs in K–12, learning to read in English means learning considerable amounts of vocabulary. Through vocabulary development, learners are expected to acquire a deep and intricate understanding of how words are used in the subject or content areas. Thus, vocabulary learning is fundamental to build their academic lexicon, which is needed for academic achievement and successful overall performance. As Nation (2009) has pointed out, ELs should be able to recognize about 98 percent of the words contained in a text for effective comprehension to take place. Therefore, much of the work that a teacher needs to do, especially when working with ELs or other at-risk learners, is to (a) assess what words they know or do not know; (b) understand how learners use words; and (c) help ELs build vocabulary across subject areas in preparation to tackle a variety of texts effectively. Vocabulary should not be taught in isolation. Rather, it should be presented to learners in meaningful contexts. It should also be an integral component of every single lesson that a teacher develops.

In learning new words at school, ELs need to know how to spell a word and its derivatives in fulfilling diverse linguistic functions, how to pronounce it, and how to properly understand and use a word in a variety of academic contexts, since words can have multiple denotations and connotations. Stated differently, "learning a new word involves an ongoing elaboration of knowledge about the word and the ability to use it" (Wesche & Paribakht, 2000, p. 198). To accomplish all of this, teachers may need to adopt a deliberate language-focused approach within a communicative framework that attends to meaning, use, and form. Nation (2009) argues for the incorporation of activities that engage language learners in the "deliberate memorization of the spelling of individual words" (p. 19). This work could entail, as he states, teaching students about the value of using analogies, analyzing word parts, visualizing the spelling of a word, deliberately presenting learners with key rules for helping them identify or recognize useful patterns as to how words are used in various academic contexts. Thus, teachers must develop the ability to properly assess the learners' social and linguistic repertoire, and provide them with a battery of vocabulary strategies that ELs may employ to enhance their language development. It is important to encourage ELs to engage in self-assessments of their own understanding of words, but these assessments need to be approached with caution. Research has shown that, at times, ELs overestimate their knowledge of words (Laufer & Yano, 2001), so teachers need to put into practice a diversified or balanced approach to diagnose EL's lexical knowledge, involving vocabulary activities that show what ELs truly know, not what they think they know.

Consequently, for teachers to develop a sense for the vocabulary knowledge that their ELs bring into the teaching and learning process, teachers can make use of well-known strategies that have shown to be quite useful for the purpose of assessing background knowledge with a focus on vocabulary. Consider for example the use of K-W-L charts (Ogle, 1986) originally introduced for helping learners prepare for reading expository texts. K-W-L charts can be used beyond the general assessment of background knowledge to more specifically assess knowledge of vocabulary. In completing a K-W-L chart with a focus on vocabulary, ELs could indicate what words they (a) know; (b) wish to know, or (c) learned after instruction and practice. This strategy could be used as a self-assessment or a peer-assessment. As a self-assessment, students could complete it individually. As a peer-assessment, students could interview or survey a classmate in regard to a list of key words identified by a teacher. Yet another variation for implementing this strategy and promoting collaborative practices and learning would be to form small groups and have students complete this as a group assessment. Students, could be assigned an additional task such as providing an example for each word they know to ensure they actually know the meaning of the word and how to properly use it in a specific context of their choice.

Another strategy that is very valuable is *Vocabulary Four Square* (Johns, Lenski, & Elish-Piper, 2002; Lenski, & Ehlers-Zavala, 2004). This strategy is intended to assess the conceptual knowledge learners have about specific words that are key to the comprehension of a passage or a story. In essence, when teachers implement this strategy, they ask learners to complete a 2 x 2 table for each word to be discussed or selected. Each cell will list one of the following four prompts: (a) Vocabulary Word, (b) What It's Like, (c) What It Means, and (d) Personal Connections.

Students then, whether individually, in pairs, or in small groups complete the table. Within highly culturally and linguistically diverse groups of students, this strategy could lead to greatly enhancing the world knowledge of each participant in a class, including the teacher. At other times, teachers may find that certain words may actually elicit vastly diverse referents. This is typically the case when words are presented without context. Consider, for example, the word "table." Depending on the grade level of ELs and their world and educational experiences, a term that may appear to be simple at first may have diverse and very distinct connotations, which may be easily demonstrated by asking ELs to draw a picture of the term as part of the Vocabulary Four Square strategy. In response to this activity and based on the previous personal and educational background of ELs, it is quite likely that some ELs might draw a four-legged table; others may draw a periodic table of elements; yet others may consider drawing a table of contents. Teachers could use this strategy to emphasize the need to understand how words need to be understood in context. So moving from using this strategy in isolation to having students refer to a particular context where the selected words appear may serve to achieve an important goal in vocabulary learning: the need to understand the meaning of words in context.

The Value of Meta-linguistic Awareness

As is the case for vocabulary acquisition, or language learning in general, metalinguistic awareness (i.e., learners' knowledge about language and their ability to reflect on it) plays a major role not only in helping learners learn to read, but also in helping them become successful readers (Koda, Lü, & Zhang, 2014), and independent learners. Schneider and Ganschow (2000) remind us that researchers have drawn a distinction between two types of metalinguistic awareness. One refers to a person's knowledge about the linguistic rule system in a given language; while the other refers to the strategies individuals deploy when learning in various contexts. Thus, language learners who become meta-cognitively aware can experience reading in highly productive ways. In fact, research shows that language learners whose bilingualism is relatively balanced and who are metalinguistically aware tend to outperform monolingual speakers "of the same age on cognitive tasks requiring high levels of analysis of knowledge and/or control of processing" (Tellier & Roehr-Brackin, 2013, p. 84). Koda, Lü, and Zhang (2014), explain that "the utility of metalinguistic awareness lies in its capacity for enabling children to analyze a word into its sub-lexical constituents, and in so doing, providing them with direct assistance in learning the specific pattern of grapheme-to-language mappings that is optimal for their language use" (p. 143). Engaging ELs in this type of activity can be quite useful for vocabulary acquisition/learning. It can, for example, contribute to developing independence in incidental vocabulary learning as they engage in extensive reading while reading for pleasure.

When considering what teachers can do to promote the development of metalinguistic awareness on the part of ELs, they can help them discover that words can be broken down into smaller units (i.e., morphemes). Teachers may help learners understand that some of these smaller units can stand alone (i.e., independent base or free morphemes, such as "tree"), while others may not (i.e., bound morphemes, such as "trees" where plural "s" is attached to the base "tree"). That is, they need to be attached to other words to make sense. As they attach to words, they can help convey additional meanings. By using examples from the texts ELs access as part of their grade-level curriculum, teachers can help ELs understand these concepts gradually, and encourage them to guess the function and meanings of words if they stop to think about the composition of a word. Think of, for example, a social studies unit, where ELs in middle school are learning about the rivers of Latin America. A typical question a middle school learner could be asked is: "What is the longest or second long*est* river in the world?" This question, as simple as it may appear to a fluent speaker of English, may not be so if presented to an EL who is developing proficiency in the language. The use of the superlative ending/ suffix (*-est*) may be enough to challenge an EL in understanding the prompt, yet once an EL grasps the concept or understands that this suffix (i.e., "*-est*") helps accomplish the meaning of "most" in the case of "short adjectives," then the EL is empowered to recognize and comprehend future questions that may contain words with this specific ending, such as: "What is the highest lake in the world?"

The Role of Background Knowledge

All readers come into the process of reading comprehension with varying degrees and types of world knowledge (i.e., funds of knowledge) about topics they read or know about in academic and nonacademic texts. This fact has been vastly accounted for in the literature of reading research. The prior knowledge an EL brings into the process of reading mediates success in reading (Bernhardt, 2011; Dehghan & Sadighi, 2011; Steffensen, Joag-Dev, & Anderson, 1979; Steffensen, Goetz, & Cheng, 1999). In referring to this type of knowledge, historically, various terms have been used to refer to the knowledge readers contribute to the reading process during the act of reading, such as "content knowledge, domain knowledge, topic knowledge, background knowledge, and readers' schema" (Brantmeier, 2005, p. 89). Regardless of the terminology a teacher adopts to refer to the prior knowledge a learner brings into the reading process, understanding its role as a key mediator of successful comprehension matters.

When the prior knowledge a learner brings into the reading process is similar to that of the target language and culture, the process of reading comprehension is likely to be highly facilitated; when the opposite happens, it may be challenged in significant ways, especially when working with novice readers who find themselves in the early stages of language development and highly dependent on their dominant language and culture. The combination of lower levels of English proficiency and lack of background knowledge on a given topic constitute some of the main obstacles of a successful reading experience. For this reason, teachers of ELs need to take a highly proactive stance in preparing these learners for reading success. When preparing to read in another language, ELs are likely to make use of their previous knowledge (Kern & Schultz, 2005) in comprehending texts. Consequently, critical to their success is the work that teachers (initially) and the learners themselves (subsequently) need to carry out to properly prepare for the act of reading and the process of effectively comprehending a text in a second or foreign language. The activation, or the building, of background knowledge prior to tackling a text is fundamental for ELs and their success in reading.

To assess ELs' prior background knowledge of reading material, teachers can make use of prereading strategies such as "anticipation guides," "knowledge-rating scales," and "possible sentences" (see Lenski & Ehlers-Zavala, 2004). Anticipation guides, for example, offer teachers the opportunity to help students form and share opinions about what they are about to read. These guides can also help teachers in assessing the factual (or mythical) knowledge ELs may have about the topics they are about to read. Once teachers develop a sense for what ELs are bringing into the act of reading, teachers can help align (or, if necessary *build*) their knowledge with the expected knowledge a text presupposes. When working with ELs that come from diverse linguistic and cultural backgrounds, this activity is key to their reading success. Imagine for example an EL who has lived most of his or her life in the tropics, he or she may have a harder time relating to a text that describes activities in the Arctic. Or consider the case of ELs who may have spent their life in a fairly dry climate of places such as Colorado, Wyoming, or New Mexico, and who have not experienced the concept of humidity others know well by virtue of living in places such as in Illinois, Iowa, or North Carolina. One can be certain that their concept of humidity practically is nonexistent. (For additional examples on how teachers can implement pre-reading activities to assess prior knowledge, such as the use of prediction or connection charts, see Lenski and Ehlers-Zavala, 2004).

The Role of Text Structure in Improving ELs' Reading Comprehension

As in the case of prior knowledge, we know enough about second and foreign language reading to also assert that, when ELs read, they make use of their knowledge of what a text is or of its rhetorical structure as experienced in their dominant, native, or first language. This is particularly true of ELs in the initial stages of second or foreign language development when they tend to rely on the knowledge they have about their dominant language(s). Then, as they develop higher levels of linguistic proficiency in the target language (e.g., English) and begin to encounter a variety of academic texts in that language, they become better prepared to delve into the process of acquiring new rhetorical frameworks for understanding text structures in the additional language (Genesee, 2005), known as textual or formal schemata. Progressively, and with the appropriate instructional support on the part of teachers, ELs can expand their experiences with various rhetorical styles or textual exigencies, and therefore become better equipped to comprehend a variety of academic texts. In other words, experiencing literacy in other languages means that learners "become familiar with new ways of signifying, new genres, new social practices, and new ways of thinking in and about the language in question" (Kern & Schultz, 2005, p. 382). Since reading research began to consider it (e.g., Carrell, 1985), interest in understanding text structure has only grown through the years. Despite the various debates, it has been acknowledged to have a positive impact in helping ELs become effective readers (Purcell-Gates, Duke, & Martineau, 2007). In fact, more recent conceptualizations of how to approach the teaching of text structure or the introduction of genre theory to learners has adopted a social-construction and communicative approach that is consistent with our most current understandings of effective language teaching and learning. As Purcell-Gates et al. (2007) explain, "the social semiotic view of language considers genres as socially constructed language practices, reflecting on community norms and expectations. These norms are not static but change to reflect changing social cultural needs and contexts" (p. 11). Thus, work in the area of genre studies does not need to be approached from a prescriptive or static perspective. Work on genre studies can certainly take a very fluid and dynamic perspective, as conceived under more recent approaches, such as the work conducted in the area of contrastive rhetoric, and more recently in its most up-to-date version: Intercultural rhetoric (e.g., Connor, 2008; LoCastro, 2008).

To assist ELs in becoming successful in reading and in tackling various types of expository or informative texts (e.g., main idea, list, order, classification, compare/contrast types of texts), through guided modeling, teachers can gradually introduce ELs to various types of expository texts depending on the subject matter they teach. For instance, when mainstream science teachers teach a unit on "Changes in Matter," they could introduce the classification type of expository texts by explaining that texts that aim at presenting information in classes or categories are known as classification texts (Bakken & Ponce, 1996). Teachers can then highlight the key words or phrases associated with these types of texts: "can be classified," "are grouped," "consist(s) of," etc. Using an authentic textual sample, teachers can model the identification of these key terms/phrases, and then provide other samples for learners to do the same. Teachers could scaffold this activity by having ELs engage in this work in small groups or in pairs before they tackle this activity at the individual level.

In addition to guided modeling, once ELs have developed an understanding for the diversity of expository types of texts, teachers can use a variety of reading strategies to help ELs understand and predict the exigencies of texts as well as their purposes. For instance, teachers could make use of prereading strategies that help learners identify text structure by previewing texts. A strategy of this sort will require that ELs examine texts before reading them to determine, or predict, what a particular type of reading material might be about based on the examination of pictures or accompanying illustrations as well as headings and subheadings. Mainstream teachers can also employ graphic organizers to guide students into the use of different strategies that connect to different text-types (for samples of graphic organizers, see Vogt and Echevarria, 2008).

Consequently, when preparing to work with diverse ELs, teachers (if necessary) may want to consider enhancing their own linguistic and rhetorical knowledge of the texts they expect their ELs to read. In doing so, they will become familiar with the demands of texts to predict what challenges ELs may face, and determine how to best support them in a proactive manner. Teachers may also want to prepare themselves to introduce their ELs to the various stylistic devices, or metadiscourse markers (also known as linking devices, linking words, connectors, connecting devices), that writers consider and use during textual production or composition. Each of these devices entails specific logical relationships. Different linguistic or stylistic devices (i.e., words that indicate chronology, contrast, addition, similarity, consequence) that writers use are intended to bring about or elicit a wide "range of mental processes" for accomplishing different "rhetorical purposes" (Sandford & Emmott, 2012, p. 1). For ELs, acquiring or developing the ability to understand how writers use these cohesive or metadiscoursive devices will be fundamental in their ability to make texts cohere in their minds. This knowledge will also have a positive impact on their ability to compose effective texts in English, not to mention the positive impact on their reading skills at higher levels (i.e., to infer information, to draw conclusions) as well as on their oral abilities. (For more on metadiscourse, see Hyland, 2005).

The Role of Reading Strategies: From Individual to Collaborative Strategic Reading

The development of the strategic competence on the part of ELs is key to their success in learning in general and for specific purposes, such as becoming effective readers. When it comes to reading, readers can enhance their ability to critically interact with texts through the use of strategies (see Bartu, 2001, for examples on how to foster critical reading). Readers who are metacognitively aware engage in self-regulated learning (Zhang, 2010), and therefore can monitor their own reading comprehension as they interact with texts through the use of reading strategies. Unlike struggling ELs who have yet to discover the benefit of reading strategies, ELs who are strategic readers typically employ or deploy different reading strategies when reading. Effective ELs have acquired strategies that allow them to enhance their vocabulary learning and their ability to tackle a variety of texts, showing success in diverse comprehension tasks or assessments, appropriate to their level of linguistic proficiency. ELs who are effective readers will also employ other strategies when encountering texts. Some of those will be used prior to reading a text as mentioned previously in this chapter (e.g., KWL Strategy; Anticipation Guides; Vocabulary Four Square); others will be put into action during reading (e.g., Fix-Up Strategies; Prediction Charts; Questioning the Author); and yet others will be activated after reading to promote self-regulated learning, and ensure that effective comprehension has taken place (e.g., Sequencing; Plus, Minus, Interesting; Two-Column Response Chart). (See Lenski and Ehlers-Zavala [2004] for a description and templates of these strategies; see Kostka and Olmstead-Wang [2014], for additional information on teaching academic reading.)

Consequently, in helping struggling readers succeed, teachers need to (1) assess whether or not ELs come to classes with awareness or command of reading strategies, and (2) if needed, teachers need to explicitly teach (and reteach when necessary) strategies. An integral component of explicit teaching is modeling and, when introducing strategies to ELs, teachers play a key role in modeling the use of reading strategies. In fact, many of the key concepts discussed in this chapter that have a positive effect in EL reading development can be modeled through the use of think-aloud strategies (e.g., to model what effective readers do, how they make use of text structure, how they describe mental processes such as imagery and affect to intensify the reading experience) (see Wilhelm [2012] for the use of think-aloud strategies to intensify readers' involvement with texts).

When it comes to strategies, teachers expand their creativity by adapting many of the strategies they already know. For instance, to assess what strategic repertoire ELs already possess, teachers can make use of an adapted form of a K-W-L chart. An adaptation could be the formulation and use of a "K-T-D" chart on which ELs indicate, next to the name of the reading strategy provided by the teacher, if they "know," "think they know," or "do not know" each listed strategy. Once teachers have identified the type of strategic support ELs need, they can then introduce strategies that can assist learners in remembering that they can draw from a variety of strategies to improve their reading. They can even implement a differentiated approach as they help ELs identify what strategies they may need to use to address their individual reading comprehension needs. Teachers can accomplish this goal by introducing ELs to "Strategy Bookmarks" that can be individualized to the needs of each particular learner. For example, if ELs fail to remember to engage in the use of prereading and during-reading strategies, they can develop their own bookmarks that they can then use to remember what strategies they need to employ before reading or during reading. Fix-up strategies are strategies that teachers can introduce to learners to help with trouble-shooting problems they face during reading. These could also be presented to ELs in the form of bookmarks that prompt the learners when, for instance, they do not know a word, of what to do (i.e., "Examine the parts of a word," "Reread the section," "Continue reading," "Stop and ask someone," or "Consult your dictionary").

In addition to the strategies that individuals may prefer to use, teachers working with ELs may also want to consider strategies that are collaborative in nature. For instance, there is a technique that has been argued to show much success in content area reading development especially when working with diverse learners at the elementary levels. This strategy is commonly known as *collaborative strategic reading* (CSR). The goal of this particular strategy is to maximize the levels of collaboration on the part of learners to positively affect language development and content acquisition (Klinger &

Vaughn, 2000, p. 73). It is based on the principles of cooperative learning, and, therefore, it requires careful structuring on the part of the teacher. CSR requires that learners work in groups to help one another as they progress through the implementation of the following specific reading strategies as defined by Klinger and Vaughn (2000, p. 73):

1. Preview: Prior to reading, students recall what they already know about the topic and to predict what the passage might be about.
2. Click and clunk: During reading, students monitor comprehension by identifying clunks, or difficult words and concepts in the passage, and using fix-up strategies when the text does not make sense.
3. Get the gist: During reading, students restate the most important idea in a paragraph or section.
4. Wrap-up: After reading, students summarize what has been learned and generate questions that a teacher might ask on a test (Palincsar & Brown, 1984).

The teacher can model the use of these strategies so that learners develop a better understanding of how to properly implement them. Student groups take into account the ELs' levels of language proficiency to assure they are provided the opportunity to meaningfully fulfill their roles within their groups. Each group will have a leader, an encourager, and a timekeeper. Each student receives explicit instruction on how to best play his or her role. These types of intervention have shown that diverse learners, as is the case of ELs, are much more academically engaged in meaningful discussion and are perfectly capable of developing and implementing new skills in helping others (Klinger & Vaughn, 2000).

The Role of Authentic Texts

Key to the success of ELs in reading, whose experience is already culturally, biculturally, or multiculturally mediated, is their exposure to authentic texts. Exposing learners to a variety of authentic texts is critical to the learning of academic discourses across subject or content areas (Purcell-Gates, Duke, & Martineau, 2007). It is through a gradual and well-supported exposure to a variety of texts (supported by relevant reading strategies) that ELs will begin to expand their rhetorical understandings of the variety of academic texts that they will encounter across the subject or content areas as well as through the grades. In this process of encountering academic texts, ELs will learn that a science informational text, for instance, is a text "written for the purpose of conveying information about the natural world, typically from one presumed to be more knowledgeable on the subject to someone presumed to be less so"

(Purcell-Gates, Duke, & Martineau, 2007, p. 15). They will also learn that a science procedural text is a "text that is written for the purpose of instructing a reader in how to conduct investigations or experiments related to science content, typically written by someone who knows how to do the procedure to someone who must rely on the written procedures to conduct the investigation appropriately" (Purcell-Gates, Duke, & Martineau, 2007, p. 15). They will learn that texts across subject areas follow different developmental and organizational patterns or rhetorical structures. They will also discover that they may or may not be similar to the ways in which texts are produced in their first or native language.

Teachers preparing to introduce ELs to the texts that pertain to their subject areas should develop, first of all, enough linguistic knowledge of the textual features in those texts, and engage in some meaningful and explicit instruction of these genre features. It is important that teachers feel comfortable making this knowledge explicit to their ELs. This explicit instruction ought to be gradually introduced to learners by having teachers first model their own practices in identifying key genre features (with greater support provided to ELs in the early stages of language learning). In doing so, teachers could consider verbalizing their mental processes to help learners understand how to work with genre features contained in content or subject area texts through the use of think-aloud protocols (see Wilhelm, 2012). Once enough modeling has been provided to students, they are ready to work with texts in pairs, and then in small groups, until teachers feel comfortable encouraging the ELs to work individually in identifying different text structures.

The Value of Building Cross-linguistic Links for Positive Transfer

In recent years, bilingual and multilingual research has embraced the opportunity to guide ELs in discovering their full linguistic potential through the exploration of cross-linguistic links or connections between or among the languages they know. Riches and Genesee (2006), upon reviewing the available published research, states that "use of the L1 [native or dominant language] does not seem to detract from ELs' L2 [second language] literacy development" (p. 69). Genesee et al. (2008) reviewed the published research on the topic of cross-linguistic relationships when it comes to second-language learners. They concluded that, while much research is still needed in certain specific areas, there is "strong evidence of the relationships and influences between English language learners' first and second languages in second-language literacy development" (p. 83).

In reviewing the work of others, Horst, White, and Bell (2010) state the following: "L2 and L1 teachers (and teachers of other subjects) would do well to take opportunities to engage school-age learners in talk about aspects of the languages they are studying" (p. 331). Sometimes, as Genesee et al. (2008) pointed out, there is still debate as to the benefits of cross-linguistic influence. Some research suggests that, depending on the languages involved in terms of their typology, cross-linguistic linkages may be more or less productive. For example, for Chinese learners of English, cross-linguistic linkages may be less productive given that English and Chinese are typologically different. For other ELs, as is the case of Spanish/English bilinguals, who share the same alphabet or may come from similar or not so distant language families, the transfer may be quite successful (see Cummins, 1979). When this is the case, ELs are thought to experience positive linguistic transfer. When this is not the case, then they are thought to experience negative transfer (as in the case of false cognates or words that look alike in two languages, but have a completely different meaning). Drawing ELs' attention to the diverse features across languages in meaningful communicative ways will contribute to maintain, and even foster, their bilingualism/biliteracy or multilingualism/multiculturalism. Thus, they can continue to be effective in two or more languages as they take advantage of their full range of linguistic knowledge.

The Role of Effective Classroom-Based Reading Assessments

Essential to a teacher's success in effectively guiding ELs to read with success is a teacher's ability to engage in proper "assessment and diagnosis" (Bernhardt, 2003, p. 115) of what students bring into the reading comprehension process. Without proper classroom-based assessments in reading, teachers will be at a significant disadvantage in being able to select strategies and reading materials that are suitable to diverse ELs. Appropriate selection of materials is likely to have a direct and significant impact on student reading engagement (Ivey & Broaddus, 2007). Teachers need to feel comfortable assessing ELs' levels of metacognitive awareness or degrees or types of background knowledge (linguistic, cultural, rhetorical) ELs bring into the process as well as their reading skills and abilities. In essence, teachers need to be prepared to assess the impact of the verbal and the nonverbal in matters of ELs' reading comprehension.

Furthermore, for teachers to obtain an even richer picture of ELs, they must also consider "assessment-based questions from a native-language perspective, and then ask those same questions again regarding individual children, taking different linguistic and social perspectives (e.g., understanding spelling regularities, syntax and morphology within and across languages)" (Ivey & Broaddus, 2007, p. 517). When working with multilingual learners, teachers will need to expand their understanding of the literacy practices these students may have experienced whether it is in previous academic or schooling contexts. These include home-literacy practices, such as the ones described by Orellana et al. (2003), which underscores the role of paraphrasing, language brokering, translating, and interpreting in the regular literacy practices of immigrant learners. Bernhardt (2003) helps educators see what they can do. She states, that for "teachers who are charged with guiding and developing literacy in children with whom they do not have a common language, explicit knowledge of the languages involved helps to fill the gap between teachers and pupils" (p. 115). (For additional information on EL assessment, see Ehlers-Zavala 2012; Lenski, Ehlers-Zavala, Daniel, & Sun-Irminger, 2010).

RECOMMENDATIONS FOR ACTION

In this section, I will offer three key recommendations for mainstream teachers working with ELs to help these students become successful readers. These are in line with what Bernhardt (2011) pointed out matters most to ELs in their journey to become effective readers. Below each recommendation, I provide suggested readings that will support teachers' work with ELs across the content areas.

First, supporting the reading development of ELs in mainstream classes requires that teachers attend to both content and language issues in an integrated fashion. It is critical that teachers see themselves as professionals who have the power to support and contribute to the EL's language development in the subjects they teach. Knowledge of the language is fundamental to assist an EL when working toward becoming an effective reader. This task cannot be exclusively delegated to ESL/EFL teachers. A collaborative approach by which ESL/EFL specialists guide content/subject areas teachers to maximize their efforts and attention to language issues considering content aspects is highly encouraged and preferred.

Second, because of the diversity of ELs, and the many factors that influence literacy development, it is important that teachers understand the ELs' previous literacy experiences through the implementation of adequate formal and informal assessments (traditional or alternative/authentic). Mainstream teachers need to connect with their ELs' family members, whenever possible, and previous teachers to gather more information about their previous literacy experiences in both their dominant and second or additional languages. Doing so allows teachers to be in a better position to assist these learners in preparing to read a text for comprehension purposes and further learning. Though experiencing a foreign or second language is perhaps the richest experience a teacher of ELs may have to understand what it means to a language learner, it is not imperative that a teacher be bilingual or multilingual to be an effective EL teacher or a teacher that is better prepared to understand the needs of ELs. What is fundamental for assisting ELs is for teachers to learn about the linguistic nature of other languages as well as the cultural experiences students may have had previously and presently. This type of learning allows us to more fully understand the types of literacy experiences that may be shaping the literacy experiences of ELs as they read in English (their non-dominant language).

Third, in as much as possible, it is critical that teachers attend to the nonverbal aspects of reading comprehension (mental imagery, attention, engagement, affect). Understanding the role of the nonverbal aspects has many instructional implications, ranging from careful selection of curriculum for ELs to the presentation of explicit guidance to make effective use of these by ELs.

RESOURCES

The following are suggested readings for further understanding how to integrate language and content instruction and enhance your knowledge on the development in academic literacy K–12:

- http://tapestry.usf.edu—This site has excellent resources that support the integration of ESL education in the preparation of all teachers.
- Brock, C., Lapp, D., Salas, R., & Townsend, D. *Academic literacy for English learners. High-Quality Instruction across content areas. Grades 1 through 5.* New York, NY: Teachers College Press. Supported by classroom examples, this book helps elementary education teachers achieve a deep understanding of the challenges ELs face as they become acquainted and immersed in the language of science, math, and history. It focuses on how to support instruction across the subject areas as ELs develop academic literacy in each of them.
- Echevarria, J., Vogt, M. E., & Short, D. (2012). *Making content comprehensible for English learners: The SIOP Model* (4th ed.). New York, NY: Pearson. A must-read for all teachers. A nice overview of all the aspects that contribute to successful instruction of ELs in the content area classroom.
- Fang, Z., & Schleppegrell, M. J. (2008). *Reading in secondary content areas.* Ann Arbor, MI: University of Michigan Press. An excellent resource for secondary teachers who are trying to more fully understand how language differs across content areas. The authors address the teaching of reading in relation to the language found in science, history, mathematics, and language arts. It guides teachers into the realm of what it means to embark in the functional analysis of language in a classroom, which is a skill teachers will appreciate reinforcing or developing.

- Schleppegrell, M. J. (2004). *The language of schooling. A functional linguistics perspective*. Mahwah, NJ: Lawrence Erlbaum Associates. Written from a functional linguistic perspective, this book introduces teachers to what they need to know when working toward helping learners develop advanced literacy in middle and secondary schools. It examines how language is used in a variety of content areas, and gives teachers tools to explicitly guide learners in acquiring advanced literacy.
- Zwiers, J. (2008). *Building academic language. Essential practices for content classrooms. Grades 5–12*. Newark, NJ: Jossey-Bass/International Reading Association.
- This book provides teachers with the fundamentals to consider when preparing to work with ELs in schools. It focuses on the development of academic languages and it addresses the four language skills (listening, speaking, reading, and writing) that are fundamental for EL schooling success.

The following are suggested readings for better understanding literacy development in other languages:

- Goodman, K., Wang, S., Iventosh, M. S., & Goodman, Y. (Eds.) (2012). *Reading in Asian languages. Making sense of written texts in Chinese, Japanese, and Korean*. New York, NY: Routledge. This edited collection helps teachers understand what it means to become literate in Asian languages. It is inspired by the work of Ken Goodman that focuses on meaning creation. It discusses the similarities and differences of what it means to read in English versus in Asian languages, such as the ones addressed in this book.
- Jones, T. G., & Fuller, M. L. (2003). *Teaching Hispanic children*. New York, NY: Pearson. A guide for teachers who want to connect more effectively with Hispanic learners. The book is well illustrated with the authors providing many activities for reflection.

Chapter 12

Socrates Returns to the Classroom

Joan Wink with Kerry Britton, Dee Hawksworth,
Tammy McMorrow, Debra Schneider, Chyllis Scott,
Ruthie Wienk, Dawn Wink

In this chapter, we share insights about how teachers can engage English learners (ELs) in deep levels of reflection to support their language development, literacy acquisition, and academic achievement outcomes.

Dear readers, I bet you are wondering, *Why Socrates?* Socrates was a thinker, and his thoughts still matter today, as he gave us inquiry-based teaching and learning. Okay, I'll admit that he did not quite use the same words that we use today, but his legacy is the use of deeper and deeper questions to enhance learning. Now, your second question will be, *How do I do it?* So, let's simply begin with an answer from Dee, who has taught in secondary schools for twenty-two years. She demonstrates one way of using Socratic Seminars with the teenagers in her class. She tells me, "I have learned from the students that there are three essentials of a Socratic Seminar. They are, *first,* you must have a thought-provoking, open-ended question; *second,* adequate source material is a must; and *third,* you need a willingness to simply plunge in."

There you have it: The mystery is gone. Three simple steps. One little problem: It is not so easy to generate a question that will capture the fancy of teenagers, is it? In addition, it can take so much time to gather adequate source materials in order to have examples or quotes ready when needed. However, plunging in can be the toughest part. Oh, the courage it takes to teach passionately, meaningfully, and authentically in this age of teaching to the test.

Socratic teaching and learning has many names: Socratic Circles, Socratic Dialogues, Socratic Seminars, and so on. Do not be confused. It is all inquiry-based teaching and learning; it uses questions to guide and empower learning. Almost always, new questions will emerge during the process. In this chapter, we will demonstrate various ways to initiate deeper learning. The reflective cycle, which is very Socratic, will be our primary guide.

The purpose of this chapter is to make visible the reflective cycle as it comes to life in diverse classrooms where the demographics are changing rapidly. The reflective cycle opens the door to using assessment to inform and empower teaching and learning for all students, and it is simultaneously very effective with non-native speakers of English. By using the reflective cycle, teachers use questioning to create deeper learning and more equitable access to the curriculum for diverse learners. In addition, I hope that you will find your own courage *to plunge in*, as Dee advises, as you read the words from the teachers in this chapter. I have a hunch that courage can be contagious.

In this chapter we will begin with the reflective cycle: "What Is It?" and "Where Did It Come From?" In the second section of this chapter, "How Do You Do It?" readers will find authentic vignettes from elementary, secondary, and higher education classrooms led by critically grounded reflective teachers. All of these teachers are joined by their commitment to Socratic learning and an emphasis on literacy for all—particularly for those who are in the process of acquiring English as a new language. History tells us that Socrates loved to ask why, and this chapter will conclude with the question, "Why Do We Do What We Do?" (Wink & Putney, 2002, p. 1).

WHAT IS REFLECTION?

Teachers reflect. A lot. We focus our deep thinking on an explicit pedagogical practice in our classroom, so that we improve our teaching and thus, the learning of the students. Reflection is how we think and learn more deeply. It is how we get smarter. It is what we, as professionals, do to understand more and better. It is focused deep thinking on a specific experience. It is when we ask ourselves: What can I learn from this? It is when we ask ourselves: What was my role in all of this? (Wink, 2011, p. 41). Often reflection will look like we are not doing anything, as we may be simply staring off in space; however, it might be some of our best work. When we focus and think deeply, it is often a path to solving problems and answering questions.

Research and Theory: What Is the Reflective Cycle?

The reflective cycle is a process to assist us with reflection as it provides guideposts, in the form of explicit verbs (see figure 12.1.), to lead us to deeper and deeper thinking (Wink, 2011, pp. 41–42). First, think about what to think about. We must *focus* intentionally and explicitly on our primary question or problem. Name it. Second, *describe* the experience or find out as much as

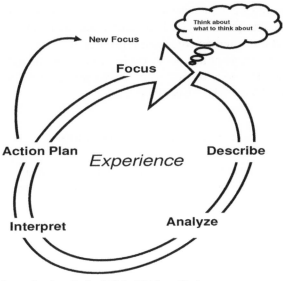

Figure 12.1 The Reflective Cycle (Wink, 2011, p. 9)

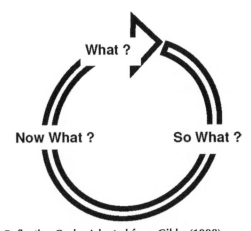

Figure 12.2 The Reflective Cycle, Adapted from Gibbs (1998)

possible about the question or the problem. Write what we know from experience or from our reading and researching. Stay on this phase of the process for as long as it takes to gather available information. Third, *analyze* the question or problem. Evaluate, investigate, dissect, probe, rethink our description of our focus. Fourth, *interpret* our focus and all that we know about it to this point on the cycle. Make meaning of our focus, our description, and our analysis of it. Fifth, *make* an action plan. It is at this point that we move toward creating a solution based on our reflection. How can we improve the situation; how can we implement an action plan, which will address the problem or answer the question? Transformation begins. In addition, remember that new questions often emerge from reflection. It is very common to have a new question emerge at this point. Gibbs (1988) contributed greatly to the reflective cycle. His body of work is often synthesized with these questions: What? So what? Now what? (see figure 12.2).

WHERE DID IT COME FROM?

> I am saying as you must say, too, that in order to see where we are
> going, we not only must remember where we have been, but we must
> understand where we have been.
>
> —Ella Baker

Socrates, it is safe to say, was a rather strange man. He wandered the streets of Athens and asked questions of anyone who would listen. When they responded, he would answer with another question. Socrates had no wealth, and apparently no shoes, as he walked the streets barefoot. He was repelled by wealth, and was surrounded by men scrambling for power and money. His message was not always well-received, as he told all who listened that they were on the wrong track. Instead of material things, he said, they should be seeking justice. He had many enemies in positions of power who did not like him, nor his ideas. In the end he was arrested and charged with ruining young minds; he was condemned as a heretic. His punishment—to drink hemlock, the poisonous plant. He drank the poisoned tea and died comforting his few friends. If you search online for images of him, you will often find him barefoot, with a woman in the background (his wife), the hemlock, and a chicken nearby. From the image of the chicken, we learn about his honor and integrity, as before drinking the hemlock, he paid off an existing debt with his chicken (Weate, 1998).

One legacy from Socrates is, of course, the Socratic dialogue, often found in more progressive and even transformational classrooms. So, what is Socratic dialogue? Think of peeling the layers off an onion; the center of the onion is the answer to our question or it shed new light on our original focus. It is where we find meaning. Socrates found truth, love, or justice. As we peel off each consecutive layer of the onion, we come to a clearer understanding. Socratic dialogue is the process of asking deeper and deeper questions.

Socratic dialogue does not cost anything. You cannot buy it in a box. It requires a terrific teacher who has the expertise and wisdom to lead students to find their own truth. For example, Sonia Nieto (2003) tells of Mr. Mannheim, a social studies teacher in a dilapidated urban public school in Brooklyn, who used Socratic dialogue with the eighth graders. The students come alive with learning and created answers worthy of the loftiest college-bound class anywhere (p. 11).

The Socratic dialogue or method is a way of bringing the knowledge out of students, even if they are not aware at the time that they know it. For example, Plato wrote on his papyrus leaf about an incident when Socrates met up with a young boy on the street. Socrates began questioning him about the Pythagorean theorem. Initially, the boy was sure that he did not know what it was. However, with Socrates's adept questions, the boy soon came to understand that he, indeed, did know it (Johnson, 2005).

In its most basic form the Socratic dialogue begins with the teacher asking a question, which on the surface may appear simple and even easy. For example, What is justice today? As the students answer, the teacher continues to respond with deeper questions. This continues until teacher and students feel that they have taken the question as deep as they are able—or, in today's world, until they run out of time.

Later Contributions from Others

Since the time of Socrates, many have contributed and continue to do so. However, it is safe to begin with *Socrates* (inquiry-based Socratic method), who influenced *Hegel* (thesis, antithesis, synthesis), who influenced *Vygotsky* (socially culturally grounded dialectical learning) who influenced, who influenced *Dewey* (experientially learning), who influenced *Lewin* (action research), who influenced *Kolb* (reflective observation to abstract conceptualization to active experimentation to concrete experiences). *Lewin* and *Kolb* also stressed the value of feedback. *Freire* initiated participatory action research (to name, to reflect critically, to act), and *Schön* is remembered for his approach: Do. Plan. Review. *Gibbs* emphasized description, feelings, evaluation, conclusion, and action plan, commonly referred to as What? So what? Now what? *Rosenblatt* emphasized the reciprocity inherent in observation and reflection. *Cochran-Smith* challenges us to (re)theorize, to (re)consider assumption to explore decision-making, develop action plans, and monitor the progress. *Eyler, Giles, Schmiede.* I have contributed the notion that for reflection to be productive, it must be continuous, challenging, connected, and contextualized. This list of names is not all-inclusive. However, it is a snapshot of the evolution of thought as it relates to reflection. (Wink, 2011, p. 41)

PRACTICAL APPLICATIONS: HOW DO WE DO IT?

We began this chapter with Dee providing a three-step process to the Socratic Seminar. In what follows, I will share another approach, which expands on Dee's but takes a slightly different progression. Next, we will see multiple approaches from the various teachers. Only Ruthie and Debra follow the reflective cycle, as I have shared it (see figure 12.1).

Another Generic Reflective Process

First, stimulating questions are at the heart of learning; good questions generate more questions. In the stories to follow, you will note that immediately Tammy, a first grade teacher, highlights the value of a specific question. Note how it is her focus. *Second*, the text represents many disciplines; rich text generates questions. Dee and Kerry bring this to light in their work with secondary students. Ruthie and Chyllis also validate the significance of which text to be used, only their examples come from higher education. *Third*, the teacher facilitates learning; good teachers generate more questions. All the teachers' vignettes, emphasize the complex professional responsibilities of the teacher. *Fourth*, the students' responsibility is to jump into the text; to share; to think aloud; to write to make meaning and to generate new ideas. As you read each teacher's example, which follow, you will see that the teacher and the students really do *plunge in.*

For the remainder of this chapter, I will highlight authentic classroom examples. We begin with Tammy, a first grade teacher, then Dee and middle school students. Kerry and the secondary students provide our guidelines next, followed by Chyllis, who prepares secondary teachers in a teacher education program. Next, we meet Ruthie as she works with Korean students, who are enrolled at a U.S. university in order to improve their academic English. Finally, we meet Debra and a group of teachers from the National Writing Project.

An Example from First Grade: Tammy

Tammy wants the students to use the number line to solve problems. She asks a professor from a local university how she can do this, but ultimately, she found the answer when she asked the students. She had the question, and she just had to *plunge in* for students to discover their own answer.

It's an exciting time to be a math teacher with so many paradigm shifts occurring in the way we think about and teach math, even in first grade. One of the most exciting shifts is presenting students with a task and allowing them the time and space to find their own strategies. Coupled with that is the invitation to explain their thinking, not only to me, but especially to the rest of the class. Recently, I met with a math professor from a local university who helped to lead our district toward better math practices. He made the point that we want our mathematicians to move toward using more efficient models, like the number line, when solving problems. I totally agreed, although in the past few years my efforts had felt a little clumsy. I asked him this question. "So my kids know what a number line is. They know how it functions with ordered numbers and appropriate spacing. *How do I now transition them to using the number line as a tool?*" (Note to Readers: That is Tammy's primary question.) It seemed like a question I should know the answer to, but I honestly wasn't sure. I wanted to nudge them toward using the number line independently. After he gave me a few pointers, I jumped right in with both feet and brought my kids along. (Note to Readers: Tammy *plunged in.*)

"Hey mathematicians, I have a problem I want you to figure out." The problem on the Smart Board read: *Amaya found 6 maple leaves. Bradley found 7. How many maple leaves did they find altogether?* After reading the problem, I simply said that I wanted them to use a number line to find the answer.

"Go for it!" I said as I passed out closed number lines copied onto paper, gave them a few minutes to draw their answers, and collected them as soon as they were finished. Once I had gathered all of their work, I quickly looked through them to find the two or three that we could analyze and that would best nudge them toward using the number line more accurately and efficiently. Going into the lesson, I wasn't expecting that many would have a good concept of how to pull this off, but all it takes is one. I quickly drew one of the student's number line on the Smart Board. This person had made thirteen hopping movements. "So what do you think this mathematician did?" Someone explained that the person had hopped six times and then seven more to land on thirteen. I drew the next chosen strategy. This person had hopped above the number line, which is a more accurate way to hop and also had added an equation. Again, "What did this mathematician do? Why do you think they hopped above the number line? Why do you think they wrote 6 + 7 = 13?" More explanations ensued. See figure 12.3.

Finally, I drew the one I had crossed my fingers for, as can be seen in Walter's first try on the number line (figure 12.3). This person had made

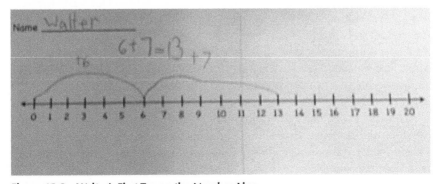

Figure 12.3   Walter's First Try on the Number Line

Figure 12.4

one big hop to six and another big one to thirteen. They had also added an equation. I questioned them about this person's strategy as well, making sure to get to the all-important question, "Why do you think they made big hops instead of individual ones?" In less than ten minutes, students were trying out their own strategies, see exemplar strategies, talk about them, and make some important shifts in their own thinking.

I repeated this same lesson two to three times per week with varying contextual problems. Soon, almost all of my students could use the number line efficiently and accurately. As an added bonus, a few days after introducing the concept, we pulled out our math journals where they solve problems in any way that makes sense to them. I secretly crossed my fingers that someone would choose to solve the problem with a number line. Sure enough, someone did. He shared it with the class, and we dubbed it, "Walter's Way," as can be seen in figure 12.4, when Walter independently drew a number line to solve a problem. All it takes is one.

An Example from Middle School: Dee

The three-step Socratic Seminars from Dee opened our chapter. Now, we see Dee as she begins to teach the Pre-Advanced Placement English (Pre-AP) classes at her junior high.

"Do anything with the curriculum you want, but you MUST do the Socratic Seminar," the previous teacher of the Pre-AP class said to Dee when the year began. "Yes, Mom, it is essential," her own children told Dee, when she asked them. Both kids had taken the same class earlier. Often her own kids were a bit vague on procedures, but this time they were unanimous in saying, "Yes, Mom, you must do Socratic Seminars." Like Tammy, Dee seeks and finds her answers with and from the students. At this point, Dee takes over and tells her own story.

All I knew was that a Socratic Seminar involved asking a *good* question to which the students respond, referring to their texts as often as possible. I knew I wanted the students to use thoughtful and analytical dialogue, rather than a debate, which turns into a "I'm right, and you're wrong" scenario, so I prepared sentence starters in the following manner: "I agree with what Teresa said and would like to add. . . ." or "Lisa, what did you mean when you said . . . ?" The goal was a deeper understanding of the topic. So, with a small touch of anxiety, I plunged in.

The first book we read in the fall was *Witch-Hunt: Mysteries of the Salem Witch Trials*, by Marc Aronson. We read it with a list of eight guiding questions in mind, including this one: *What is moral courage, and what forms did it take during the Salem Witch Trials?* Since then, we've answered other questions such as (1) Should our school participate in a Shut-Down-Your-Screen Week? (2) Is a utopian society possible to create, and if so, what would it involve? and (3) Why is dystopian literature so popular? It's important that the questions be open-ended and thought-provoking. After reading a book or nonfiction articles somewhat independently, my two Pre-AP classes voted on which questions they would like as the topics of their Socratic Seminars. Because my classes were large (thirty to thirty-four students), I needed to divide the class into two groups, with each group set to answer a different question.

On the day of the seminars, they walked in the classroom to see desks rearranged into two circles, one inside the other. The first team sat down in the inner circle, with their books at hand and a list of reminders about polite, thoughtful discourse taped to each desk. The second team sat down in the outer circle, making sure they had a clear view of the person they would be observing. Each student was given an observation checklist and a self-evaluation form for after the seminar.

My own personal goal was to remain quiet during the seminars, a challenge I embraced. I suggested to the students that their personal goals should be deeper understandings of the topic and to participate, participate, participate! Reminding them that each team had one period (of our two-period block), I asked for a volunteer to start the discussion. The first team began, talking slowly and hesitantly at first, and the second team began furiously taking notes and recording checkmarks every time their designated partner spoke, referred to the text, asked a question, and so on. As we watched, the conversation picked up, and occasionally, temporary leaders emerged. I kept track of how many times each student talked, having forewarned my eighth graders I expected them to each contribute a minimum of three comments or questions.

#Fun #Educational #Let'sDoItAgain!

Everyone participated, and I can't emphasize this enough, but *every* single self-evaluation form was positive. I will admit that in my twenty-two-year teaching career, it has been rare to find that 100 percent of the students liked an activity. One boy wrote on the bottom of his feedback form, "#Fun #Educational #Let'sDoItAgain!" Even the shy students (while not raving with Twitter-esque hash tags) still appreciated the chance to speak their minds and hear others' opinions. A strong majority of the eighth graders were articulated how their understanding had grown or how their views had changed.

"The Socratic Seminar is a great learning experience. It gives people that deep thinking on one subject. I believe it helps us all. [It] helps me think about my opinions and how to express them," Anna explained to her classmates. "I feel good about the Socratic Seminar overall. I really liked this activity. I rethought the situation, listening to what everyone had to say using the text and their own ideas," Arianna replied. Later, she added, "My individual part in the Socratic Seminar was scary, having everyone's eyes on you. It was easier having the text to refer to." Smart girl! The text gave her confidence to participate.

I altered the observation and self-evaluation forms slightly each time, but I usually asked the students to acknowledge someone who stood out during the Seminar, someone who made a positive difference in the conversation. Jason wrote, "I think Risa did a great job of citing evidence from the texts, using logic, and asking good questions." I was pleased they could easily identify these role models, and even more pleased that names varied from seminar to seminar.

When evaluating their own performance, they were often extremely insightful. Sara said, "For me, I feel that I need to change *how* I say things." "I felt that I made some valid points, maybe talked too many times, and other than the time I criticized someone, I thought that I did pretty well," Ray explained. "I could work on asking a question every now and then instead of just commenting," Maggie wrote, "I think the Socratic Seminar is very useful because not only do we interact with our classmates, we also learn a lot about our chosen topic or focus. However, I should have referred to the text more often."

Since my first nerve-wracking experience with Socratic Seminar, I have continued and adapted my methodology several times. However, it doesn't matter which rules or procedures are implemented. The students, especially teenagers, will run with it. As one girl wrote, "In how many classes do you get to talk to each other for a whole period, and it's educational?"

An Example from Junior High: Kerry

As Kerry reflects on her own learning about the use of Socratic Seminars with secondary students, she illuminates the complex responsibilities of the teacher. We began this chapter with Dee's three guidelines, but in Kerry's sharing, we see that we, as teachers, also must focus on many tasks in our preparation to assist students in focusing on the text and the emerging questions.

Socratic Seminars from Kerry

In preparing for doing a Socratic Seminar, use a text that involves inquiry and critical-thinking skills. During the seminar, students use the text again and again to discuss, explore, and generate new ideas. The students experience knowledge from the text with their classmates. In addition, teachers must plan for time to encourage students to read, reread, and rethink the text. Students need time to negotiate their own understandings. It is helpful for them to use sticky notes or a journal to take notes about their thinking. Students need to be taught to write the main idea, key words, specific details, and holistic thoughts. They are encouraged to use highlighters and other tools to outline thoughts and ideas.

When preparing the questions, the students' role has primacy: Questions are based on the text. Opinions are based on the text. References to evidence in the text are made throughout the seminar. Many questions evolve during the student dialogue of the text, and students need to be encouraged to write down their questions. The teacher must have strategies prepared to assure that students keep notes about their thinking; the teacher also needs strategies to maintain equity and balance during the dialogue among students. It is helpful to share guidelines with students about what is expected during the Socratic Seminar; for example, only one student talks at a time; respect one another's thinking and questions; be prepared to discuss and question, which will generate more discussion and more questions. In addition, students need to know what the role of the teacher will be, as students may have limited experience with being in charge of the dialogue. Take time to assess the Socratic seminar and process, which can be done in a variety of ways. Use open-ended questions during the seminar and assessment. For example, What worked well? What could have gone better? Did your partner offer questions or discussion? What is the author's purpose? Where do you find evidence for that in the text? Can you clarify what you meant by . . . ? How does imagery help you understand the text? What symbolism is used and why? I don't understand what is said by. . . . Take time to have students assess the seminar; rubrics, questionnaires, discussion times, and self and partner assessments work well for the assessment.

An Example from Higher Education, Preservice, and Inservice: Chyllis and Ruthie

These two teachers take Socratic teaching and learning to the university level. In addition, both are focused on literacy development, but the needs of their students are quite different. Chyllis focuses on teacher-preparation students, and Ruthie focuses on students who are speakers of English as a new language.

Content-Area Instruction and Literacy Development: Chyllis

Teachers are told that their classrooms should be student-centered, riddled with evidence that students are actively learning and engaged in higher-level thinking. Typically, this is asked of teachers and their classrooms on a daily basis, but in reality, is this something that is taught by and asked of our preservice and inservice teachers? As an educator of future and current teachers, I felt the need to reflect on my own teaching and instruction; this was achieved by asking myself how I could help my students to be better teachers?

Donahue (2003) evaluates how new teachers engage in discussions about teaching reading within content area instruction. It was this concept and research that sparked an idea and an assignment to use with my own instruction and students. From Donahue's study, I adapted his idea and implemented what I titled the Disciplinary Reading Journal Project (DRJP) (see table 12.1, Chyllis's Implementation and Donahue's Model) in two literacy courses (a Language and Reading course for preservice teachers at the university where I am a beginning assistant professor, and a Content Area Literacy for inservice teachers and graduate-level students). I asked students to take part in an ongoing several-week-long assignment that would stretch them as learners, readers, writers, thinkers, and teachers. I introduced the DRJP during the first week of the semester. The initial task was to select a text to use in their discipline area (e.g., English language arts, math, science, social studies, art). The text selection needed to be a new read and an adult-level text (Donahue, 2003) as opposed to a text for adolescents. Additionally, text selection was not limited to genre, textbooks, or trade books—the choice was up to the students. Next, each student was paired with another student from the class, preferably someone from a different content area or area of interest. Once the text and partners were selected, the assignment moved forward.

The students were assigned to read their text of choice for approximately three weeks and to keep a journal of his or her reading. They were to write in their journals a minimum of twice a week and apply a strategy taught during the weekly class (e.g., note taking, sticky notes, or types of questions [Tovani, 2000]). In addition, they could also use prompts given in the class, questions provided in the assignment directions, or questions posed by their partners during the journal trade. I told the students that they must focus on what they had read and use the following prompts for writing in their journals: Is there a connection to instruction, class, or personal experiences? How or why did you choose the text? What strategies are you using as you read? What strategies work best or do not work for you? How are you gaining knowledge from the text?

Each week the students were provided class time to meet with their partners. During this time, the partners traded journals and read each other's writing and provided feedback, asked questions about the readings, made connections to the text content, the course content, or the journaling experience. This time of journaling and peer interaction promoted deeper dialogue and thinking.

Table 12.1   Differences between Chyllis's Implementation and the Donahue (2003) Model

Chyllis	Donahue	Comparison
Assignment name: Disciplinary Reading Journal Project (DRJP)	Reading apprenticeship portfolio	Similar
Similar purpose and questions of assignment	Similar purpose and questions of assignment	Same
First year: preservice (elementary level)	Preservice (fifth year students and secondary) in English and math.	A little different
Second year: inservice (elementary and secondary)		
Second year: content area literacy class	Content area literacy class	Same (my second year)
The first year I did this was more challenging when using elementary ed students, but still valuable.		
Partners with different disciplines	Partners with different disciplines	Same
Book selection process	Book selection process	Same
Journal trade with partner—during class, because we only meet once a week and I wanted the students to keep their journals so that they could use their own weekly journals. Therefore, the journals were only traded during class time (approximately twenty minutes). The journal was also a final product turned in at the end of the assignment.	"The logs were exchanged weekly with the partner who responded in writing with comments and questions."	Different
Journal for own notes, strategies, and writing, as well as dialogue with their partner.	Writing log was a way to write and communicate with their partner. But student also reflected and wrote about the strategies used throughout the process	Similar, but different
Second book chosen by the partner	Second book chosen by the partner	Same
I provided prompts for journals.	Donahue provided prompts for journals	Same
Read journals for grading purpose and feedback	Coded journals for the purpose of his research	Different
Meta-reflection paper	n/a—writing from journal	Different

Similar to Donahue's original study, for the second half of the project, and after the completion of the first book, the students read a second book. However, the second text was selected by the partner and vice versa. The purpose of the second text was to introduce, challenge, or push the students' partners out of their comfort zones and to introduce the students to a new book, genre, or academic discipline that they would not have chosen on their own. During this time, I provided additional scaffolding and discussion: How do I read a book that does not interest me? What do I do if I don't understand or if I lack the skills to read or comprehend? Am I required to read the text, or may I choose another text to read? These questions provided a foundation for rich dialogue and engaging interaction between the students.

In the final component of the assignment, a variation of Donahue's original project, I required the students to write a meta-reflection paper. This paper was a culminating reflection of the assignment, the journaling, the reading selections, and the experience as a whole. Possibly due to the dynamic of the classes or the class environment with their peers, the meta-reflections were thoroughly honest and candid, and several themes emerged: the assignment (in general), their like or dislike of the assignment, their growth as learners (much to their surprise), and the practicality of learning and applying reading strategies to their own learning.

As a new professor, I work hard to keep my own learning and instruction current. In a desire to make my class and instruction valuable, I welcome and appreciate the feedback of my students. Through this assignment, I observed many types of learners. The journal component of the assignment often made the students think outside the box and stretch themselves as learners. Since the students were applying strategies to their own learning, they often expressed in their journals and in class discussion that they were also implementing the strategies into their own classes and instruction. It was the guided instruction, the independent practice, and the practical application of their learning that made this assignment relevant and appreciated.

An Example from Higher Education, Academic English Program: Ruthie

Ruthie also works at the university level, but the students in her classes are non-native speakers of English, whose primary goal is to improve their English. Ruthie is a TESOL educator (Teacher of English to Speakers of Other Languages) and focuses primarily on languages, literacies, and linguistics. Ruthie, like Debra, who will be immediately after Ruthie's vignette, follow the reflective cycle as seen in figure 12.1.

The Reflective Cycle: A Tuning Fork

The reflective cycle is an integral aspect of my course development and lesson planning process. In my job as the head teacher for the Academic English

Preparation (AEP) program for international students at a publicly funded Midwestern university, I develop both the program as a conceptual whole as well as the individual classes I teach. The program is high stakes for students; their progression into academic, credit-bearing coursework is dependent on their English language development and their performance in the AEP.

As such, a cacophony of voices clamor to inform the decisions I make. I find myself accountable to future faculty members, administrators here at my university, and administrators at students' home universities. Like all TESOL professionals, I must also answer to the heroes of our profession who have blazed trails and developed foundational hypotheses, which must be remembered in creating programs, syllabi, and lessons. Most loudly, I must listen to the voices of the adult students, frequently successful in their home universities, who hold firmly ensconced ideas about English education and how they best learn languages. These, all too frequently discordant voices, must be harmonized if I am to perform my job well. In what seems an over-whelming task, it is the reflective cycle, which provides me with an instru-ment to create balance from the dissonance and develop educational practices to best meet the needs of the students.

Focus

Reading. If there is any facet of language learning that needs to be the focus of reflection and assessment, it is in the reading class. Not coincidentally, academic reading is also the area that has been simultaneously the most prob-lematic and the least popular for the students who come to our AEP program. At the end of each semester, I engage in a process of program analysis and try to measure where the courses were the most and least effective. Time and again, the reading class emerges as the one that needs the most attention. To prepare students for the postsecondary classroom, I require them to read longer passages in my class. This is problematic because the majority of my students have never read anything longer than two or three pages in English. Even those students with the highest levels of English proficiency struggle with reading extended texts.

Describe

Students often do not read. The problem is as simple as it is complex. Students' preparation for the academic environment has often focused on test prepara-tion rather than actual skill development. So not only do students routinely not read, many of them have never engaged in either serious academic reading or enjoyable pleasure reading in English. Furthermore, the skills needed to score well on an English proficiency test are different from those needed to perform well in an academic English context where students must manage hundreds of pages, evaluate the arguments presented, and construct critical responses.

When I initially established the academic reading course, I selected a typical reading textbook. It was and remains an anthology of academic articles covering a variety of topics that the editors presumably thought should be interesting to postsecondary English for Academic Purposes (EAP) students. After using the textbook for two consecutive semesters, I came to the conclusion that it was not working. Students would submit their TOEFL (an English language test used throughout the world) scores before admission into the program and would then take the TOEFL again upon program completion. While their scores in speaking, writing, and listening would increase dramatically, their reading scores remained stagnant. I saw this pattern with student after student. Moreover, after the students had exited the program and started studying in the regular credit-bearing coursework in order to earn their degrees, reading was the one reason that they would come back to my door and ask for help. They could not keep up with their assigned readings. Too many pages were required, and the syntax was too dense. They did not have the skills to learn from their assigned readings.

Analyze

The analysis section of the reflective cycle drives the decisions that I will later make. In this section, I intently listen to the different voices of those individuals who have an interest in the outcomes of the program. Here is the area of the reflective cycle where I systematically assess the preconceptions, needs, and values of the various stakeholders of the reading course:

University faculty report that the students do not have the discipline to read multiple pages of text nor do they possess the reading comprehension skills to grasp the nuances and implications of the shorter texts that are assigned. University administrators use the post-program test scores as well as student performance in the regular coursework to evaluate program efficacy. International university administrators (officials responsible for sending students to our program if they think it has value) state time and again that they do not want a great deal of students' instruction to focus on reading. TESOL experts believe extensive reading of full-length novels and a wide variety of text is the best way to increase both reading ability and overall language proficiency. Students as a group do not want to read. The majority of them resent the assignment of long passages and being held accountable for reading them. Students overtly state that they come to our university to socialize rather than develop their English reading skills.

Interpret

In this phase of the reflective cycle process, I critically evaluate the discordant ideologies about reading and its necessity in English language development. In a truly Hegelian sense, this is the power of the reflective cycle as I look at the different theses held by stakeholders (which are truly antithetical to each other) and try to harmonize them into a synthesis. I could also describe this in terms of English language teaching by explaining the interpretive aspect of the reflective cycle as the area where I negotiate meaning between conflicting reading dogmas and establish an approach toward reading instruction that will best meet the needs of the students.

When synthesizing the different opinions to develop the academic reading course, I have to make value judgments about which of the different views on academic reading should drive pedagogy. While each different perspective needs to be answered and acknowledged, they cannot all provide justifiable rationale for instructional choices. Consequently, for my academic reading course, the opinions that drive my instruction must come from the practical needs of students and the research-based findings of TESOL professionals. While the preconceptions of both students and home universities must be factored into the plan, that placement must be strategic.

Action Plan

To continue with the music analogy, the action plan is the song harmonized by the reflective cycle. This is where all of the steps come together and I create a meaningful melody out of the previously discordant voices. In the academic reading course, I determined that students need to start the course by reading short, academic, nonfiction texts to more easily acculturate to the U.S. university classroom. Starting the semester with novels would be too far outside of the students' comfort zones and schema. While the course does not focus on those types of readings for more than a couple of weeks, during that time, I focus on teaching the literature circle and questioning techniques which will be the structure for their later explorations into longer texts. I then assign at least two novels each semester. This is because of the research that supports this type of reading as a major component of language and skill development. Language learners need recycled language, they need extensive input, and they need to develop the disciple of tolerance of ambiguity to make sense of future texts that their professors will assign. To answer to the students' home universities, very little class time is devoted to actual reading. Instead, I give mini-lessons on either the skill of reading or a language objective, which will help students negotiate meaning in the text. The vast majority of each class session is student-led discussion of the text and its implications to world issues and broader themes.

Ruthie Reflects

The reflective cycle is a cyclical procedure of self-assessment and course evaluation. While I have shared with you one revolution through the process, the decisions that I make in my action plan will become the focus of my next inquiry into course development. For example, because of the robust literature on the importance of students' choice in reading development, next semester, I plan to substitute the second assigned novel for an extensive list of novels from which students can select what they want to read based on what fits their interests and intended fields of study. In this way, my courses evolve to better meet the needs of students, and I evolve as a more confident and deliberate teacher who makes stronger daily decisions.

An Example from Professional Development in the Teachers' Writing Project: Debra

Know ELLs Takes a Ride on the Inquiry Cycle

The EL Inquiry Group from the Great Valley Writing Project (GVWP) manages a virtual community, *Know ELLs* (knowells.ning.com), for teachers of ELs. We created it to fill our need to communicate with teachers who are passionate about equity, language, and students acquiring English as a new language. It is an inquiry-based community of learners. We quickly had hundreds of members from all over the United States (mostly writing-project teacher-consultants) but almost no consistently active members. We didn't know how to create more participation on the site. Our writing-project work had taught us to inquire into our classrooms, and we decided to apply the Reflective Cycle (see figure 12.1.) to our work with Know ELLs. We met for four hours on a Saturday morning at one member's house and invited new leadership to participate in the inquiry group.

We used the verbs of the Reflective Cycle to spark the discussion. We started with some questions that would help us *describe Know ELLs*: What is the purpose of our virtual community? Who is it for? How should it be used? What does it need? Fueled by strong coffee and Norwegian apple cake, we talked through the phases of *description* to *action* and back again. (Note to readers: Dee would say that they simply *plunged in*.)

The cycle was extremely dynamic and organic: Questions followed ideas followed suggestions followed actions. We knew Know ELLs was easy to find, easy to navigate, had a diverse membership, and had new content almost weekly. But that wasn't enough. We focused our *analysis* on what we knew about why teachers weren't using Know ELLs. Sometimes, district filters block our electronic posts. In addition, we knew teachers were busy or perhaps tech-anxious, but, mostly, we realized by looking at the site that we weren't *essential* to teachers. That led us to *interpret*: What would it mean for us to be essential? We discussed what was essential to us: We needed strategies and materials in our classrooms, but we also needed the support and encouragement to persist in work that is often undervalued or even ignored in our workplaces. Immediately, we thought of ways to change the groups within Know ELLs to be more focused on essential elements of support and encouragement. Our new question: How can we become essential to teachers of ELLs? (Readers, we know that a new question will often suddenly emerge: see figure 12.1, The Reflective Cycle).

Next, we went back to the list of *actions* that we had been recording all through the morning. We added new ones, revised old ones, and began to divide the work among us and other supportive colleagues. We thought of ways to bring more members to the site by making sure that Know ELLs is part of every GVWP presentation and meeting. We created new groups that aligned with teachers' essential needs, such as finding good professional-development and instructional materials. We highlighted groups with the most members, the ones showing teachers' personal accounts of their own classrooms and their students' work. We committed to weekly blogging and identified new voices to bring onto the blogging schedule.

We didn't use the reflective cycle as a one-shot strategy; we use it regularly to deal with issues in our classrooms, departments, school sites, and projects. We know it's effective. And that Saturday in March, in four short hours, we had revitalized Know ELLs and recommitted ourselves to using the verbs to keep up a continuous cycle of reflection and action.

WHY DO WE DO WHAT WE DO?

The purpose of reflecting is to learn deeply; to think new thoughts; to get smarter; to solve problems; to create a more just context. If this is true, then a more challenging question is Why do we do what we do (Wink & Putney, 2013, p. 1)?

In this chapter, we have looked at the reflective cycle as a way to progressively improve our pedagogy. It is a tool that we use to be better teachers. But if the chapter were to end here, that simply would not be sufficient to make us *great* teachers. The reflective cycle must also be applied to ourselves, as teachers. It can serve as a microscope to magnify the fundamental inner motivations that drive our choices and reactions. In doing this, we remember why we wanted to be teachers in the first place; we rekindle our love for our students and our desire to make the world better by promoting ideals of social justice, democracy, and equal access to excellent education for every student regardless of race, ethnicity, language, or religion.

In what follows, Dawn shares her adaptations of the reflective cycle when working with teachers and teacher-educators nationally and internationally. Dawn beautifully demonstrates the power of the reflective cycle as a tool for intrapersonal assessment. She finds that through the process of the structured reflection teachers gain insight into how all experiences, whether we feel them to be positive, negative, or somewhere in between, hold the potential to improve our efficacy as educators. As with the examples from teachers and teacher-educators previously used in this chapter, the reflective cycle deepens ELL teacher-educators' pedagogy, thus initiating a more engaged learning experience for the students. In the following vignette, Dawn, who works at a community college and specializes in teacher preparation for emergent bilinguals, shares one example of her use of the reflective cycle to capture the essence of student learning.

A Final Example from Dawn: Reflection to Efficacy

We arrived in Puebla, Mexico, to work with seventy-five teacher-educators for a three-day intensive professional development session, focusing on workshop design, characteristics of adult learners, and teaching based in the reflective cycle, in which events in the classroom are described, reflected upon, interpreted, and acted upon. When teacher-educators are ELLs themselves, the reflective cycle lifts pedagogy out of the paradigm of the traditional and ineffective hierarchical paradigm of "teacher talks; students listen and memorize" and deepens learning for the teacher and the students. These teacher-educators, like the others mentioned within the chapter, focus on teaching and learning in English; this group differs from the previous examples in that they are teacher-educators outside of the United States.

My colleagues from Centro Espiral Maná (www.espiralmana.org/) spent these days delving deeply with our students into the required content, which we shared through engaged and reflective, interactive methods. The students responded with new ideas, conversation, noise, movement, and laughter. As our final hours approached, we reflected together about everything that these teacher-educators had experienced. As we planned our final class experience, our focus was on deep reflection. We wanted them to take what they had learned as they moved forward on their continuing professional journey. It had been an intense few days together, as we felt compelled to share all of the content while still maintaining a reflective pedagogical experience for the students. Finally, we asked the students to use the reflective cycle to guide them as they synthesized their own individual learning. Our intention was for these teacher-educators to create personal and professional relevancy and meaning based on deeper learning.

The concept of focusing on the question, *Why Do We Do What We Do?* is used widely in motivational, psychological, and educational circles. However, for our final activity, I used the ideas from *Why Do You Do What You Do?* (http://wdydwyd.ning.com/photo), where posting photos of ourselves with a single phrase or word that conveys that, beyond strategies, theory, and methodology—at the heart of it all, why we do what we do. We gave each teacher-educator a piece of paper and magic marker. We asked that everyone be silent as people sank deeply into this idea and wrote a single phrase or word on their piece of paper. When all were finished, we each held our piece of paper in front of us and stood in a circle as we quietly read what those around us had written. It was a time of deep humility and inspiration to read of people's sacred paths in education. Here are some quotes: "To give life back what she has given me," "Because it makes me feel alive," "Teaching can change someone's life," and "To provide people with the magic power of communicating in another language." I wrote, "To create beauty in the world."

We took individual photos of the teacher-educators holding their signs in front of them so that each was left with a tangible memory of our special time together. The photos of each person with his or her *Why Do We Do What We Do?* provides community and honors the voice of each individual. This also provides them with a reminder of the essence of deep learning. We all need these reminders sometimes. Then, all seventy-five of us took a photo on some steps we found outside. What a marvelous feeling to read seventy-five sacred understandings of education and gather in one place. We uploaded the photos to http://wdydwyd.ning.com/photo.

To integrate reflection at its deepest level for this closure activity ended our time together with a sense of both individual dedication and shared passion within the teaching profession. The reflective cycle grounds all components of teaching ELL teacher-educators in ways that open and encourage Socratic learning, deeper learning, reflective learning. When teacher-educators experience reflective, deep learning, they pay it forward to the ELs in their own classrooms.

Chapter 13

Mainstream Literacy Teachers in Multilingual and Transnational Learning Communities

Making a Case for Transliteracy

David Schwarzer

In this chapter, I introduce the concept of *transliteracy* as an alternative ideology to the traditional notion of literacy development and show how this reconceptualization can more effectively support the language and literacy development of English learners (ELs) in the mainstream classroom.

> Jewel is a child in motion. A member of a family who emigrated to the US from Bangladesh, Jewel moves across languages (Bengali, English), identities (e.g. Bengali girlhood, kindergartener), and, when her family is able to make the trip to Bangladesh for a summer or longer, national borders. . . . In school, we can see the movement in her literacies as she writes, draws and designs texts on pages and screens during the daily writer's workshop in her classroom, and in the weekly digital writer's workshop held in the school's computer lab. Across these social spaces, Jewel shifts her body, her texts, and her identities in ways that offer a glimpse of the fluid meanings literacy has for this child of globalization. (Siegel, Kontovourki, Schmier & Enriquez, 2008, p. 89).

I begin the chapter by revisiting the definition of literacy development or *literacies-in-motion* to better suit millions of children like Jewel. In other words, to make school literacy ready for Jewel and children like her in today's multilingual and transnational learning communities. I will first make a case for the need of *transliteracy* development as a concept needed in a globalized world. Then I will explore the concept as a phenomenon of study, as an ideology and as a pedagogy. Finally, I will offer practical ways to promote transliteracy practices in the mainstream classroom.

RESEARCH AND THEORETICAL BACKGROUND

I claim that the traditional definitions of literacy development are based on a static monolingual and monocultural view. Siegel, Kontovourki, Schmier, and Enriquez (2008) state:

> The school curriculum continues to treat literacy as monomodal, monolinguistic, and monocultural, and thus appears to have more in common to what children learned about literacy a generation ago than with the literacies needed for the world in which Jewel lives. In this sense, school literacy is not ready for Jewel. (p. 97)

Why Is a Reconceptualization Needed?

In this chapter I argue that the curriculum treats literacy in these particular ways since disciplinary structures in place do not facilitate the conversations among and between areas of expertise that share a great deal of insight once the phenomenon of study, literacy, is redefined. However, the movement of immigrants and migrant populations between contiguous countries like the Mexican-U.S. border has been broadly studied in the area of transnational studies and borderline epistemologies (Abes, 2009; Enright, 2011; Rosario-Ramos, 2009; Warriner, 2007).

Universities and teacher education programs are not prepared to help teachers who teach children like Jewel. Cummins (2009a) tells us, "Curriculum is typically developed with a 'generic' student in mind, and this generic student is usually from a middle-class, monolingual, and monocultural background" (p. 59). Literacy development is not different. It is always defined and based on a de facto monolingual and monocultural and static view of literacy. Teachers sometimes make decisions to separate languages in the classroom environment by using blue for English and red for Spanish. The color coding and the separation of languages in the environmental print of the classroom environment is one example of the conceptualization of literacy as a static phenomenon. To better serve our multilingual and transnational students researchers and teachers must challenge the assumptions behind the traditional and self-imposed compartmentalization of disciplinary knowledge (ESL, Foreign Language, Bilingual Ed, Multilingual Studies, etc.). I also contend that the different definitions of literacy (offered in the next section) needs to be reconceptualized as transliteracy development under these new globalized circumstances.

MAKING A CASE FOR TRANSLITERACY DEVELOPMENT

There have been five concepts used to describe language and literacy development in the classroom. All of these concepts define this phenomenon in a static and discrete way from more static to the most fluid. The following is a short overview of those five concepts:

Language and Literacy Development (Unmarked)

Most teacher education programs contain some classes about language development, literacy development, or child development (Villegas & Lucas, 2002b). These classes are designed to provide an overview of typical children and adolescent development. However, they assume that the typical child is monolingual, monoliterate, and monocultural. Literacy development in the bilingual or multilingual learner is not a concern (unmarked). Sometimes there is one lesson or chapter at the end of the class in which all the atypical situations are portrayed (students with disabilities, emergent bilingual/ English learners, multiracial children, etc.). This situation is troublesome for two distinct reasons—by conceptualizing this class as an unmarked language development class, a subtle message is sent that the norm is language development in one language only; literacy development in one language only, and monolinguicism is typical—bilingualism/multilingualism is a rarity (Cummins, 2007; Schwarzer, 2007; Skutnabb-Kangas, 2009).

LANGUAGE AND LITERACY DEFINED BY ITS CONTEXT

Another important concept and body of research has centered on language and literacy development in the context of student and family experiences. Depending on the location of the teacher education program, and the proximity to migrant and/or immigrant populations, the program may have classes on how to teach language and literacy to students from those particular backgrounds. What is more, teacher education programs near the Mexico-U.S. border tend to include classes that deal particularly with the language and literacy practices of children and families living in a border area between two nations in transitory conditions. The concept of borderland epistemology (understanding the development of literacy in a border town or in a border area where people move back and forth between countries and therefore between language and cultures as a completely different phenomenon than literacy development in mainstream United States is a way to explain how language, literacy, and identities are defined while transacting with physical country boundaries in areas of contact (Anzaldúa, 2007; Clandinin & Murphy, 2007; Enright, 2011; McLean, 2010).

POLITICAL POWERS OF ENGLISH

One more central concept that is available to teacher candidates particularly in the area of English education and language arts is defined by the centrality and focus on English as the main goal of language and literacy education. The importance and implications of the term used to frame the experience of acquiring language and literacy in a different language in school than at home is key to this concept. The federal government uses the term Limited English Proficiency (LEP) to define this type of students. Although some scholars may disagree with the following assertion, limited English proficient could be perceived as a term that describes what the student is lacking and therefore is centered on a deficit view of the students' ability. It emphasizes what *is not* there yet (the deficit), instead of highlighting what is already accomplished (in this case, the mother tongue). There is another group of terms to acknowledge the student population that are more descriptive in nature—English as a second language (ESL), English as an additional language (EAL), and English learners (ELs). Each one of these terms emphasizes the centrality of English as the target language. It also implies the power of the English language as the lingua franca of the postmodern world—or as others have framed it, as the "killer" language (Robertson, 2003; Skutnabb-Kangas, 2009). This terminology suggests that native tongues spoken by small communities are being eliminated while English is succeeding and embraced as an important commodity (Phillipson, 1992; Mohanty, 2009; Skutnabb-Kangas, 2009).

Beyond Monolingual Views of Language and Literacy Development

In many teacher education programs, teacher candidates are expected to complete a class or at least a module about how to adapt instruction to ELs. As part of these educational experiences, a teacher candidate may be exposed to some theoretical and practical insights about second language and literacy development—this time clearly labeled and marked (Johnson & Parrish, 2010; Robertson, 2003; Taylor, 2009).

Within these experiences, teacher candidates may also learn about additive ways of looking at language learning with a bilingual, trilingual, or multilingual environment. This is an important concept since it highlights the centrality of multiple languages as a possible goal of the public education system. Bilingual and multilingual experiences are central to bilingual teacher education programs. Biliteracy development is a concept that bilingual teachers have studied as an area of expertise. However, mostly monolingual teachers with no training or basic understanding on biliteracy development teach bilingual and multilingual students in mainstream classrooms (Villegas & Lucas, 2002b).

Attempts for More Fluid Conceptualizations of Multiple Languages

The first premise of this conceptualization is the idea that language and literacy development in multilingual and transnational settings are fluid phenomena.

That implies that code-switching (i.e., when a speaker or a writer alternates between the use of two or more languages or language varieties, in the context of a single conversation or text and it emphasizes linguistic performance) (Sarkar & Winer, 2006; Schwarzer, 2004; Sollors, 1998), code-meshing (i.e., when a writer purposefully alternates between Standard Written Englishes and other languages, or language varieties as a way to expand the definition of academic writing as a monolithic entity) (Alim, 2009), and code-mixing (i.e., when the alternation between languages, or language varieties is accepted as an unmarked linguistic choice, for example, in Spanglish mixing Spanish and English) (Auer, 1999; Sarkar, 2009) are intrinsic parts of the development of language and literacy of bilingual/multilingual communities. Examples of this more fluid view of language and literacy are apparent in the work of Ofelia Garcia and her descriptions of students as emergent bilinguals (Garcia, 2011; Garcia & Kleifgen, 2010).

Another concept that has a more fluid view of languages and literacies in contact is the concept of hybridity (Gutierrez, Baquedano-López, & Tejeda, 1999; Kumaravadivelu, 2008; Werbner & Modood, 1997). An example of a hybrid language and literacy experience is Spanglish. This hybrid language implies an *in between* space in which both and none of the assumptions made by neither Spanish nor English can fully explain this radically new phenomenon. Additionally, the crafting of a *third space*, a place that is neither *here* nor *there*—it is a new space of *in-between-ness* that promotes a more fluid conceptualization of the language and literacy needed for such a position. For classroom teachers, school and home may be first and second space. Meeting with the parents of a student at a local community event in their church creates a third space. Some of the hallmarks of a third space are: highly accessible, welcoming and comfortable; food and drinks may be available, it involves regulars, and it is free. In most cases, a meeting in the first or second space will be very different than a meeting in this third space. Moreover, there is a third space as a psychological metaphor—If English is the first space and Spanish is the second space, Spanglish is the third space that teachers can use in their practice.

A whole new set of concepts developed around the idea of the prefix *trans-* instead of the more commonly used *bi-* or *multi-* ones. Transnational identities have been explored also around imagined crossings through the help of new technologies. For example, the idea of a student talking to a family member through Skype in another country while having breakfast at home in the United States, then going to a bilingual school, coming back home in the evening, and texting students in other languages is also considered a transnational experience (Haglund, 2010; Lam, 2009; Lam & Rosario-Ramos, 2009).

Finally, the work of Garcia about *translanguaging* is an important addition to this discussion. She describes how bilingual teachers not only purposefully mix languages as they instruct ELs, but they mimic some of the linguistic

behaviors bilinguals use in their daily life to explain or emphasize information. The parent may say something in English first, move to Spanish second,
and then repeat part of the Spanish message again in English to ensure understanding as well as to maximize the communicative potential of the situation.
According to Garcia (2009):

> Translanguaging is the act performed by bilinguals of accessing different
> linguistic features or various modes of what are described as autonomous
> languages, in order to maximize communicative potential. It is an approach to
> bilingualism that is centered, not on languages, as has often been the case, but
> on the practices of bilinguals that are readily observable in order to make sense
> of their multilingual worlds. Translanguaging, therefore, goes beyond what has
> been termed code-switching, although it includes it. (p. 140)

Most recently, Canagarajah (2013) expanded and contributed to the conceptualization of translingualism. He states:

> Existing terms such as *multilingual* or *plurilingual* keep languages somewhat
> separated . . . the term translingual enables a consideration of communicative
> competence as not restricted to predefined meanings of individual languages,
> but the ability to merge different language resources in situated interactions for
> new meaning construction. (pp. 1–2)

PRACTICAL APPLICATIONS: TRANSLITERACY
IN MAINSTREAM CLASSROOMS

In this section I elaborate on translingualism and transliteracy as a more
appropriate concept to suit children like Jewel in the mainstream classroom.
I will then provide a definition of transliteracy development as a phenomenon
of study, as an ideology and as pedagogy. Each section will include one classroom application for teachers to explore.

Transliteracy Development as a Phenomenon of Study

Schwarzer, Petron, and Luke (2011) offer a possible first definition for emergent translingual/transliteracy development as:

> The development of several languages and literacies in a dynamic and fluid way
> across the life span while moving back and forth between real and imagined
> border and transacting with different cultural identities within a unified self.
> (p. 210)

A more in-depth description of each part of this new conceptualization
considers that the development of several languages and literacies at the

same time could be viewed both as biliteracy development or multiliteracy development. However, both terms elicit the idea of two languages or multiple languages competing and compacted in one person's head. Transliteracy better encapsulates the dynamic and fluid movements of moving back and forth between the different languages, registers, and dialect variations as a commonplace daily occurrence.

The concept of emergent literacy as something that happens only in early childhood needs to be expanded (Clay, 1991; Goodman, Reyes, & McArthur, 2005). I believe that the conceptualization of emergent transliteracy development as an activity across the life span better explains how young adults, adults, and senior citizens may learn how to use languages in different modalities (e.g., Hebrew as a foreign language while also using e-mail [in Hebrew] to communicate with the instructor). That is why the word literacies in the plural is part of this definition to signal both different languages and different modalities.

Research on transnational education discusses the challenges and advantages of educating children that cross the *real borders* between countries on a daily basis. I would like to expand this borderline concept to *imagined borders*. I contend that many of the students in our learning communities wake up in a Mexican American household that has a grandmother that speaks Nahuatl (an Indian language from Mexico), take classes in an English only school, have lunch in the Spanish-speaking area of town, and get their medical services in an English-only clinic—but far away from an established border between two countries, they cross these *imagined borders* several times during their days. The idea of an imagined border (or a psychological one) is widely used by Anzaldúa (2007) in her depiction of her own identity crossing in the "psychological, sexual and spiritual borderlands" (p. 21).

Transactional views of literacy have been extended to a transactional view of identity development. The way I make this transaction of identities and languages clearer to many of our monolingual students and teachers is by describing their possible interactions at the dinner table. They may be talking to their children (in a particular register, voice, and intonation as their mother), they may also talk to their partners (in another register, voice, and intonation as their spouse), and they may be interrupted by a phone call with their parents (in another register, voice, and intonation as their children). They are moving and transacting with different identities, contexts, language registers within a *unified self.*

Linguistic Landscape as a Phenomenon of Study

Multilingual and transnational students live in communities where language use is fluid. By asking teacher candidates to photograph the linguistic landscape of their communities, they become aware of the phenomenon of study and how is relevant to their lives.

According to (Ben-Rafael, Shohamy, Amara, & Trumper-Hecht, 2006) a linguistic landscape is a collection of photos that depict a particular linguistic reality of a community. Researching public spaces such as local grocery stores, marquees, or environmental print is a good way to begin to widen teacher candidates' worldviews. Moreover, the placement of languages for view by the community also provides information about the status of the languages in the community (Cenoz & Gorter, 2008). Candidates may start noticing that English is usually placed first and in larger text, followed by the Spanish translation (placed below and in smaller fonts). Some languages are only present in certain areas of town (church signage) while completely absent in other sections (public schools). More important, it becomes evident that sometimes languages are not separated, rather they interact with each other in the linguistic landscape: some signs have code-switched words that may suggest a more inclusive environment. Another important feature of a linguistic landscape is the distinction between private signs that are written by individual and are short lived in nature (e.g., a computer printed advertisement for tutoring services, apartments for rent, babysitting) versus and public signs (usually written by government municipalities or other public agencies as well as marquees for stores). These signs are permanent and intended to last for many years. The public signs need to be approved by the agencies or the owner of the establishment. When candidates pay attention to how languages behave in their local community, they have opportunities to become aware of the powerful forces of globalization and transnationalism that are part of their own local community.

As part of this activity, I encourage teacher candidates in my classes, to take twenty to twenty-five digital pictures of multilingual artifacts representing the languages in the community where they live. They analyze the pictures and find some common trend among them. Places where students can take pictures of languages in action are local ethnic restaurants and their menus, signs in public places such as parks, churches, or schools. Moreover, I encourage my students to interview parents and neighbors about religious sites, specialty food stores, or other local festivals where multilingual signage may abound.

Following are pictures that were part of a linguistic landscape projects carried out in urban school districts in the Central New Jersey geographical area. This particular linguistic landscapes centers on Jersey City—the second most populous city in New Jersey (after Newark) with around 250,000 citizens. It is part of the New York metropolitan area since it lies across from Lower Manhattan. The city is very diverse with 32 percent white, 25 percent African American, 14 percent Native American, and 12 percent Pacific Islander.

Hispanics of any race are 18 percent of the population. Important to note is that 21 percent of the city population is under the age of 18 and 28 percent of them live below the poverty line.

Students often find that sometimes storeowners decide to place items in the same store facing in different ways to showcase both languages available (see figure 13.1). In the first case the soymilk package is facing the English side next to the one written in Korean. Using the same strategy; in the second picture, the containers arranged in the right were arranged facing the Spanish version, while in the left they were arranged facing the English one.

This is a very savvy move employed by the storeowner to appeal to both the broader audience of clients (who speak English) and also the minority language speakers (Korean and Spanish respectively). We called it bilingual juxtaposition.

The more traditional bilingual signage is the situation in which the English version is bigger and written first followed by the Spanish version in smaller font and second. In some very specialized stores, the signage is only in a minority language. For example in Spanish in a grocery store that is intended only for Spanish-speaking clients. This is an unusual occurrence since storeowners' interest is to appeal to the broadest costumer population not for linguistic reasons but for economical ones.

Figure 13.1   Example of Bilingual Juxtaposition Signage

Figure 13.2   Example of Translingual Signage

Finally, sometimes we find real translingual signage in which languages and literacies interact in very fluid ways (see figure 13.2).

In this picture there are at least four languages represented: English (Chinese food take out), Spanish (*Pollo a la Brasa*), Chinese (Chinese characters above the logo), and French (*Rotisserie*). More importantly, unlike the other signs, there is no clear intention to translate all the aspects of the sign to all the languages; some content is only in one language with no apparent translation. This signage design may be a stylistic device to show authenticity.

I believe that in order to transform educational practices, we need to show students how translingualism and transliteracy is all around them in their daily lives. Moreover, we can acknowledge that a linguistic landscape project may help candidates understand language usage in their communities and lives as a fluid phenomenon.

Translingualism as an Ideology

The question that we want educators to ask is: what do I believe is the best way to help ELs become multilingual and multiliterate? Sometimes, bilingual teachers may have a monolingual ideology about language and literacy development. Not to confuse their students, they separate the language and literacy experiences. On the other hand, some monolingual teachers have adopted a translingual ideology about language and literacy development. They act as jazz band directors in their multilingual and transnational learning communities—they only know how to play one instrument (English), but they create spaces in their classrooms where many different instruments can be played together in harmony. Unlike the director of an orchestra (with preassigned roles that should follow one particular version), the jazz band director crafts a space for students' improvisation. Therefore, teachers who adopt a translingual ideology, create an overarching structure that is conducive to learning while crafting a space where students experiment with their languages and literacies.

FAMILY LANGUAGE USAGE AND COMMUNITY LANGUAGE USAGE TREES

A Family Language Usage Tree (FLUT) and a Community Language Usage Tree (CLUT) are two interesting activities that promote the understanding of translingualism in general and transliteracy in particular as an ideology. Teachers can ask their students to research their own family language backgrounds as well as their own community (Schwarzer, 2001; Schwarzer, Haywood, & Lorenzen, 2003). These activities help students (monolingual, bilingual and multilingual) to see how translingualism and transliteracy is part of their lives. Both activities center on using a list of easy to complete forms, followed by some questions designed to elicit students' knowledge about their families' and their neighbors' language usage. The questions focus on food items, nicknames, and family language stories in addition to local community resources that can help all students make authentic and real-life connections to multilingualism in their own family and community structures. The FLUT is different from the language survey used by many school districts to determine eligibility for services. The FLUT should be explained as a catalyst to promote students' interest and proficiency in their heritage languages. Following are some of the questions used in a FLUT:

1. What languages do your family members use?
2. What are these family members called? (El abuelo, la abu, madre, mom, padre, etc.) Why?
3. What do these names tell us about your family background?

Sometimes, after concluding a FLUT, some candidates are disappointed to find English as the only language of the family. For these situations a Community Language Usage Tree (CLUT) might be beneficial (Schwarzer, 2007).

In a CLUT, students ask questions about language usage from the immediate community: neighbors, school personnel, or friends from religious institutions. Following are some of the questions that students may utilize:

1. Who uses languages other than English in your immediate environment (in the school setting, in the family setting, in your neighborhood, in your community, etc.)?
2. What languages do they use?
3. What language is the most used?
4. What language is the least used?

Many monolingual students are surprised to find many languages spoken in their immediate community. This insight is extremely important since it shows how common languages other than English are part of their daily lives experiences.

Following is an example of some insights gained from a FLUT and CLUT (for more information, please see Schwarzer and Acosta [2014]).

One of the questions used in the FLUT relates to students comfort foods. Acosta found that his favorite food *ñoquis de papa* (potato gnocchi) had an interesting story. The name of this food is written in a code-switched Spanish version (*ñoquis* instead of *gnocchi*). More importantly, it is a translingual experience since it is a double plural (not *ñoqui* but *ñoquis*)—a very unusual linguistic occurrence that went unnoticed until this analysis. Several years ago, another student realized that her family's comfort food, ambrosia, which is an early American dish that originated in the nineteenth century.

Creating a bridge between students' lives outside and inside the school is a crucial aspect of these activities. Finally, for the bilingual and multilingual students in particular, these activities provide a way to empower them and to help them see translingualism and transliteracy as an ideology to be cherished.

Translingualism as a Pedagogy

Translingualism as a pedagogy and methodology is an area that needs to be addressed to create a bridge between the theoretical underpinnings being explored in this chapter, and the practical applications needed both in teacher preparation programs and classroom settings.

Pedagogical changes in the classroom are the best way to make complex and theoretical ideas a daily practice for ELs. In traditional classrooms there is an overemphasis of English-only strategies for ELs. In the next section I will discuss some practical ways in which traditional activities in language arts classroom can become a translingual practice.

RECOMMENDATIONS FOR ACTION

Language arts teachers have a repertoire of language and literacy activities to promote and support literacy and language development of all students. In the following section, I will select two well-established language arts activities and suggest extension scenarios that incorporate translingual pedagogies.

Word walls is an established activity teachers use to promote reading and writing among early grade readers (Harmon, Wood, Hedrick, Vintinner, & Willeford, 2009; Jackson, Tripp, & Cox, 2011; Larson, Dixon, & Townsend, 2013). In a traditional word wall, teachers and students include words that have been studied or explained while reading or writing in the class. Some teachers have bilingual word walls and in a few cases, I have observed multilingual words being used in classrooms. In those cases, a clear separation between languages is expected, sometimes by having the word wall in spatial separate location or by using different colors to separate between them. A translingual word wall will allow students to play with words and create more fluid spaces in the classroom where languages interact with each other. This is important since it provides a real-life translingual experience within the school context to mirror the fluid use of literacy in the surrounding community.

A set of Daily Language Routines is another important activity that language art teachers use to support children's language and literacy development. Teachers may start each day by greeting students in English with sentences such as: "Good morning! How are you? Today is Wednesday August 15, 2014." Some of these routines can be established in a bilingual or a multilingual fashion. Teachers and students would be encouraged to greet each other in all the languages represented in the classroom. For example: "*Buenos días! Cómo estás? Hoy es el quince de agosto del 2014.*" However, a translingual pedagogy will encourage students to play with the languages, mix them in interesting ways exactly as they witness them in their daily lives.

A translingual pedagogy invites monolingual, bilingual, and multilingual teachers to embrace the fluid space between languages as in real life. It involves talking about *ñoquis de papa* or why the marquee of the local Chinese restaurant uses four different languages and does not translate them word-by-word.

RESOURCES

The following two sets of teacher resources are helpful in understanding of literacy development in a multilingual classroom and in eliciting conversations about multilingualism and immigration experiences.

Academic Resources

Multilingual Education in Practice: Using Diversity as a Resource by S. Schecter & J. Cummins (2003). I recommend this book to teachers interested in using translingual approaches to language and literacy instruction in the classroom. The book describes collaborative projects that help ELs with their academic success in two different schools. The book describes practical suggestions to develop policies to promote multilingualism in schools. Moreover, it provides specific strategies for public school teachers interested in working effectively in transnational and multilingual learning environment. The chapters include important topics to promote ELs' academic engagement and provide many examples and pictures of students' artwork, poetry, and projects in the language arts classroom.

Teaching Reading in Multilingual Classrooms by D. Freeman & Y. Freeman (2000). This book helps clarify the goals of literacy instruction while providing useful and concrete strategies to promote reading in multilingual and diverse learning communities. The book includes a user-friendly checklist to promote reading in a multilingual environment. Theory and practice are the hallmark of this book, in each chapter a theoretical as well as a practical explanation is used to illustrate examples from eight different teachers who work effectively and efficiently with ELs. Examples of teachers' lessons, children's literature, as well as their daily schedules are available to be used as models for other teachers. Finally, questions about testing, phonics, and standards are addressed in the last chapter to promote an important conversation in each school and school district.

Young Adult Resources

As a teacher, I find that making a connection to students' lives is crucial to promote a translingual approach to literacy. In this section I will present three young author resources I found useful in my class to help students develop a personal connection to multilingualism and immigration.

The first book *Dancing Home* (Ada & Zubizarreta, 2011) is the story of two cousins (one born in the United States and the other just came from Mexico) and their experiences in their fifth grade classroom. Margie Ceballos-Gonzalez, the U.S.-born cousin, is very proud of being American. Lupe's presence in the class brings immediate attention to the things Margie has been trying to avoid. As the relationship between the cousins becomes closer, Margie begins to appreciate in a different way parts of her family's Mexican American heritage. Of particular importance is the realization of the importance of her name—Margarita and its connection to the Nicaraguan Poet Rubén Darío's poem. This book is very useful to promote a translingual approach in the classroom to promote serious discussions about linguistic and cultural identities among young adult students in the class.

The second book *A Step from Heaven* (An, 2001) is about a Korean child's journey (Young Ju) from the age of four to her college years. The name of the book is based on the assumption that Young Ju has that they are moving to America (Mi Gook), a place that everyone describes as being a paradise or very close to heaven. Interestingly in the story, Young Ju's mother wants her to forget about her Korean heritage. However, as soon as she becomes aware of the new culture, her parents realize the price. Young Ju is embarrassed by her parents' poverty and culture. Therefore, she lies both to her parents and to her friends about the situation and becomes more and more isolated and lonely. Finally, her father's alcoholism gets out of control and soon she fears for her and her mother's lives in the new country. This book is useful to students and teachers interested in looking at a complex immigration story and make connections to other immigration stories in their classroom.

The third and final book *First Crossing Stories about Teen Immigrants* (Gallo, 2004) is an edited collection that includes eleven stories written by well-known authors on the topic of teenagers' experiences as new immigrants to the United States. Stories varied from Amina and her family leaving Venezuela, to Sarah, an adopted child who is interested to know her Korean birth parents. It also includes stories about Adrian, a Rumanian boy whose friends hold interesting misconceptions about his birthplace. All the accounts in this book have moved from one known context to a new and unfamiliar one. The challenges and opportunities the characters face in their journey are unique and useful for teachers and classrooms interested in promoting a translingual discussion about identity and language use.

References

Abedi, J., & Hejri, F. (2004). Accommodations for students with limited English proficiency in the national assessment of educational progress. *Applied Measurement in Education, 17*(4), 371–92.

Abedi, J., & Herman, J. (2010). Assessing English language learners' opportunity to learn mathematics: Issues and limitations. *The Teachers College Record, 112*, 723–46.

Abedi, J., & Lord, C. (2001). The language factor in mathematics tests. *Applied Measurement in Education, 14*(3), 219–34.

Abes, E. S. (2009). Theoretical borderlands: Using multiple theoretical perspectives to challenge inequitable power structures in student development theory. *Journal of College Student Development, 50*(2), 141–56.

Abraham, L. B. (2008). Computer-mediated glosses in second language reading comprehension and vocabulary learning: A meta-analysis. *Computer Assisted Language Learning, 21*(3), 199–226.

Ada, A. F., & Zubizarreta, G. M. (2011). *Dancing home* (1st ed.). New York, NY: Atheneum Books for Young Readers.

Afflerbach, P., Pearson, P. D., & Paris, S. (2008). Skills and strategies: Their differences, their relationships, and why it matters. In K. Mokhtari & R. Sheorey (Eds.), *Reading strategies of first and second language readers: See how they read.* Norwood, MA: Christopher-Gordon Publishers.

Albers, P., & Harste, J. C. (2007). The arts, new literacies, and multimodality. *English Education, 40*(1), 6–20.

Alim, H. S. (2009). Straight outta compton, straigh aus Munchen: Global linguistic flows, identities, and the politics of language in a global hip hop nation. In H. S. Alim, A. Ibrahim, & A. Pennycook (Eds.), *Global linguistic flows: Hip hop cultures, youth identities, and the politics of language* (pp. 1–24). New York, NY: Routledge.

Allexsaht-Snider, M., & Hart, L. E. (2001). "Mathematics for all": How do we get there? *Theory into Practice, 40*(2), 93–101.

Allington, R. L. (2007). Intervention all day long: New hope for struggling readers. *Voices from the Middle, 14*(4), 7–14.

Alvermann, D. (Ed.). (2002). *Adolescents and literacies in a digital world.* New York: Peter Lang.

Amer, A. N. (2003). Teaching EFL/ESL literature. *The Reading Matrix, 3*(2), 63–73.

An, N. (2001). *A step from heaven.* Asheville, NC: Front Street.

Anderson-Inman, L., & Horney, M. A. (1998). Transforming text for at-risk readers. In D. Reinking, M. McKenna, L. Labbo, & R. Keiffer (Eds.), *Handbook of literacy and technology: Transformations in a post-typographic world* (pp. 15–44). Mahwah, NJ: Lawrence Erlbaum Associates.

Anderson, N. J. (2003). Scrolling, clicking, and reading English: Online reading strategies in a second/foreign language. *Reading Matrix: An International Online Journal, 3*(3), 460–72.

Anzaldúa, G. (2007). *Borderlands/La frontera: The new mestiza* (3rd ed.). San Franciso, CA: Aunt Lute Books.

Anzaldúa, G. (2014). *Prietita and the ghost woman/Prietita y la llorona.* Bilingual edition. San Francisco, CA: Children's Book Press.

Atkinson, T., & Swaggerty, E. (2011). Empowering fourth grade researchers: Reaping the rewards of Web 2.0 student-centered learning. *Language Arts, 89*(2), 99–112.

Auer, P. (1999). From code-switching via language mixing to fused lects: Toward a dynamic typology of bilingual speech. *International Journal of Bilingualism, 3*(4), 309–32.

August, D., Calderón, M., & Carlo, M. (2002). Transfer of skills from Spanish to English: A study of young learners. Retrieved from http://www.cal.org/acquiring-literacy/pdfs/skills-transfer.pdf.

August, D., Carlo, M., Dressler, C., & Snow, C. (2005). The critical role of vocabulary development for English language learners. *Learning Disabilities Research and Practice, 20*(1), 50–57.

August, D., & Hakuta, K. (1997). *Improving schooling for language-minority children: A research agenda.* Washington, DC: National Research Council.

August, D., & Shanahan, T. (Eds.). (2006). *Developing literacy in second language learners: Report of the national literacy panel on language minority youth and children.* Mahwah, NJ: Erlbaum.

August, D., & Shanahan, T. (Eds.). (2008). *Developing reading and writing in second-language learners: Lessons from the Report of the National Literacy Panel on language-minority children and youth.* New York, NY: Taylor & Francis.

Austen, J. (1813/1990). *Pride and Prejudice.* New York: Oxford University Press.

Baker, C. (2011). *Foundations of bilingual education and bilingualism* (5th ed.). Buffalo, NY: Multilingual Matters.

Baker, S., Lesaux, N., Jayanthi, M., Dimino, J., Proctor, C. P., Morris, J., . . . Newman-Gonchar, R. (2014). *Teaching academic content and literacy to English learners in elementary and middle school* (NCEE 2014-4012). Washington, DC: National Center for Education Evaluation and Regional Assistance (NCEE), Institute of Education Sciences, U.S. Department of Education. Retrieved from the NCEE website:gov/ncee/wwc/publications_reviews.aspx.

Bakken, J. P., & Ponce, F. (1996). *Teaching text structure in the foreign language classroom*. Paper presented at the Summer Conference on Foreign Languages and Interdisciplinary Curricula, University of Illinois, Urbana, IL.

Ballantyne, K. G., Sanderman, A. R., Levy, J. (2008). *Educating English Language Learners: Building teacher capacity*. Washington, DC: National Clearinghouse for English Language Acquisition. Available at http://www.ncela.gwu.edu/practice/maisntreamteachers.htm.

Bartlett, E. J. (1982). Learning to revise: Some component processes. In M. Nystrand (Ed.), *What writers know: The language, process, and structure of written discourse* (pp. 345–63). New York, NY: Academic Press.

Bartolomé, L. I. (2002). Creating an equal playing field: Teachers as advocates, border crossers, and cultural brokers. In Z. E. Beykont (Ed.), *The Power of Culture: Teaching across language difference* (pp. 167–91). Cambridge, MA: Harvard Education Publishing Group.

Barton, D., & Potts, D. (2013). Language learning online as a social practice. *TESOL Quarterly, 47*(4), 815–20.

Bartu, H. (2001). Can't I read without thinking? *Reading in a Foreign Language, 13*(2), 593–614.

Beach, R., & Friedrich, T. (2006). Response to writing. In C. A. Arthur, S. Graham, J. Fitzgerald (Eds.), *Handbook of writing research* (pp. 222–34). New York, NY: Guilford.

Beach, R., Hull, G., & O'Brien, D. (2011). Transforming English language arts in a Web 2.0 world. In D. Lapp & D. Fisher (Eds.), *Handbook of Research on Teaching the English Language Arts* (pp. 161–67). New York, NY: Routledge.

Beck, I. L., & McKeon, M. G. (2001). Test talk: Capturing the benefits of read-aloud experiences for young children. *The Reading Teacher, 55*(1), 10–20.

Beck, I. L., McKeon, M. G., & Kucan, L. (2002). *Bringing words to life: Robust vocabulary instruction*. New York, NY: Guilford Press.

Ben-Rafael, E., Shohamy, E., Amara, M. H., & Trumper-Hecht, N. (2006). Linguistic landscape as symbolic construction of the public space: The case of Israel. *International Journal of Multilingualism, 3*(1), 7–30.

Bennett, A. T. (1983). Discourses of power, the dialectics of understanding, the power of literacy. *Journal of Education, Boston, 165*(1), 53–74.

Bennett, S., Maton, K., & Kervin, L. (2008). The "digital natives" debate: A critical review of the evidence. *British journal of educational technology, 39*(5), 775–86.

Benson, C. (2008). *Summary Overview: Mother tongue-based education in multi-lingual contexts found in Improving the Quality of Mother Tongue-based Literacy and Learning: Case Studies from Asia, Africa and South America*. Bangkok: UNESCO Asia and Pacific Regional Bureau for Education.

Bernhardt, E. (2003). Challenges to reading research from a multilingual world. *Reading Research Quarterly, 38*(1), 112–17.

Bernhardt, E. (2011). *Understanding advanced second-language reading*. New York, NY: Routledge.

Berninger, V. W., & Richards, T. L. (2002). Brain literacy for educators and psychologists. San Diego, CA: Academic Press.

Biancarosa, G., & Snow, C. (2004) *Reading Next—A vision for action and research in middle school and high school literacy: A report to Carnegie Corporation of New York.* Washington, DC.

Bishop, R. S. (1990). Mirrors, windows, and sliding glass doors. *Perspectives: Choosing and Using Books for the Classroom, 6*(3), ix–xi.

Bishop, R. S. (1992). Multicultural literature for children: Making informed choices. In V. Harris (Ed.), *Teaching multicultural literature in grades K-8* (pp. 37–54). Norwood, MA: Christopher-Gordon.

Black, R. W. (2005). Access and affiliation: The literacy and composition practices of English-language learners in an online fanfiction community. *Journal of Adolescent & Adult Literacy, 49*(2), 118–28.

Black, R. W. (2006). Language, culture, and identity in online fanfiction. *E-learning, 3*(2), 170–84.

Black, R. W. (2009). English-language learners, fan communities, and 21st-century skills. *Journal of Adolescent & Adult Literacy, 52*(8), 688–97.

Bley-Vroman, R. (1989). What is the logical problem of foreign language learning. *Linguistic Perspectives on Second Language Acquisition, 4*, 1–68.

Bloch, J. (2007). Abdullah's blogging: A generation 1.5 student enters the blogosphere. *Language Learning & Technology, 11*(2), 128–41.

Boaler, J. (2008). Creating mathematical futures through an equi teaching approach: The case of Railside school. *Teachers College Record, 110*(3), 608–45.

Borsheim, C., Merritt, K., & Reed, D. (2008). Beyond technology for technology's sake: Advancing multiliteracies in the twenty-first century. *Clearing House: A Journal of Educational Strategies, Issues and Ideas, 82*, 87–90.

Boyd-Batstone, P. (2013). *Helping English language learners meet the Common Core: Assessment and instruction.* New York, NY: Eye on Education/Routledge.

Boyles, N. (2012/2013). Closing in on close reading. *Educational Leadership, 70*(4), 36–41.

Brantmeier, C. (2005). Effects of reader's knowledge, text type, and test type on L1 and L2 reading comprehension in Spanish. *Modern Language Journal, 89*(1), 37–53.

Brisk, M., & Harrington, M. M. (2007). *Literacy and bilingualism* (2nd ed.). Mahwah, NJ: Elrbaum.

Britton, K. (2014, January). *Classroom experience and assessment tool.* Hill City Middle School, Hill City, SD.

Brock, C. H., Case, R., Pennington, J. L., Li, G., & Salas, R. G. (2008). Using a multimodal theoretical lens to explore studies pertaining to English learners in the visual and communicative arts. In J. Flood, S. Brice-Heath, & D. Lapp (Eds.), *The handbook of research on teaching literacy through the communicative and visual arts* (pp. 51–64). New York: Lawrence Erlbaum.

Brown, D., & Warschauer, M. (2006). From the university to the elementary classroom: Students' experiences in learning to integrate technology in instruction. *Journal of Technology and Teacher Education, 14*(3), 599–621.

Brown, H. D. (2007). *Principles of language learning and teaching* (5th ed.). White Plains, NY: Pearson and Longman.

Brown, R., Waring, R., & Donkaewbua, S. (2008). Incidental vocabulary acquisition from reading, reading-while-listening, and listening to stories. *Reading in a Foreign Language, 20*(2), 136–63.

Brown, S., & Kappes, L. (2012). *Implementing the Common Core State Standards: A primer on "close reading of text."* Washington, DC: The Aspen Institute.

Buckingham, D. (2013). *Media education: Literacy, learning and contemporary culture.* John Wiley & Sons.

Bunyi, A. (2010, November 19). Higher order comprehension: The power of Socratic seminar. Retrieved from http://www.scholastic.com/teachers/top_teaching/2010/11/ higher-order-comprehension-the-power-of-socratic-seminar.

Butler-Pascoe, M. E. (1997). Technology and second language learners: The promise and the challenge ahead. *American Language Review, 1*(3), 20–22.

Butler, F. A., Lord, C., Stevens, R., Borrego, M., & Bailey, A. L. (2003/2004). *An approach to operationalizing academic language for language test development purposes: Evidence from fifth-grade science and math.* (IES, Contract No. R305B960002). (CSE Tech. Rep. No. 626). Los Angeles, CA: University of California, National Center for Research Evaluation, Standards, and Student Testing.

Cai, M., & Bishop, R. S. (1994). Multicultural literature for children: Towards a clarification of concept. In A. H. Dyson & G. Genishi (Eds.), *The need for story: Cultural diversity in classroom and community* (pp. 57–71). Urbana, IL: National Council of Teachers of English.

California Department of Education (2012). California English Language Development Standards. Sacramento, CA: Author. Retrieved from http://www.cde.ca.gov/ sp/el/er/eldstandards.asp.

California Department of Education. (1999). English language development standards for California public schools: Kindergarten through Grade 12. Retrieved from www.cde.ca.gov/ be/st/ss/documents/englangdevstnd.pdf.

California Department of Education. (2014). "CELDT 101." Retrieved from www. celdt.org/documents/CELDT_101.pdf.

Calkins, L. M. (1983). *Lessons from a child: On the teaching and learning of writing.* Portsmouth, NH: Heinemann.

Callahan, M., & King, J. M. (2011). Classroom remix: patterns of pedagogy in a techno-literacies poetry unit. *Journal of Adolescent & Adult Literacy, 55*(2), 134–44.

Canagarajah, A. S. (2013). *Literacy as translingual practice: Between communities and classrooms.* New York, NY: Routledge.

Carel, S. (1999). Developing awareness of French pragmatics: A case study of students' interactive use of a foreign language multimedia program. *Journal of Educational Computing Research, 20*(1), 11–24.

Carger, C.L. (2004). Art and literacy with bilingual children. *Language Arts, 81*(4), 283–92.

Carrell, P. L. (1985). Facilitating ESL reading by teaching text structure. *TESOL Quarterly, 19*(4), 727–52.

Carroll, L. (1992/1865). *Alice's Adventures in Wonderland.* Illustrated by John Tenniel. New York, NY: William Morrow.

Cary, S. (2004). *Going graphic: Comics at work in the multilingual classroom.* Portsmouth, NH: Heinemann.

Caskey, M. M., & Anfara, V. A., Jr. (2007). *Research summary: Young adolescents' developmental characteristics.* Westerville, OH: National Middle School Association. Retrieved from http://www.nmsa.org/Research/ResearchSummaries/DevelopmentalCharacteristics/tabid/1414/Default.aspx.

Cazden, C. B. (1998, March). *Two meanings of "Discourse."* Paper presented at the Annual Meeting of the American Association for Applied Linguistics, Seattle, WA.

Cazden, C. (2001). *Classroom discourse: The language of teaching and learning.* Portsmouth, NH: Heinemann.

Cenoz, J., & Gorter, D. (2008). The linguistic landscape as an additional source of input in second language acquisition. *International Review of Applied Linguistics in Language Teaching (IRAL), 46*(3), 267–87.

Chall, J. S., Jacobs, V. A., & Baldwin, L. E. (1990). *The reading crisis: Why poor children fall behind.* Cambridge, MA: Harvard University Press.

Chenhansa, S., & Schleppegrell, M. (1998). Linguistic features of middle school environmental education texts. *Environmental Education Research, 4*(1), 53–66.

Cheung, A., & Slavin, R. E. (2012). Effective reading programs for Spanish-dominant English language learners (ELLs) in the elementary grades: A synthesis of research. *Review of Educational Research, 82*(4), 351–95.

Christie, F. (2002). *Classroom Discourse Analysis.* New York, NY: Continuum.

Christie, F., & Maton, K. (2011). *Disciplinarity: Functional linguistic and sociological perspectives.* London: Continuum.

Chval, K. B., & Khisty, L. L., (2009). Bilingual Latino students, writing, and mathematics: A case study of successful teaching and learning. In R. Barwell (Ed.). *Multilingualism in mathematics classrooms: Global perspectives.* (pp. 128–44). Bristol, UK: Multilingual Matters.

Clandinin, D. J., & Murphy, M. S. (2007). Mapping in a landscape of narrative inquiry: Borderland spaces and tensions. In D. J. Clandinin (Ed.), *Handbook of narrative inquiry: Mapping a methodology* (pp. 35–75). Thousand Oaks, CA: Sage.

Clay, M. M. (1991). *Becoming literate: The construction of inner control.* Portsmouth, NH: Heinemann.

Cloud, N., Genesee, F., & Hamayan, E. (2009). *English language learners: A teacher's guide to research-based practices.* Portsmouth, NH: Heinemann.

Coffin, C. (2006). *Historical discourse: The language of time, cause and evaluation.* London: Continuum.

Cognition and Technology Group and Vanderbilt Learning Technology Center. (1993). Examining the cognitive challenges and pedagogical opportunities of integrated media systems: Toward a research agenda. *Journal of Special Education Technology, 12*(2), 118–24.

Cohn, N. (2014). The architecture of visual narrative comprehension: The interaction of narrative structure and page layout in understanding comics. *Frontiers in Psychology, 5,* 1–9.

Coiro, J., Knobel, M., Lankshear, C., & Leu, D. J. (2008). *The handbook of research in new literacies.* Mahwah, NJ: Lawrence Erlbaum.

Collier, V., & Thomas, W. (1987). How quickly can immigrants become proficient in school English? *Journal of Educational Issues of Language Minority Students, 5,* 26–38.

Common Core State Standards Initiative. (2014). Common Core State Standards Initiative. Retrieved from http://www.corestandards.org/.

Common Core State Standards-Other Resources: http://www.corestandards.org/assets/application-for-english-learners.pdf.

Connor, U. (2008). Mapping multidimensional aspects of research: Reaching to intercultural rhetoric. In U. Connor, E. Nagelhout, & W.V. Rozycki (Eds.), *Contrastive rhetoric: Reaching to Intercultural Rhetoric* (299–315). Philadelphia, PA: John Benjamins.

Cope, B., & Kalantzis, M. (2000). Designs for social futures. *Multiliteracies: Literacy Learning and the Design of Social Futures*, 203–34.

Cox, B. E., Shanahan, T., & Tinzmann, M. B. (1991). Children's knowledge of organization, cohesion, and voice in written exposition. *Research in the Teaching of English*, 179–218.

Crowe, C. (2003). *Getting away with murder: The true story of the Emmett Till case*. New York, NY: Phyllis Fogelman Books.

Crystal, D. (2001). *Language and the Internet*. Cambridge: Cambridge University Press.

Crystal, D. (2003). *English as a global language*. Ernst Klett Sprachen.

Cuban, L. (2001). *Oversold and underused computers in the classroom*. Cambridge, MA: Harvard University Press.

Cummins, J. (1979). Cognitive/academic language proficiency, linguistic interdependence, the optimum age question and some other matters. *Working Papers on Bilingualism, 19*, 121–29.

Cummins, J. (1981). Immigrant second language learning. *Applied Linguistics, 11*, 132–49.

Cummins, J. (1984). *Bilingual education and special education: Issues in assessment and pedagogy*. San Diego, CA: College Hill.

Cummins, J. (1991). Language Development and Academic Learning. In L. Malave, and G. Duquette, *Language, Culture and Cognition* Clevedon: Multilingual Matters.

Cummins, J. (2000). Biliteracy, empowerment, and transformative pedagogy. In J. V. Tinajero & R. A. DeVillar (Eds.). *The power of two languages 2000: Effective dual-language use across the curriculum*. New York, NY: McGraw Hill.

Cummins, J. (2003). Reading and the bilingual students: Fact and friction. In G. G. Garcia (Ed.), *English learners: Reaching the highest level of English literacy* (pp. 2–33). Newark, DE: International Reading Association.

Cummins, J. (2007). Rethinking monolingual instructional strategies in multilingual classrooms. *Canadian Journal of Applied Linguistics, 10*(2), 221–40.

Cummins, J. (2008). BICS and CALP: Empirical and theoretical status of the distinction. In B. Street & N. H. Hornberger (Eds.), *Encyclopedia of language and education* (vol. 2: Literacy) (pp. 71–83). London: Springer.

Cummins, J. (2009a). Pedagogies of choice: Challenging coercive relations of power in classrooms and communities. *International Journal of Bilingual Education and Bilingualism, 2*(3), 261–71.

Cummins, J. (2009b). Transformative multiliteracies pedagogy: School-based strategies for closing the achievement gap. *Multiple Voices for Ethnically Diverse Exceptional Learners, 11*(2), 38–56.

Cummins, J. (2011). Literacy engagement—fueling academic growth for english learners. *The Reading Teacher, 65*(2), 142–46.

Cummins, J. (2014). Beyond language: Academic communication and student success. *Linguistics and Education, 26*, 145–54.

Cummins, J., & Swain, M. (1986). *Bilingualism in education: Aspects of theory, research and policy.* London: Longman.

Cutler, L., & Graham, S. (2008). Primary grade writing instruction: A national survey. *Journal of Educational Psychology, 100,* 907–19.

Dalton, B., & Strangman, N. (2006). Improving struggling readers' comprehension through scaffolded hypertexts and other computer-based literacy programs. In D. Reinking, M. C. McKenna, L. D. Labbo, & R. D. Keiffer (Eds.), *Handbook of literacy and technology* (2nd ed.). Mahwah, NJ: Lawrence Erlbaum Associates.

Darling-Hammond, L. (1999). *Teacher Quality and Student Achievement: A Review of State Policy Evidence.* Seattle: Center for the Study of Teaching Policy. University of Washington.

Davis, D., Spraker, J. & Kushman, J. (2005). *Improving adolescent reading: Findings from research.* Portland, Oregon: Northwest Regional Education Laboratory.

DeKeyser, R. M. (1998). Beyond focus on form: Cognitive perspectives on learning and practicing second language grammar. In C. Doughtly & J. Williams (Eds.), *Focus on form in classroom second language acquisition* (pp. 42–63). New York: Cambridge University Press.

Deci, E. L., & Flaste, R. (1996). *Why do we do what we do: Understanding self-motivation.* New York, NY: Penguin. (Reprinted from *Why do we do what we do: Understanding self-motivation,* by E. L. Deci & R. Flaste, 1995, New York, NY: G. P. Putnam's Sons.)

de Jong, E.J., & Harper, C.A. (2005). Preparing mainstream teachers for English language learners: Is being a good teacher good enough? *Teacher Education Quarterly, 32,* 101–24.

de Jong, E.J., Harper, C.A., & Coady, M. (2013). Enhanced knowledge and skills for elementary mainstream teachers of English language learners. *Theory into Practice, 52*(2), 89–97.

Dehghan, F., & Sadighi, F. (2011). On the cultural schema and Iranian EFL Learners' reading performance: A case of local and global items. *Pan-Pacific Association of Applied Linguistics, 15*(2), 97–108.

DeKeyser, R. (1995). Learning second language grammar rules: An experiment with miniature linguistic system. *Studies in Second-Language Acquisition, 17,* 379–410.

Delgado-Gaitan, C. (1993). Researching changing the researcher. *Harvard Educational Review, 63*(4), 389–411.

Derewianka, B. (1990). *Exploring how texts work.* Rozelle, NSW: Primary English Teaching Association (PETA).

Dewey, J. (1933). *How we think.* New York, NY: D. C. Heath.

Dodge, A., Husain, N., & Duke, N. (2011). Connected kids? K–2 children's use and understanding of the Internet. *Language Arts, 89*(2), 86–98.

Donahue, D. (2003). Reading across the great divide: English and math teachers apprentice one another as readers and disciplinary teachers, *Journal of Adolescent and Adult Literacy, 47*(1), 24–37.

Donato, R. (1994). Collective scaffolding in second language learning. In J. P. Lantolf & G. Appel (Eds.), *Vygotskyian approaches to second language research* (pp. 33–56) Norwood, NJ: Ablex.

Donovan, S., & Bransford, J. (2005). *How students learn: History, mathematics, and science in the classroom.* Washington, DC: National Academies Press.

Draper, M. C., Barksdale-Ladd, M. A., & Radencich, M C. (2000). Reading and writing habits of preservice teachers. *Reading Horizons, 40*(3), 185–203.

Duke, N. K. (2004). The case for informational text. *Educational Leadership, 61*(6), 40–45.

Duke, N. K., Bennett-Armistead, V. S., & Roberts, E. M. (2003). Bridging the gap between learning to read and reading to learn. In D. M. Barone & L. M. Morrow (Eds.), *Literacy and young children: Research-based practices* (pp. 226–42). New York: Guilford.

Duke, N. K., & Pearson, P. (2002). Effective Practices for developing reading comprehension. In Alan E. Farstrup & S. Jay Samuels (Eds.), *What research has to say about reading instruction*, 3rd ed. (pp. 205–42). Newark, DE: International Reading Association.

Duke, N. K., & Purcell-Gates, V. (2003). Genres at home and at school: Bridging the known to the new. *The Reading Teacher, 57,* 30–37.

Dukes, C. (2005). Best practices for integrating technology into English language instruction. *Seir-Tec News Wire, 7*(6), 3–6.

Dyson, A. (2003). *Brothers and sisters learn to write.* New York, NY: Teachers College Press.

Dyson, A., & Genishi, C. (2007). Human diversity and curricular uniformity: Young children in "real" classroom time and space. Paper presented at *NCTE*, New York, NY.

Echevarria, J. (2012). Language and content instruction (English immersion, SIOP, SDAIE). In J. Banks (Ed.), *Encyclopedia of diversity in education* (pp. 1317–20). Thousand Oaks, CA: Sage.

Echevarria, J., Vogt, M., & Short, D. J. (2008). *Making content comprehensible for English language learners: The SIOP Model* (3rd ed.). Boston: Allyn & Bacon.

Egbert, J., Huff, L., McNeil, L., Preuss, C., & Sellen, J. (2009). Pedagogy, process, a classroom context: Integrating teacher voice and experience into research on technology-enhanced language learning. *Modern Language Journal, 93*(1), 754–68.

Eggins, S. (1994). *An introduction to systemic functional linguistics.* London: Pinter.

Ehlers-Zavala, F. (2008). Teaching adolescent English language learners. In S. Lenski, & J. Lewis (Eds.), *Reading success for struggling adolescent learners* (pp. 74–89). New York, NY: Guildford Press.

Ehlers-Zavala, F. (2012). Assessing special populations of students. In E. Ortlieb & E. H. Cheek, Jr. (Eds.), *Using informative assessments towards effective literacy instruction* (pp. 221–47). Bingley, UK: Emerald Group Publishing.

Ehlers-Zavala, F., & Azcoitia, L. (2009). How can teachers help adolescent English language learners attain academic literacy? In J. Lewis (Ed.), *Essential questions in adolescent literacy* (pp. 132–55). New York, NY: Guilford Press.

Eisner, E. (2000). *The arts and the creation of mind.* New Haven, CT: Yale University Press.

Ellis, R. (1984). *Classroom second language development.* Oxford: Pergamon Press.

Ellis, R. (1993). The structural syllabus and second language acquisition. *TESOL Quarterly, 27,* 91–113.

Ellis, R. (2005). Principles of instructed language learning. *System, 33*(2), 209–24.

Englert, C. S., Berry, R., & Dunsmore, K. (2001). A case study of the apprenticeship process: Another perspective on the apprentice and the scaffolding metaphor. *Journal of Learning Disabilities, 34*(2), 152–71.

Englert, C. S., Mariage, T. V., & Dunsmore, K. (2006). Tenets of sociocultural theory in writing instruction research. *Handbook of Writing Research*, 208–21.

Enright, K. A. (2011). Language and literacy for a new mainstream. *American Educational Research Journal, 48*(1), 80–118.

Erben, T., Ban, R., & Castañeda, M. (2009). Teaching English Language Learners through technology. New York: Routledge Taylor & Francis Group.

Ernst, K. (1994). *Picturing learning: Artists and writers in the classroom*. Portsmouth, NH: Heinemann.

Escamilla, K. (2012). *Building trajectories toward biliteracy*. Paper presented at the 36th Annual Statewide Conference for Teachers Serving Linguistically and Culturally Diverse Students, Oakbrook, Illinois.

Eyler J., Giles D. E., & Schmiede, A. (1996). *A practitioner's guide to reflection in service-learning: Student voices and reflections*. A technical assistance project funded by the Corporation for National Service. Nashville, TN: Vanderbilt University. Retrieved from http://www.compact.org/disciplines/reflection/bibliography/.

Faigley, L., & Witte, S. (1981). Analyzing revision. *College Composition and Communication, 32*, 400–14.

Fang, Z. (2010). *Language and literacy in inquiry-based science classrooms, grades 3–8*. Thousand Oaks, CA: Corwin Press and Arlington, VA: National Science Teachers Association.

Fang, Z. (2012a). Language correlates of disciplinary literacy. *Topics in Language Disorders, 32*(1), 19–34.

Fang, Z. (2012b). The challenges of reading disciplinary texts. In T. Jetton & C. Shanahan (Eds.), *Adolescent literacy in the academic disciplines: General principles and practical strategies* (pp. 38–68). New York, NY: Guilford.

Fang, Z., & Schleppegrell, M. J. (2008). *Reading in secondary content areas: A language-based pedagogy*. Ann Arbor, MI: University of Michigan.

Fang, Z., & Schleppegrell, M. J. (2010). Disciplinary literacies across content areas: Supporting secondary reading through functional language analysis. *Journal of Adolescent & Adult Literacy, 53*(7), 587–97.

Figueiredo, C. (2005, Spring). An exploration of Socratic dialogues in the secondary English learner science classroom. Unpublished master's thesis, California State University, Stanislaus, Turlock, California.

Filkens, S. (2014). *Socratic seminars. Read, write, think*. NCTE. Retrieved from http://www.readwritethink.org/professional-development/strategy-guides/socratic-seminars-30600.html.

Fillmore, L., & Fillmore, C. (January, 2012). *What does text complexity mean for English learners and language minority students?* Paper (and video) presented at the Understanding Language Conference at Stanford University, California.

Fisher, D. & Frey, N. (2012). Close reading in elementary schools. *The Reading Teacher, 66*(3), 179–88.

Fisher, D. & Frey, N. (2014). Content area vocabulary learning. *The Reading Teacher, 67*(8), 594–99.

Fisher, D., Frey, N., & Lapp, D. (2012). *Text complexity: Raising rigor in reading.* Newark, DE: International Reading Association.

Fitzgerald, J. (1987). Research on revision in writing. *Review of Educational Research, 57,* 481–506.

Fleming, D. (1996). *Where once there was a wood.* New York, NY: Holt and Company.

Flores, A. (2007). Examining disparities in mathematics education: Achievement gap or opportunity gap? *The High School Journal, 91*(1), 29–42.

Flynne, K., & Hill, J. (2005). *English language learners: A growing population.* Denver, CO: Midcontinent Research for Education and Learning (McREL).

Forrest-Pressley, D. L., & Waller, T. G. (1984). Cognition, metacognition and reading. New York, NY: Springer-Verlag.

Fought, C. (2003). *Chicano English in Context.* New York, NY: Palgrave Macmillan.

Frantzen, D. (2002). Rethinking foreign language literature: Towards an integration of literature and language at all levels. In V. M. Scott & H. Tucker (Eds.), *SLA and the literature classroom: Fostering dialogues* (pp. 109–30). Boston, MA: Heinle & Heinle.

Freeman, D. E., & Freeman, Y. S. (2000). *Teaching reading in multilingual classrooms.* Portsmouth, NH: Heinemann.

Freire, P. (1970). *Pedagogy of the oppressed.* New York, NY: Continuum.

Freire, P. (1998). *Pedagogy of the oppressed.* New York, NY: Continuum.

Freire, P., & Macedo, D. (1987). *Reading the word and the world.* Westport, CT: Bergin & Garvey.

Gallas, K. (1994). *The languages of learning: How children talk, write, dance, draw, and sing their understanding of the world.* New York, NY: Teachers College Press.

Gallas, K. (2003). *Imagination and literacy: A teacher's search for the heart of learning.* New York, NY: Teachers College Press.

Gallo, D. R. (2004). *First crossing: Stories about teen immigrants.* Cambridge, MA: Candlewick Press.

Garcia, L. B. O. (2011). *Additive schooling in subtractive times: Bilingual education and Dominican immigrant youth in the Heights.* Nashville, TN: Vanderbilt University Press.

Garcia, O. (2009a). Bilingual education in the 21st century: A global perspective. West Sussex, UK: Wiley Blackwell.

Garcia, O. (2009b). Education, multilingualism and translanguaging in the 21st century. In T. Skutnabb-Kangas, R. Philips, A. Mohanty, & M. Panda (Eds.), *Social justice through multilingual education* (pp. 140–58). Tonawanda, NY: Multilingual Matters.

García, O., & Flores, N. (2014). Multilingualism and Common Core Standards in the United States. In S. May (Ed.), *The multilingual turn.* New York, NY: Routledge.

Garcia, O., & Kleifgen, J. A. (2010). *Educating emergent bilinguals: Programs, policies, and practices for English language learners.* New York, NY: Teachers College Press.

Gebhard, M., & Willett, J. (2008). Supporting teacher learning and the academic literacy development of ELLs in changing times. *The Journal of Staff Development, 29*(1), 41–45.

Gebhard, M., Harman, R., & Seger, W. (2007). Reclaiming recess in urban schools: The potential of systemic functional linguistics for ELLs and their teachers. *Language Arts, 84*(5), 319–430.

Gebhard, M., Shin, D., & Seger, W. (2011). Blogging, systemic functional linguistics, and L2 academic literacies in an urban elementary school. *CALICO Journal, 28*(2), 278–307.

Gee, J. P. (2000). Identity as an analytic lens for research in education. *Review of Research in Education*, 99–125.

Gee, J., & Hayes, E. (2011). *Language and learning in the digital age.* New York, NY: Routledge.

Genesee, F. (2005, January). *Literacy development in ELLs: What does the research say?* Paper presented at the annual meeting of the National Association for Bilingual Education, San Antonio, Texas.

Genesee, F. (Ed.). (2006). *Educating English language learners: A synthesis of research evidence.* New York: Cambridge University Press.

Genesee, F., & Riches, C. (2006). Literacy: Instructional Challenges. In F. Genesee, K. Lindholhm-Leary, W. M. Saunders, & D. Christian (Eds.), *Educating English language learners: A synthesis of research evidence* (pp. 14–63). New York, NY: Cambridge University Press.

Genesee, F., Geva, E., Dressler, C., & Kamil, M. (2008). Cross-linguistic relationships in second language learners. In D. August & T. Shanahan (Eds.), *Developing reading and writing in second language learners. Lessons from the Report of the National Literacy Panel on Language-Minority Children and Youth* (pp. 61–93). New York, NY: Routledge.

Genesee, F., Lindholm-Leary, K., Saunders, B., & Christian, D. (Eds.). (2006). *Educating English language learners.* New York, NY: Cambridge University Press.

Gersten, R., Baker, S. K., Shanahan, T., Linan- Thompson, S., Collins, P., & Scarcella, R. (2007). *Effective literacy and English language instruction for English learners in the elementary grades: A practice guide* (NCEE 2007-4011). Washington, DC: National Center for Education Evaluation and Regional Assistance, Institute of Education Sciences, U.S. Department of Education. Retrieved from http://ies.ed.gov/ncee/.

Gibbs, G. (1988). *Learning by doing: A guide to teaching and learning methods.* Oxford, England: Oxford Polytechnic, Further Education Unit.

Glasswell, K. (2001). Matthew effects in writing: The patterning of difference in writing classrooms K–7. *Reading Research Quarterly, 36*, 348–49.

Goldenberg, C. (2008). Teaching English language learners: What research says— and does not—say. *American Educator, 32*(2), 8–44.

González, N., Moll, L., & Amanti, C. (Eds.) (2005). *Funds of knowledge for teaching in Latino households.* Mahwah, NJ: Lawrence Erlbaum Associates.

Goodman, Y., Reyes, I., & McArthur, K. (2005). Emilia Ferreiro: Searching for children's understanding about literacy as cultural object. *Language Arts, 82*(4), 6–318.

Goodman, Y., Watson, D., & Burke, C. (1987). *Reading miscue inventory: Alternative procedures.* Katonah, NY: Richard C. Owen.

Graham, S., Bollinger, A., Booth Olson, C., D'Aoust, C., MacArthur, C., McCutchen, D., & Olinghouse, N. (2012). *Teaching elementary school students to be effective writers: A practice guide* (NCEE 2012-4058). Washington, DC: National Center for Education Evaluation and Regional Assistance, Institute of Education Sciences, U.S. Department of Education. Retrieved from http://ies.ed.gov/ncee/wwc/publications_reviews.aspx#pubsearch.

Graham, S., Harris, K. R., Fink-Chorzempa, B., & MacArthur, C. A. (2003). Primary grade teachers' instructional adaptations for struggling writers: A national survey. *Journal of Educational Psychology, 95*, 279–92.

Graves, M. F. (2006). *The vocabulary book: Learning and instruction.* New York, NY: Teachers College Press.

Green, T. (2005) Using technology to help English language students develop language skills: A home and school connection. *Multicultural Education, Winter,* 56–59.

Greene, J. P. (1997). A meta-analysis of the Rossell & Baker review of bilingual education research. *Bilingual Research Journal, 21*(2/3).

Greenhow, C., Robelia, B., & Hughes, J. E. (2009). Learning, teaching, and scholarship in a digital age Web 2.0 and classroom research: What path should we take now? *Educational Researcher, 38*(4), 246–59.

Gregg, M., & Sekeres, D. (2006). Supporting children's reading of expository text in the geography classroom. *The Reading Teacher, 60*, 102–109.

Grigg, W., Donahue, P., & Dion, G. (2007). *The nation's report card: 12th grade reading and mathematics 2005 (NCES 2007-468).* U.S. Department of Education, National Center for Education Statistics. Washington, DC: U.S. Government Printing Office.

Grosjean, F. (2008) *Studying bilinguals.* New York, NY: Oxford University Press.

Guiberson, B. (1991). *Cactus hotel.* New York, NY: Henry Holt.

Guthrie, J. T., & Wigfield, A. (2000). Engagement and motivation in reading. In M. L. Kamil, P. B. Mosenthal, P. D. Pearson, & R. Barr (Eds.), *Handbook of Reading Research*, vol. 3 (pp. 403–22). Mahwah, NJ: Lawrence Erlbaum Associates.

Guthrie, J. T., McGough, K., Bennett, L., & Rice, M. E. (1996). Concept-oriented reading instruction: An integrated curriculum to develop motivations and strategies for reading. In L. Baker, P. Afflerbach, & D. Reinking (Eds.), *Developing engaged readers in school and home communities* (pp. 165–90). Mahwah, NJ: Erlbaum.

Guthrie, J. T., McGough, K., & Wigfield, A. (1994). *Measuring reading activity: An inventory* (Instructional Resource No. 4). Athens, GA: National Reading Research Center.

Guthrie, J. T., Wigfield, A., Barbosa, P., Perencevich, K. C., Taboada, A., Davis, M. H., . . . Tonks, S. (2004). Increasing reading comprehension and engagement through concept-oriented reading instruction. *Journal of Educational Psychology, 96*(3), 403–23.

Gutierrez, K. D., Sengupta-Irving, T., & Dieckmann, J. (2010). Developing a mathematical vision: Mathematics as a discursive and embodied practice. In J. N. Moschkovich (Ed.). *Language and mathematics education: Multiple perspectives and directions for research* (pp. 29–71). Charlotte, NC: Information Age Publishing.

Gutierrez, K. D., Baquedano-López, P., & Tejeda, C. (1999). Rethinking diversity: Hybridity and hybrid language practices in the third space. *Mind, Culture, and Activity, 6*(4), 286–303.

Gutierrez, K., & Rogoff, B. (2003). Cultural ways of learning: Individual traits and repertoires of practice. *Educational Researcher, 32*(5), 19–25.

Hadaway, N. L., Vardell, S. M., & Young, T. (2002). *Literature-based instruction with English language learners.* Boston: Allyn & Bacon.

Haglund, C. (2010). Transnational identifications among adolescents in suburban Sweden. In P. Quist, & Svendsen, B.A. (Ed.), *Multilingual urban Scandinavia: New linguistic practices* (pp. 96–110). Tonawanda, NY: Multilingual Matters.

Hakuta, K., Butler, Y. G., & Witt, D. (2000). How long does it take English learners to attain proficiency? (Policy Report 2000–1.) Santa Barbara, CA: University of California Linguistic Minority Research Institute.

Hall, G. (2005) *Literature in language education.* New York, NY: Palgrave.

Halliday, M. A. K. (1985). *An Introduction to Functional Grammar.* London: Edward Arnold.

Halliday, M. A. K., & Matthiessen, C. (2004). *An introduction to functional grammar* (3rd ed.). London: Arnold.

Haneda, M. (2014). Why should we care about academic language? *Linguistics and Education, 26,* 88–91.

Harmon, J. M., Wood, K. D., Hedrick, W. B., Vintinner, J., & Willeford, T. (2009). Interactive word walls: More than just reading the writing on the walls. *Journal of Adolescent & Adult Literacy, 52*(5), 398–408.

Healey, D., & Klinghammer, S. J. (2002). Constructing meaning with computers. *TESOL Journal, 11*(3), 3–3.

Heath, S. (1983). *Ways with words.* Cambridge, England: Cambridge University Press.

Heckman, W. (2004). Reading heroes for a new generation. *Florida Media Quarterly, 29*(3), 3–4.

Hedgcock, J. S., & Ferris, D. R. (2009). *Teaching readers of English.* New York, NY: Routledge.

Hefzallah, I. M. (2004). *The new educational technologies and learning: Empowering teachers to teach and students to learn in the information age.* Springfield, IL: Charles C. Thomas Publisher.

Henry, L. A., Castek, J., O'Byrne, W. I., & Zawilinski, L. (2012). Using peer collaboration to support online reading, writing, and communication: An empowerment model for struggling readers. *Reading & Writing Quarterly, 28*(3), 279–306.

Herrera, S. G., & Murry, K. G. (2011). *Mastering ESL and bilingual methods: Differentiated instruction for culturally and linguistically diverse (CLD) students* (2nd ed.). Boston, MA: Pearson.

Herrera, S. G., Perez, D. R., & Escamilla, K. (2010). *Teaching reading to English language learners: Differentiated literacy.* Boston, MA: Allyn & Bacon.

Herz, S. K., & Gallo, D. R. (2005). *From Hinton to Hamlet: Building bridges between young adult literature and the classics* (2nd ed.). London, England: Greenwood Press.

Hickman, P. & Pollard-Durodola, S. D. (2009). *Dynamic read-aloud strategies for English Learners.* Newark, DE: International Reading Association.

Hiebert, E. H. (2014). *Knowing what's complex and what's not: Guidelines for teachers in establishing text complexity.* Santa Cruz, CA: TextProject, Inc.

Hiebert, E. H., & Grisham, S. L. (2012). What literacy teacher educators need to know about supporting teachers in understanding text complexity within the Common Core State Standards. *Journal of Reading Education, 37*(3), 5–12.

Higgins, S., Smith, H. J., Wall, K. & Miller, J. (2005). Interactive white boards: Boon or bandwagon? A critical review of the literature. *Journal of Computer Assisted Learning, 21*, 91–101.

Hillocks, G. (1986). *Research on written composition: New directions for teaching.* Urbana, IL: NCTE/NCRE.

Hopman, M., & Glynn, T. (1989). The effect of correspondence training on the rate and quality of written expression of four low achieving boys. *Educational Psychology, 9*, 197–213.

Horrigan, J. B. (2010). *Broadband adoption and use in America.* Federal Communications Commission.

Horst, M., White, J., & Bell, P. (2010). First and second language knowledge in the language classroom. *The International Journal of Bilingualism, 14*(3), 331–49. doi: 10.1177/1367006910367848.

Horwitz, A. R., Uro, G., Price-Baugh, R., Simon, C., Uzzell, R., Lewis, S., & Casserly, M. (2009). Succeeding with English language learners: Lessons learned from the Great City schools. *Council of the Great City Schools.*

Hubbard, P., & Levy, M. (2006). The scope of CALL education. *Teacher education in CALL*, 3–20.

Hubbard, P., & Levy, M. (Eds.). (2006). *Teacher education in CALL* (vol. 14). John Benjamins Publishing.

Hyland, K. (2005). *Metadiscourse.* New York, NY: Continuum.

Hyland, K., & Hyland, F. (2006). Feedback on second language students' writing. *Language Teaching, 39*, 83–101.

Ibrahim, A. (1999). Becoming black: Rap and hip-hop, race, gender, identity, and the politics of ESL. *TESOL Quarterly, 33*(3), 349–68.

Institute of Education Sciences. (2014). *Teaching academic content and literacy to English learners in elementary and middle school.* J. Lesnick & D. McCallum (Eds.), Retrieved from http://ies.ed.gov/ncee/wwc/PracticeGuide.aspx?sid=19.

Ivey, G., & Broaddus, K. (2007). A formative experiment investigating literacy engagement among adolescent Latina/o students just beginning to read, write, and speak English. *Reading Research Quarterly, 42*(4), 512–45.

Jackson, J., Tripp, S., & Cox, K. (2011). Interactive word walls: Transforming content vocabulary instruction. *Science Scope, 35*(3), 45–49.

Johns, J. L., Lenski, S. D., & Elish-Piper, L. (2002). *Teaching beginning readers: Linking assessment and instruction* (2nd ed.). Dubuque, IA: Kendall/Hunt.

Johnson, J. A., Musial, D., Hall, G. E., Gollnick, D. M., & Dupuis, V. L. (2005). *Introduction to the foundations of American education.* New York, NY: Pearson.

Johnson, K. A., & Parrish, B. (2010). Aligning instructional practices to meet the academic needs of adult ESL students. *TESOL Quarterly, 44*(3), 618–27.

Kamil, M. L., Borman, G. D., Dole, J., Kral, C. C., Salinger, T., and Torgesen, J. (2008). Improving adolescent literacy: Effective classroom and intervention practices: A practice guide. Washington, DC: National Center for Education Evaluation and Regional Assistance, Institute of Education Sciences, U.S. Department of Education.

Kanno, Y. & Cromley, J. (2013). English language learners' access to and attainment in postsecondary education. *TESOL Quarterly, 47*(1), 89–121.

Karegianes, M. J., Pascarella, E. T., & Pflaum, S. W. (1980). The effects of peer editing on the writing proficiency of low-achieving tenth grade students. *Journal of Educational Research, 73*(4), 203–206.

Kelley, M., Wilson, N. S., & Koss, M. D. (2012). Using young adult literature to motivate and engage the disengaged. In J. A. Hayn & J. S. Kaplan (Eds.) *Teaching young adult literature today: insights, considerations and perspectives for the classroom teacher* (77–98). Lanham, MD: Rowman & Littlefield.

Kelly, I. (2007). *It's a butterfly's life*. New York, NY: Holiday House.

Kennedy, G. E., Judd, T. S., Churchward, A., Gray, K., & Krause, K. L. (2008). First year students' experiences with technology: Are they really digital natives. *Australian Journal of Educational Technology, 24*(1), 108–22.

Kern, R., & Schultz, J. (2005). Beyond orality: Investigating literacy and the literary in second and foreign language instruction. *Modern Language Journal, 89*(3), 381–92.

Khisty, L. L. (1995). Making inequality: Issues of language in mathematics teaching with Hispanic students. In W. G. Secada, E. Fennema, & L. B. Adajean (Eds.). *New directions for equity in mathematics education.* Cambridge, UK: Cambridge University Press.

Kiefer, B. (1995). *The potential of picturebooks: From visual literacy to aesthetic understanding.* Englewood Cliffs, NJ: Merrell.

Kintsch, W. (1992). A cognitive architecture for comprehension. In H. L. Pick, P. van den Broek, & D. C. Knill (Eds.), *The study of cognition: Conceptual and methodological issues* (pp. 143–64). Washington, DC: American Psychological Association.

Kist, W., Doyle, K., Hayes, J., Horwitz, J., & Kuzior, J. T. (2010). Web 2.0 in the elementary classroom: Portraits of possibilities. *Language Arts 88*(1), 62–68.

Klinger, J. K., & Vaughn, S. (2000). The helping behaviors of fifth graders while using collaborative strategic reading during ESL content classes. *TESOL Quarterly, 34*(1), 69–98.

Knapp, P., & Watkins, M. (2005). *Genre, text, grammar: Technologies for teaching and assessing writing.* Sydney: UNSW Press.

Knobel, M., & Lankshear, C. (2009). Wikis, digital literacies, and professional growth. *Journal of Adolescent and Adult Literacy, 52*(7), 631–34.

Koda, K., & Zehler, A. (2008). *Learning to read across languages: Cross-linguistic relationships in first- and second-language literacy development.* New York, NY: Routledge.

Koda, K., Lü, Ch., & Zhang, D. (2014). L1-Induced facilitation in biliteracy development in Chinese and English. In X. Chen, Q. Wang, & Y.C. Luo (Eds.), *Reading development and difficulties in monolingual and bilingual Chinese children* (pp. 141–69). New York, NY: Springer.

Koehler, M., & Mishra, P. (2009). What is technological pedagogical content knowledge (TPACK)? *Contemporary Issues in Technology and Teacher Education, 9*(1), 60–70.

Kolb, A., & Kolb, D. A. (2001). Experiential learning theory bibliography. Englewood Cliffs, NJ: Prentice Hall.

Kostka, I., & Olmstead-Wang, S. (2014). *Teaching English for academic purposes.* Alexandria, VA: TESOL Press.

Krashen, S. (1981). *Second language acquisition and second language learning.* Oxford: Pergamon Press.

Krashen, S. (1982). *Principles and practice in second language acquisition* (pp. 65–78). Oxford: Pergamon Press.

Krashen, S. (1985). *The input hypothesis: Issues and implications.* London: Longman.

Krashen, S. (1994). The input hypothesis and its rivals. In N. Ellis (Ed.), *Implicit and explicit learning of languages* (pp. 45–77). London: Academic.

Krashen, S. D. (2005). The "decline" of reading in America, poverty and access to books, and the use of comics in encouraging reading. *Teachers College Record.* Retrieved from http://www.sdkrashen.com/content/articles/decline_of_reading.pdf.

Kress, G. (2003). *Literacy in the new media age.* Psychology Press.

Kress, G. (2009). *Multimodality: A social semiotic approach to contemporary communication.* Routledge.

Kress, G., & Van Leeuwen, T. (2001). *Multimodal discourse: The modes and media of contemporary communication.* Edward Arnold.

Kruger, J., & Dunning, D. (1999). Unskilled and unaware of it: Difficulties in recognizing one's own incompetence lead to inflated self-assessments. *Journal of Personality and Social Psychology, 77*(60), 1121–34.

Kumaravadivelu, B. (2008). *Cultural globalization and language education.* New Haven, CT: Yale University Press.

Kuroneko (2008). The basics: chalkboards, flipcharts, whiteboards, and overhead projectors. Retrieved December 1, 2013 from blog.classroomteacher.ca.

Kuroneko, K. (2008). *SMART Board—Pros and cons of using a digital, interactive whiteboard (in the classroom).* Retrieved November 3, 2008, from http://ezinearticles.com/?SMART-Board---Pros-and-Cons-of-Using-a-Digital,-Interactive-Whiteboard-(In- theClassroom)&id=1399407.

Labbo, L. D., & Reinking, D. (1999). Negotiating the multiple realities of technology in literacy research and instruction. *Reading Research Quarterly, 34,* 478–92.

Lagerf, C. (2006). Types of mathematics-language reading interactions that unnecessarily hinder algebra learning and assessment. *Reading Psychology, 27*(2–3), 165–204.

Lam, W. S. E. (2000). L2 literacy and the design of the self: A case study of a teenager writing on the Internet. *TESOL Quarterly, 34*(3), 457–82.

Lam, W. S. E. (2009). Literacy and learning across transnational online spaces. *E-Learning, 6*(4), 303–23.

Lam, W. S. E. E. R.-R. (2009). Multilingual literacies in transnational digitally mediated contexts: An exploratory study of immigrant teens in the United States. *Language and Education, 23*(2), 171–90.

Lam, W. S. E., & Rosario-Ramos, E. (2009). Multilingual literacies in transnational digitally mediated contexts: An exploratory study of immigrant teens in the United States. *Language and Education, 30*(1), 213–37.

Lam, W. S. E., & Warriner, D. (2012). Transnationalism and literacy: Investigating the mobility of people, languages, texts, and practices in contexts of migration. *Reading Research Quarterly, 47*(2), 191–215.

Landt, S. M. (2006). Multicultural literature: A kaleidoscope of opportunity. *Journal of Adolescent and Adult Literacy, 46*, 690–98.

Landt, S. M. (2011). Integration of multicultural literature in primary grade language arts curriculum. *Journal of Multiculturalism in Education, 7*, 1–27.

Langer, J. (1997). Literacy acquisition through literature. *Journal of Adolescent and Adult Literacy, 40*, 602–14.

Langer, J. A. (2011). *Envisioning knowledge: Building literacy in the academic disciplines.* New York, NY: Teachers College Press.

Larson, L., Dixon, T., & Townsend, D. (2013). How can teachers increase classroom use of academic vocabulary? *Voices from the Middle, 20*(4), 16–21.

Lau, S. M. C. (2012). Reconceptualizing critical literacy teaching in ESL classrooms. *The Reading Teacher, 65*(5), 325–29.

Laufer, B., & Yano, Y. (2001). Understanding unfamiliar words in a text: Do L2 learners understand how much they don't understand? *Reading in a Foreign Language, 13*(2), 549–66.

Leach, J. M., Scarborough, H. S., & Rescorla, L. (2003). Late-emerging reading disabilities. *Journal of Educational Psychology, 95*(2), 211–24.

Lear, E. (1871). The Owl and the Pussycat. In *Nonsense songs, stories, botany, and alphabets.* Boston, MA: James R. Osgood and Company.

Lee, C. D. (2007). *Culture, literacy, and learning: Taking bloom in the midst of the whirlwind.* New York, NY: Teachers College Press.

Lee, J., Grigg, W., & Donahue, P. (2007). *The nation's report card: Reading 2007 (NCES 2007-496).* U.S. Department of Education, National Center for Education Statistics. Washington, DC: U.S. Government Printing Office.

Leu, D. J. (2000). Literacy and technology: Deictic consequences for literacy education in an information age. *Handbook of Reading Research, 3*, 743–70.

Leu, D. J., O'Byrne, W. I., Zawilinski, L., McVerry, J. G., & Everett-Cacopardo, H. (2009). Comments on Greenhow, Robelia, and Hughes: Expanding the new literacies conversation. *Educational Researcher, 38*(4), 264–69.

Lenski, S., & Ehlers-Zavala, F. P. (2004). *Reading strategies for Spanish speakers.* Dubuque, IA: Kendall-Hunt.

Lenski, S., Ehlers-Zavala, F., Daniel, M. C., & Sun-Irminger, X. (2010). Assessing English language learners in mainstream classrooms. In R. M. Bean, N. Heisey, & C. M. Roller (Eds.), *Preparing reading professionals* (2nd ed.) (pp. 184–95). Newark, DE: International Reading Association.

Lesaux, N. K., Crosson, A. C., & Pierce, M. (2010). Uneven profiles: Language minority learners' word reading, vocabulary, and reading comprehension skills. *Journal of Applied Developmental Psychology, 31*(6), 475–83.

Lesaux, N. K., Rupp, A. A. & Siegel, L. S. (2007). Growth in reading skills of children from diverse linguistic backgrounds: Findings from a 5-year longitudinal study. *Journal of Educational Psychology, 99*(4), 821–34.

Lesh, R., Galbraith, P., Haines, C. R., & Hurford, A. (2010). International perspectives on the teaching and learning of mathematical modeling: Modeling students' mathematical competencies: ICTMA 13. New York, NY: Springer.

Leu, D. J., O'Byrne, W. I., Zawilinski, L., McVerry, J. G., & Everett-Cacopardo, H. (2009). Expanding the new literacies conversation. *Educational Researcher, 38*(4), 264–69. doi: 10.3102/0013189X09336676.

Lewin, K. (1943). Defining the field at a given time. *Psychological Review, 50,* 292–310.

Lewin, K. (1997). Field theory and learning. In D. Cartwright, (Ed.). *Field Theory in Social Science and Selected Theoretical Papers* (pp. 212–30). Washington, DC: American Psychological Association (Original work published 1942).

Lewin, K. (2008, April 3). Kurt Lewin. *New world encyclopedia.* Retrieved from http://www.newworldencyclopedia.org/p/index.php?title=Kurt_Lewin&oldid=686706.

Lillie, K. E., Markos, A., Arias, M. B., & Wiley, T. G. (2012). Separate and not equal: Implementation of structured English immersion in Arizona's classrooms. *Teachers College Record, 114,* 1–33.

Littlewood, W. (1984). *Foreign and second language learning: Language acquisition research and its implications for the classroom.* Cambridge, MA: Cambridge University Press.

Liu, M., Moore, Z., Graham, L., & Lee, S. (2002). A look at the research on computer-based technology use in second language learning: A review of the literature from 1990–2000. *Journal of Research on Technology in Education, 34*(3), 250–73.

Livingstone, S. (2004). Media literacy and the challenge of new information and communication technologies. *The Communication Review, 7*(1), 3–14.

Lobel, A. (1975). *Owl at home.* New York: HarperCollins.

LoCastro, V. (2008). "Long sentences and floating commas": Mexican students' rhetorical practices and the sociocultural context. In U. Connor, E. Nagelhout, & W. V. Rozycki (Eds.), *Contrastive rhetoric: Reaching to intercultural rhetoric* (pp. 195–217). Philadelphia, PA: John Benjamins.

Long, M. (1996). The role of linguistic environment in second language acquisition. In W. Ritchie and T. Bhatia (Eds.), *Handbook of second language acquisition* (pp. 413–68). San Diego, CA: Academic Press.

Long, M. H. (2006). *Problems in SLA.* Mahwah, NJ: Lawrence Erlbaum Associates.

Lyster, R., & Ranta, L. (1997). Corrective feedback and learner uptake: Negotiation of form in communicative classrooms. *Studies in Second Language Acquisition, 28,* 321–41.

Ma, J. Y., & Singer-Gabella, M. (2011). Learning to teach in the figured world of reform mathematics: Negotiating new models of identity. *Journal of Education, 62*(1), 8–22.

Marsh, D. (2008). Language awareness and CLICL. In J. Cenoz and N. Hornberger (Eds.). *Encyclopedia of language and education* (pp. 233–46). New York, NY: Springer.

Martin, J. R., & Rose, D. (2008). *Genre relations: Mapping culture.* London: Equinox.

Maxwell, L. A. (2014). Test supports for ELLs: Differences between PARCC and Smarter Balanced. *Education Week.* Retrieved from http://blogs.edweek.org/edweek/learning-the-language/2014/04/test_supports_for_english-lear.html.

McGreevy, P. (2014). Calif. Senate panel advances bill to restore bilingual education *L.A. Times.* Retrieved from http://www.latimes.com/local/political/la-me-pc-calif-senate-panel-advances-bill-to-restore-bilingual-education-20140430-story.html.

McHoul, A. W. (1993). *A Foucault primer: Discourse, power, and the subject.* New York, NY: New York University Press.

McLaughlin, M., & Overturf, B. J. (2013). *The common core: Teaching K–5 students to meet the reading standards.* Newark, DE: International Reading Association.

McLean, C. A. (2010). A space called home: An immigrant adolescent's digital literacy practices. *Journal of Adolescent and Adult Literacy, 54*(1), 13–22.

McMorrow, T. (2013, September 11). What are you full of? *Forever in First.* Retrieved from http://foreverin1st.blogspot.com/2013/09/what-are-you-full-of.html.

McVerry, J. G. (2012). New literacies: Online reading comprehension, online collaborative inquiry, and online content construction. *Connecticut Reading Association Journal.*

Meminger, N. (2011). Getting diverse books into the hands of teen readers: How do we do it? *Young Adult Library Services, 9*(3), 10–13.

Mendoza, M., & Garza, A. (2010). Critical literacy: Changing the world through the word. *McNair Scholars Research Journal, 6*(1), 39–44.

Meskill, C. (1999). Computers as tools for sociocollaborative language learning. *Computer-assisted language learning (CALL): Media, design and applications,* 144–52.

Michaels, S. (1981). "Sharing time": Children's narrative styles and differential access to literacy. *Language in Society, 10*(3), 423–42.

Mikow-Porto, V., Humphries, S., Egelson, P., O'Connell, D., Teague, J., & Rhimm, L. (2004). *English language learners in the Southeast: Policy, research and practice.* Greensboro, NC: University of North Carolina SERVE.

Miller, D. (2001). ESL reading textbooks vs. university textbooks: Are we giving our students the input they may need? *Journal of English for Academic Purposes, 10*(1), 32–46.

Mohanty, A. K., Mishra, M. K., Reddy, N. U., & Ramesh, G. (2009). Overcoming the language barrier for tribal children: Multilingual education in Andhra Pradesh and Orissa, India. In T. Skutnabb-Kangas, R. Philips, A. Mohanty, & M. Panda (Eds.), *Social justice through multilingual education* (pp. 283–97). Tonawanda, NY: Multilingual Matters.

Mohr, K. A. J. (1999). Variations in a theme: Using thematically framed language experience activities for ESL instruction. In O. G. Nelson & W. M. Linek (Eds.). *Practical classroom applications of language experience: Looking back and looking forward* (pp. 237–47). Boston, MA: Allyn and Bacon.

Mohr, K. A. J. (2012, November). *Perceptions of writing among second graders in an exemplary school: Gender and language issues.* Grand Rapids, MI: Association of Literacy Educators and Researchers.

Mohr, K. A. J. (2014, June). *Maximizing academic opportunities by extending ELL engagement.* Region 10 Bilingual/ESL/Migrant Conference, Plano, Texas.

Mohr, K. A. J., Robles-Goodwin, P. J., & Wilhelm, R. W. (2009). A study of optimism among Latinos in a successful urban elementary school. *Tapestry Journal, 1*(1), 1–14. Accessed online at http://journals.fcla.edu/tapestry/article/view/81778.

Mokhtari, K., & Reichard, C. (2002). Assessing students' metacognitive awareness of reading strategies. *Journal of Educational Psychology, 94*(2), 249–59.

Mokhtari, K. & Sheorey, R. (2002). Measuring ESL students' awareness of reading strategies. *Journal of Developmental Education, 25*(3), 2–10.

Moll, L. C., & González, N. (2003). Engaging life: A funds-of-knowledge approach to multicultural education. In J. A. Banks & C. A. M. Banks (Eds.), *Handbook on multicultural education* (2nd ed.). Boston, MA: Jossey-Bass.

Moll, L., Amanti, C., Neff, D., & Gonzales, N. (1992). Funds for knowledge for teaching: Using a qualitative approach to connect homes and classrooms. *Theory into Practice, 31*(4), 132–41.

Monseau, V. S., Gary. (2000). *Reading their world: The young adult novel in the classroom.* (2nd ed.). Portsmouth, NH: Heinemann.

Morrow, L., Shanahan, T., & Wixson, K. K. (2014). *Teaching with the common core state standards for English language arts: What educators need to know.* New York, NY: Guilford.

Moschkovich, J. (2010). Recommendations for research on language and mathematics education. In J. Moschkovich (Ed.), *Language and mathematics education: Multiple perspectives and directions for research* (pp. 151–70). Charlotte, NC: Information Age Publishing.

Myles, F., Mitchell, R., & Hooper, J. (1999). Interrogative chunks in French L2: A basis for creative construction? *Studies in Second Language Acquisition, 21*, 49–80.

Nation, I. S. P. (2009). *Teaching ESL/EFL reading and writing.* New York, NY: Routledge.

National Assessment of Educational Progress (NAEP). (2009). The nation's report card: Reading grade 4 national results. Washington, DC: Author. Retrieved from http://nationsreportcard.gov/reading_2009/nat_g4.asp?subtab_id=Tab_7&tab_id=tab1#tabsContainer.

National Center for Education Statistics. (2012). *What does the NAEP Writing Assessment measure?* Washington, DC: National Center for Educational Statistics, Institute of Education Sciences, U.S. Office of Education. Retrieved from http://nces.ed.gov/nationsreportcard/writing/whatmeasure.aspx.

National Center for Education Statistics. (2013a). *The condition of education 2013.* Washington, DC: U.S. Department of Education.

National Center for Educational Statistics. (2013b). National Assessment of Educational Progress. Retrieved from http://nces.ed.gov/nationsreportcard/about/.

National Commission on Teacher and America's Future (NCTAF). (2010). *Team up for 21st century teaching and learning: What research and practice reveal about professional learning.* Washington, DC: NCTAF.

National Governors Association Center for Best Practices (NGA) & Council of Chief State School Officers (CCSSO). (2010). *Common Core State Standards for English language arts and literacy for history/social studies, science, and technical subjects.* Washington, DC: Author.

National Institute of Child Health and Human Development. (2000). *The report of the National Reading Panel. Teaching children to read: An evidence-based assessment of the scientific literature on reading and its implications for reading instruction.* Washington, DC: U.S. Government Printing Office.

Neill, J. (2010, November 14). Experiential learning cycles: Overview of 9 experiential learning cycle models. Retrieved from http://www.wilderdom.com/experiential/elc/ExperientialLearningCycle.htm.

New London Group. (1996). A pedagogy of multiliteracies: Designing social features. *Harvard Educational Review*, 66(1), 60–92.

Nieto, S. (2003). *What keeps teachers going?* New York, NY: Teachers College Press.

No Child Left Behind. (2002). Act of 2001, Pub. L. No. 107-110, § 115. *Stat, 1425*, 107–10. Retrieved from http://www.kings.k12.ca.us/EdServices/SiteAssets/Categoricals/legalServicesHandbook.pdf.

O'Byrne, W. I. (2012). *Facilitating critical evaluation skills through content creation: Empowering adolescents as readers and writers of online information.* Unpublished doctoral dissertation, Storrs. CT.

O'Byrne, W. I. (2013). Online content construction: Empowering students as readers and writers of online information. In K. Pytash & R. Ferdig (Eds). *Exploring Technology in Writing and Writing Instruction.*

O'Byrne, W. I., & McVerry, J. G. (2015). Online research and media skills: An instructional model to support students as they search and sift online informational text. In T. Rasinky, K. Pytash & R. Ferdig (Eds). *Comprehension of informational texts.* Bloomington, IN: Solution Tree Press.

O'Grady, C. (Ed.). (2012). *Integrating service learning and multicultural education in colleges and universities.* New York, NY: Routledge.

Office of English Language Acquisition, Language Enhancement and Academic Achievement for Limited English Proficient Students (OELA). (2010). *The growing number of English learner students 1997/98–2007/08.* Washington, DC: U.S. Department of Education.

Ogle, D. (1986). K-W-L: A teaching model that develops active reading of expository text. *The Reading Teacher, 39*, 564–70.

Ogle, D., & Correa-Kovtun, A. (2010). Supporting English-language learners and struggling readers in content literacy with the "Partner Reading and Content, Too" routine. *The Reading Teacher, 63*(7), 532–42.

Orellana, M. F., Reynolds, J., Dorner, L., & Meza, M. (2003). In other words: Translating or "para-phrasing" as a family literacy practice in immigrant households. *Reading Research Quarterly, 38*(1), 12–38.

Painter, C., Martin, J. R., & Unsworth, L. (2013). *Reading visual narrative: Image analysis of children's picture books.* Bristol, CT: Equinox.

Pajares, F. (2003). Self-efficacy beliefs, motivation, and achievement in writing: A review of the literature. *Reading and Writing Quarterly, 19*, 139–258.

Pajares, F., Miller, M. D., & Johnson, M. J. (1999). Gender differences in the writing self-beliefs of elementary school students *Journal of Educational Psychology, 91*, 50–61.

Pajares, F., & Valiante, G. (1999). Grade level and gender differences in the writing self-beliefs of middle school students. *Contemporary Educational Psychology, 24*, 390–405.

Pajares, F., & Valiante, G. (2001). Gender differences in the writing motivation and achievement of middle school students: A function of gender orientation? *Contemporary Educational Psychology, 26*, 366–81.

Palincsar, A. S., & Brown, A. L. (1984). Reciprocal teaching of comprehension-fostering and comprehension-monitoring activities. *Cognition and Instruction, 1*(2), 117–75.

Parkinson, B., & Reid Thomas, H. (2000) *Teaching literature in a second language.* Edinburgh, Scotland: Edinburgh University Press.

Pearson, P. D., & Gallagher, M. C. (1983). The instruction of reading comprehension. *Contemporary Educational Psychology, 8*, 317–44.

Peregoy. S. F., & Boyle, O. F. (2013). *Reading, writing, and learning in ESL: A resource book for teaching K–12 English learners* (6th ed.). Boston, MA: Pearson.

Peregoy. S. F., & Boyle, O. F. (2015). *Reading, writing, and learning in ESL: A resource book for teaching K-12 English learners* (6th ed.). Boston, MA: Pearson.

Phillipson, R. (1992). *Linguistic imperialism.* Oxford, UK: Oxford University Press.

Ponce, F. (1994). *Mental imagery in second language reading.* Unpublished master's thesis, Illinois State University, Normal.

Ponce, F., & Steffensen, M. (1996, March). *Mental imagery in second language reading.* Paper presented at the annual meeting of TESOL International. Chicago, Illinois.

Prensky, M. (2001). Digital natives, digital immigrants part 1. *On the Horizon, 9*(5), 1–6.

Pressley, M. (2000). What should comprehension instruction be the instruction of? In M. L. Kamil, P. B. Mosenthal, P. D. Pearson, & R. Barr (Eds.), *Handbook of reading research*, vol. 3 (pp. 545–61). Mahwah NJ: Erlbaum.

Proctor, C. P., Dalton, B., & Grisham, D. L. (2007). Scaffolding English language learners and struggling readers in a universal literacy environment with embedded strategy instruction and vocabulary support. *Journal of Literacy Research, 39*(1), 71–93.

Proctor, C. P., Dalton, B., Uccelli, P., Biancarosa, G., Mo, E., Snow, C., & Neugebauer, S. (2011). Improving comprehension online: Effects of deep vocabulary instruction with bilingual and monolingual fifth graders. *Reading and Writing, 24*(5), 517–44.

Purcell-Gates, V., Duke, N. K., & Martineau, J. A. (2007). *Learning to read and write genre-specific text: Roles of authentic experience and explicit teaching, 42*(1), 8–45. doi: 10.1598/RRQ.42.1.1.

Quality Counts. (2009). Portrait of a population: How English language learners are putting schools to the test. *Education Week, 28*(17).

Ramsey, A., & O'Day, J. (2010). *Title III Policy: State of the States.* Washington, DC: American Institutes for Research.

RAND Reading Group (2002). Reading for Understanding: Toward an R&D Program in Reading Comprehension. Published by RAND, 1700 Main St., Santa Monica, CA.

Ray, K. W. (1999). *Wondrous words: Writers and writing in the elementary classroom.* Urbana, IL: National Council of Teachers of English.

Readf, S. (2005). Nonlinear nonfiction writing and the I-chart: Scaffolding for success. *2005 College Reading Association Yearbook, 27*, 170–81.

Reich, J., Murnane, R., & Willett, J. (2012). The state of wiki usage in U.S. K–12 schools: Leveraging Web 2.0 data warehouses to assess quality and equality in online learning environments. *Educational Researcher, 41*(1), 7–15.

Reiss, J. (2012). *120 content strategies for English language learners: Teaching for academic success in secondary school* (2nd ed.). Boston, MA: Pearson.

Richards, F. (2010). Enabling key stage 3 students to make improvements to their own writing. *Changing English: Studies in Culture and Education, 17*(1), 79–92.

Richardson, W. (2006). *Blogs, wikis and podcasts: And other powerful tools for classrooms*. Thousand Oaks, CA: Corwin Press.

Riches, C., & Genesee, F. (2006). Literacy: Crosslinguistic and crossmodal issues. In F. Genesee, K. Lindholm-Leary, W. M. Saunders, & D. Christian (Eds.), *Educating English Language Learners: A Synthesis of Research Evidence* (pp. 64–108). New York, NY: Cambridge University Press.

Robertson, I. H. (2003). *Opening the mind's eye: How images and language teach us how to see* (1st U.S. ed.). New York, NY: St. Martin's Press.

Robinson, E., & Robinson, S. (2003). *What does it mean? Discourse, text, culture: An introduction.* Sydney, Australia: McGraw-Hill.

Reinking, D. (1997). Me and my hypertext: A multiple digression analysis of technology and literacy (sic). *The Reading Teacher*, 626–43.

Rodgers, C. (2002). Defining reflection: Another look at John Dewey and reflective thinking. *Teachers College Record, 4*(4), 842–66. Retrieved from http://teachandreflect.com/.

Rogers, L. A., & Graham, S. (2008). A meta-analysis of single subject design writing intervention research. *Journal of Educational Psychology, 100*, 879–907.

Rosario-Ramos, W. S. E. L. E. (2009). Multilingual literacies in transnational digitally mediated contexts: an exploratore study of immigrant teens in the United States. *Language and Education, 23*(2), 171–90.

Rose, D. H., & Meyer, A. (2002). *Teaching every student in the digital age: Universal design for learning.* Alexandria, VA: ASCD. Retrieved December 25, 2009, from http://www.cast.org/teachingeverystudent/ideas/tes/.

Rosenblatt, L. M. (1995). *Literature as exploration* (5th ed.). New York, NY: Modern Language Association of America.

Rudiger, H. M. (2006). Reading lessons: Graphic novels 101. *The Horn Book Magazine*, 126–34.

Ruiz, T. (2014). Integrating content and language. *Language Magazine.* Retrieved from http://languagemagazine.com/?page_id=47991.

Rumberger, R. W., & Tran, L. (2010). State language policies, school language practices, and the English learner achievement gap. In P. Gándara & M. Hopkins (Eds.), *Forbidden language: English learners and restrictive language policies* (pp. 86–101). New York, NY: Teachers College Press.

Ryan, A. M., & Patrick, H. (2001). The classroom social environment and changes in adolescents' motivation and engagement during middle school. *American Educational Research Journal, 38*(2), 437–60.

Rylant, C. (1987). *Henry and Mudge: The first book.* New York, NY: Simon & Schuster.

Rylant, C. (1993). *The relatives came.* New York, NY: Aladdin.

Sadoski, M. (2004). *Conceptual foundations of teaching reading.* New York, NY: Guilford Press.

Salvner, G. M. (2000). Time and tradition: Transforming the secondary English class with young adult novels. In V. R. Monsea & G. M. Salvner (Eds.), *Reading their world: The young adult novel in the classroom* (pp. 85–99). Portsmouth, NH: Boynton/Cook–Heinemann.

Sandford, A. J., & Emmott, C. (2012). *Mind, brain and narrative.* New York, NY: Cambridge University Press.

Saponaro, T. (2013, December 6). Apps for inquiry-based learning. *Teaching with iPad in a flipped classroom.* Retrieved from http://tsaponar.blogspot.com/2013/12/apps-for-inquiry-based-learning.html.

Sarkar, M. (2009). "Still reppin' por mi gente": The transformative power of language mixing in Quebec hip hop. In H. S. Alim, A. Ibrahim, & A. Pennycook (Eds.), *Global linguistic flows: Hip hop cultures, youth identities, and the politics of language* (pp. 139–58). New York, NY: Routledge.

Sarkar, M., & Winer, L. (2006). Multilingual code-switching in Quebec rap: Poetry, pragmatics, and performativity. *International Journal of Multilingualism, 3*(3), 173–92.

Sato, E., Langunoff, R., Worth, P., Baily, A. L., & Butler, F. A. (2005). *ELD standards linkage and test alignment under title III: A pilot study of the CELDT and the California ELD content standards.* Final report (June) to the California Department of Education, Sacramento, California.

Schecter, S. R., & Cummins, J. (2003). *Multilingual education in practice: Using diversity as a resource.* Portsmouth, NH: Heinemann.

Scheibe, C., & Rogow, F. (2011). *The teacher's guide to media literacy: Critical thinking in a multimedia world.* Thousand Oaks, CA: Sage.

Schleppegrell, M. (2004). *The language of schooling: A functional linguistic perspective.* Mahwah, NJ: Lawrence Erlbaum Associates.

Schleppegrell, M. J., & O'Halloran, C. L. (2011). Teaching academic language in L2 secondary settings. *Annual Review of Applied Linguistics, 31*, 3–18.

Schon, D. (1983). *The reflective practitioner.* New York, NY: Basic Books.

Schmidt, R. (2001). Attention. In P. Robinson (Ed.), *Cognition and second-language instruction* (pp. 3–32). Cambridge, MA: Cambridge University Press.

Schmitt, N., & Carter, R. (2000). The lexical advantages of narrow reading for second language learners. *TESOL Journal,* 4–9.

Schneider, E., & Ganschow, L. (2000). Dynamic assessment and instructional strategies for learners who struggle to learn a foreign language. *Dyslexia, 6,* 72–82.

Schwarzer, D. (2001). *Noa's ark: One child's voyage into multiliteracy.* Portsmouth, NH: Heinemann.

Schwarzer, D. (2004). Student and teacher strategies for communicating through dialogue journals in Hebrew: A teacher research project. *Foreign Language Annals, 37*(1), 77–84.

Schwarzer, D. (2007). Monolingual teachers fostering students' native literacies. In P. Martens & Y. Goodman (Eds.), *Critical issues in early literacy development: Research and pedagogy.* Mahwah, NJ: Lawrence Erlbaum Associates.

Schwarzer, D., & Acosta, C. (2014). Multilingual students in monolingual class-rooms: Two activities to bridge between them. *Journal of Multilingual Education Research.*

Schwarzer, D., Haywood, A., & Lorenzen, C. (2003). Fostering multiliteracy in a linguistically diverse classroom. *Language Arts, 80*(6), 453–60.

Schwarzer, D., Petron, M., & Luke, C. (2011). *Research informing practice—practice informing research: Innovative teaching methologies for world language teachers. Research in second language learning.* Greenwich, CT: Information Age Publishing.

Scollon, R., Scollon, S. W., & Jones, R. H. (2011). *Intercultural communication: A discourse approach.* New York, NY: John Wiley & Sons.

Selfe, C. L. (1999). Technology and literacy: A story about the perils of not paying attention. *College Composition and Communication, 50*, 411–37.

Selfe, C. L. (1999). *Technology and literacy in the 21st century: The importance of paying attention.* SIU Press.

Selinker, L. (1972). Interlanguage. *International Review of Applied Linguistics in Language Teaching, 10*(1–4), 209–32.

Shanahan, L. E. (2013). Composing "kid-friendly" multimodal text: When conversations, instruction, and signs come together. *Written Communication, 30*(2), 194–227.

Shanahan, T. (2012). What is close reading? Retrieved August 25, 2014, http://www.shanahanonliteracy.com/2012/06/what-is-close-reading.html.

Shanahan, T. (2013). Letting the text take center stage. *American Educator* (Fall), 4–11.

Shanahan, T., & Beck, I. L. (2006). Effective literacy teaching for English language learners. In D. August & T. Shanahan (Eds.), *Developing literacy in second-language learners: Report of the National Literacy Panel on language-minority children and youth* (pp. 415–88). Mahwah, NJ: Lawrence Erlbaum Associates.

Shetzer, H., & Warschauer, M. (2000). An electronic literacy approach to network-based language teaching. *Network-based language teaching: Concepts and practice*, 171–85.

Shiga, J. (2007). Copy-and-persist: The logic of mash-up culture. *Critical Studies in Media Communication, 24*(2), 93–114.

Shin, D. (2014). Web 2.0 tools and academic literacy development in a US urban school: A case study of a second grade English language learner. *Language and Education, 28*(1), 68–85.

Short, D., & Fitzsimmons, S. (2007). *Double the work: Challenges and solutions to acquiring language and academic literacy for adolescent English language learners: A report to the Carnegie Corporation of New York.* Washington, DC: Alliance for Excellent Education.

Short, K. G., Kauffman, G., & Kahn, K. H. (2000). "I just need to draw": Responding to literature across multiple sign systems. *The Reading Teacher, 54*(2), 160–71.

Siegel, M., Kontovourki, S., Schmier, S., & Enriquez, G. (2008). Literacy in Motion: A Case Study of a Shape-Shifting Kindergartener. *Language Arts, 86*(2), 89–98.

Sims Bishop, R. (1990). Mirrors, windows, and sliding glass doors. *Perspectives*, ix–xi.

Sims Bishop, R. (1992). Multicultural literature for children: Making informed choices. In V. Harris (Ed.), *Teaching multicultural literature in grades K–8* (pp. 37–54). Norwood, MA: Christopher-Gordon.

Skehan, P. (1998). *A Cognitive approach to language learning.* Oxford: Oxford University Press.

Skutnabb-Kangas, T., Phillipson, R., Panda, M., & Mohanty, A. K. (2009). Multilingual education concepts, goals, needs and expense: English for all or achieving justice? In T. Skutnabb-Kangas, R. Philips, A. Mohanty, & M. Panda (Eds.), *Social justice through multilingual education* (pp. 320–44). Tonawanda, NY: Multilingual Matters.

Smith, H. J., Higgins, S., Wall, K. & Miller, J. (2005). Interactive whiteboards: boon or bandwagon? A critical review of the literature. *Journal of Computer Assisted Learning, 21,* 4.

Smolkin, L. B., & Donovan, C. A. (2001). The contexts of comprehension: The information book read aloud, comprehension acquisition, and comprehension instruction in a first-grade classroom. *The Elementary School Journal, 102*(2), 97–122.

Snow, C., & O'Connor, C. (2013). *Close reading and far-reaching classroom discussion: Fostering a vital connection* (A policy brief from the Literacy Research Panel of the International Reading Association). Newark, DE: International Reading Association.

Snow, C., & Uccelli, P. (2009). The challenge of academic language. In D. R. Olson & N. Torrance (Eds.), *The Cambridge handbook of literacy* (pp. 112–33). New York, NY: Cambridge University Press.

Snow, C., Burns, M. S., & Griffin, P. (1998). *Preventing reading difficulties in young children.* Washington, DC: National Academy Press.

Sollors, W. (1998). Introduction: After the culture wars—from "English only" to "English plus." In W. Sollors (Ed.), *Multilingual America: transnationalism, ethnicity and the languages of American literature* (pp. 1–16). New York, NY: New York University Press.

Stahl, S. A. (1986). Three principles of effective vocabulary instruction. *Journal of Reading, 29,* 662–68.

Stahl, S. A., & Stahl, K. A. D. (2004). Word wizards all: Teaching word meaning in pre-school and primary education. In J. F. Baumann & E. J. Kamenui (Eds.) *Vocabulary instruction: Research to practice* (pp. 59–78). New York, NY: Guilford Press.

Steffensen, M. A., & Cheng, X. (1997, October). *Chinese/English readers: The images they form, the emotions they experience, the methods that help in reading.* Paper presented at the Third Symposium on Language Teaching in China.

Steffensen, M. A., Joag-Dev, C., & Anderson, R. C. (1979). A cross-cultural perspective of reading comprehension. *Reading Research Quarterly, 15*(1), 10–29.

Steffensen, M. S., Goetz, E. T., & Cheng, X. (1999). A cross-linguistic perspective on imagery and affect in reading: Dual coding in Chinese and English. *Journal of Literacy Research, 31*(3), 293–99.

Stover, L. (2001). The place of young adult literature in secondary reading programs. In B. O. Ericson (Ed.), *Teaching reading in high school English classes* (pp. 115–38). Urbana, IL: National Council of Teachers of English.

Strong, W. J. (1994). *Sentence combining: A composing book* (3rd ed.). New York, NY: McGraw-Hill.

Strong, W. J. (2001). *Coaching writing: The power of guided practice.* Portsmouth, NH: Heinemann.

Strong, C. J., & Strong, W. J. (1999). *Strong rhythms and rhymes: Language and literacy development through sentence combining.* Eau Claire, WI: Thinking Publications.

Strangman, N., & Dalton, B. (2005). Technology for struggling readers: A review of the research. In D. Edyburn, K. Higgins, & R. Boone (Eds.), *The handbook of special education technology research and practice* (pp. 545–69). Whitefish Bay, WI: Knowledge by Design.

Supporting secondary reading through functional language analysis. *Journal of Adolescent and Adult Literacy, 53*(7), 587–97.

Susag, D. (1998). *Roots and branches: A resource of Native American literature—themes lessons and bibliographies.* Urbana, IL: National Council of Teachers of English.

Swain, M. (1995). Three functions of output in second language learning. In G. Cook and B. Seidlhofer (Eds.), *Principle and practice in applied linguistics* (pp. 125–44). Oxford: Oxford University Press.

Tayebipour, F. (2009). In defence of teaching literature to EFL students in the era of globalization. In L. J. Zhang, R. Rubdy, & Alsagoff (Ed.), *English and literatures-in-English in a globalized world: Proceedings of the 13th international conference on English in Southeast Asia* (pp. 213–19). Singapore: National Institute of Education, Nanyang Technological University

Taylor, B. M., Pearson, P. D., Peterson, D. S., & Rodriguez, M. C. (2003). Reading growth in high-poverty classrooms: The influence of teacher practices that encourage cognitive engagement in literacy learning. *The Elementary School Journal, 104*(1), 3–28.

Taylor, S. K. (2009). The caste system approach to multilingualism in Canada: Linguistic and cultural minority children in French immersion. In T. Skutnabb-Kangas, R. Philips, A. Mohanty, & M. Panda (Eds.), *Social justice through multilingual education* (pp. 177–98). Tonawanda, NY: Multilingual Matters.

Tellier, A., & Roehr-Brackin, K. (2013). Metalinguistic awareness in children with differing language learning experience. *EUROSLA Yearbook, 13,* 81–108.

TESOL Standards: http://www.tesol.org/docs/books/bk_prek-12elpstandards_framework_318.pdf?sfvrsn=2.

Thomas, W. P., & Collier, V. P. (2002). *A national study of school effectiveness for language minority students long-term academic achievement.* Santa Cruz, CA: Center for Research on Education, Diversity, and Excellence, University of California Santa Cruz. http://repositories.cdlib.org/crede/final/rpts/1_1_final/.

Thomas, W., & Collier, V. (1997). *School effectiveness for language minority students.* Washington, DC: National Clearinghouse for Bilingual Education.

Thompson, D. R., Kersaint, G., Richards, J. C., Hunsader, P. D., & Rubinstein, R. N. (2008). *Mathematical literacy: Helping students make meaning in the middle grades.* Portsmouth, NH: Heinemann.

Thorne, S. L. (2008). Mediating technologies and second language learning. In J. Coiro, M. Knobel , C. Lankshear, & D. Leu (Eds.), *Handbook of research on new literacies* (pp. 417–49). Mahwah, NJ: Lawrence Erlbaum.

Torres, M., & Mercado, M. (2006). The need for critical media literacy in teacher education core curricula. *Educational Studies, 39*(3), 260–82.

Tovani, C. (2000). *I read it, but I don't get it: Comprehension strategies for adolescent readers.* Portland, ME: Steinhouse.

Triplett, C. F., & Buchanan, A. (2005). Book talk: Continuing to rouse minds and hearts to life. *Reading Horizons, 46*(2), 63–76.

Troia, G. A., & Olinghouse, N. G. (2013). The Common Core State Standards and evidence- based educational practices: The case of writing. *School Psychology Review, 42*, 343–57.

Twain, M. (1876/2001). *The adventures of Tom Sawyer.* New York: Modern Library.

Uro, G., & Barrio, A. (2013). *English language learners in America's great city schools: Demographics, achievement, and Staffing.* Washington, DC: Council of Great City Schools.

Van Houten, R., & McKillop, C. (1977). An extension of the effects of the performance feedback system with secondary school students. *Psychology in the Schools, 14*, 480–84.

Van Houten, R., Morrison, E., Jarvis, R., & McDonald, M. (1974). The effects of explicit timing and feedback on compositional response rate in elementary school children. *Journal of Applied Behavior Analysis, 7*, 547–55.

Veel, R. (1997). Learning how to mean—scientifically speaking: Apprenticeship into scientific discourse in the secondary school. In F. Christie & J. R. Martin (Eds.), *Genre and institutions: Social processes in the workplace and school* (pp. 161–95). London: Continuum.

Villegas, A. M., & Lucas, T. (2002a). *Educating culturally responsive teachers: A coherent approach*: Ithaca, NY: State University of New York Press.

Villegas, A. M., & Lucas, T. (2002b). Preparing culturally responsive teachers: Rethinking the curriculum. *Journal of Teacher Education, 53*(1), 20–32.

Viorst, J. (1987). *If I were in charge of the world and other worries.* New York, NY: Aladdin.

Vogt, M. E., & Echevarria, J. (2008). *99 ideas and activities for teaching English learners with the SIOP model.* Boston, MA: Allyn and Bacon.

Vygotsky, L. (1962). *Thought and language.* (E. H. G. Vakar, Trans.). Cambridge, MA: MIT Press.

Vygotsky, L. (1978). Interaction between learning and development. *Readings on the Development of Children, 23*(3), 34–41.

Wallace, C. (2007). Vocabulary: the key to teaching English Language Learners. *Reading Improvement, 44*(4), 189–93.

Ware, P. (2008). Language learners and multimedia literacy in and after school. *Pedagogies: An International Journal, 3*, 37–51.

Warriner, D. S. (2007). Transnational literacies: Immigration, language learning, and identity. *Linguistics and Education, 18*(3–4), 201–14.

Warschauer, M. (2006). *Laptops and literacy: Learning in the wireless classroom.* New York, NY: Teachers College Press.

Warschauer, M., & Meskill, C. (2000). Technology and second language learning and teaching. In J. Rosenthal (Ed.), *Handbook of undergraduate second language education* (pp. 303–18.). Mahwah, NJ: Lawrence Erlbaum Associates.

Watts, E. L. (1999). Using young adult literature with adolescent learners of English. *ALAN Review, 26*(3), Retrieved from http://scholar.lib.vt.edu/ejournals/ALAN/spring99/watts.html.

Weate, J. (1998). *A young person's guide to philosophy: I think therefore I am.* New York, NY: DK Publishing.

Weaver, C. A., Ill, & Kintsch, W. (1991). Expository text. In R. Barr, M. L. Kamil, P. B. Rosenthal, & P. D. Pearson (Eds.), *Handbook of reading* (pp. 230–45). New York: Longman.

Werbner, P., & Modood, T. (1997). *Debating cultural hybridity: Multi-cultural identities and the politics of anti-racism.* Highlands, NJ: Zed Books.

Wesche, M. B., & Paribakht, T. S. (2000). Reading-based exercises in second language vocabulary learning: An introspective study. *Modern Language Journal, 84*(2), 196–213.

Weygant, A. D. (1981). *The effects of specific instructions and a lesson on the written language expression of learning disabled elementary school children.* Unpublished doctoral dissertation, University of Virginia.

Whitehurst, G. J., Falco, F. L., Lonigan, C. J., Fischell, J. E., DeBaryshe, B. D., Valdez-Menchaca, M. C., & Caulfield, M. (1988). Accelerating language development through picture book reading. *Developmental Psychology, 24*(4), 552–59.

WIDA. (2014). World-class instructional design and assessment. Retrieved from http://www.wida.us/.

Wilhelm, J. (2001). Improving comprehension with think-aloud strategies. New York: Scholastic Professional Books.

Wilhelm, J. D. (2012). *Improving comprehension with think-aloud strategies: Modeling what good readers do. Theory and practice.* New York, NY: Scholastic.

Willems, M. (2010). *Cat the cat, who is that?* New York, NY: HarperCollins.

Willig, A. (1985). A meta-analysis of selected studies on the effectiveness of bilingual education. *Review of Educational Research, 55*(3), 269–317.

Wilson, E. O. (2014). *A window on eternity: A biologist's walk through Gorongosa National Park.* New York: Simon & Schuster.

Winerip, M. (2005). *SAT Essay Test Rewards Length and Ignores Errors.* The New York Times, May, 4, 2005. Retrieved from http://www.nytimes.com/2005/05/04/education/04education.html?_r=0.

Wink, J. (2011). *Critical pedagogy: Notes from the real world* (4th ed.). Upper Saddle River, NJ: Pearson Education.

Wink, J. (2006, June–July). Socratic dialog. *WinkWorld.* Retrieved from http://www.joanwink.com/newsletter/2006/news0706.pdf.

Wink, J., & Putney, L. G. (2002). *A vision of Vygotsky.* Boston, MA: Pearson Education.

Wink, J., & Putney, L.G. (2013). *A vision of Vygotsky.* Howes, SD: Authors. (Reprinted from *A vision of Vygotsky,* by J. Wink & L. G. Putney, 2002, Boston, MA: Pearson Education).

Wolfe, L. H. (1997). *Effects of self-monitoring on the on-task behavior and written language performance of elementary students with learning disabilities.* Unpublished master's thesis, Ohio State University.

Wong-Fillmore, L., & Valadez, C. (1986). Teaching bilingual learners. In M. C. Wittrock (Ed.), *Handbook of research on teaching* (3rd Ed.). New York: Macmillan.

World-class Instructional Design & Assessment (2003). http://www.tesol.org/docs/books/bk_prek-12elpstandards_framework_318.pdf?sfvrsn=2.

Yi, Y. (2007). Engaging literacy: A biliterate student's composting practices beyond school. *Journal of Second Language Writing, 16*(1), 23–39.

Yolen, J. (1987). *Owl moon.* New York, NY: Philomel Books.

Young, K. A. (2005). Direct from the source: The value of 'think-aloud' data in understanding learning. *Journal of Educational Enquiry, 6*(1), 19–33.

Zehler, A. M., Fleischman, H. L., Hopstock, P.J., Stephenson, T. G., Pendzick, M. L., and Sapru, S. (2003). *Descriptive study of services to LEP students and LEP students with disabilities.* Volume I: Research Report. Submitted to the U.S. Department of Education, OELA. Arlington, VA: Development Associates Inc.

Zhang, L. J. (2010). A dynamic metacognitive systems account of Chinese university students' knowledge about EFL reading. *TESOL Quarterly, 44*(2), 320–53.

Zhao, Y., Pugh, K., Sheldon, S., & Byers, J. (2002). Conditions for classroom technology innovations. *The Teachers College Record, 104*(3), 482–515.

Index

About the Editors

Dr. Mayra C. Daniel, associate professor in the Department of Literacy and Elementary Education at Northern Illinois University, serves as the Bilingual ESL Coordinator for NIU's College of Education. Her research focuses on preparing teachers to work with bilingual and multilingual populations in the United States and in Latin America. Prior to her work with teachers in postgraduate programs, she worked to help learners (at levels K–12) from diverse linguistic and cultural backgrounds to transition and adapt to the cultural norms of life in schooling within rural communities in the state of Illinois. She is chair of the Literacy, Diversity, and Multiculturalism Committee of the International Reading Association, and past-chair of the TESOL International Organization's Interest Section Leadership Council. She is a member of the Board of Examiners of CAEP and a TESOL Program Auditor.

Mayra emigrated with her family to the United States at age ten to escape communism and live in a free country. As a young child she spoke Spanish, the language of her country, Cuba, a land colonized by Spaniards long ago. When she arrived to the United States she was an English learner (EL) who received no assistance to acquire English. This was at the very beginning of the educational movement that seeks to validate linguistic and cultural diversity. Mayra was a lucky immigrant because she came from a highly educated family, she was an avid reader, and had completed her school years from K–6 in a school system that had provided her a solid education. Many, if not the majority of EL in U.S. schools today, are not this lucky. These personal experiences are a factor in Mayra's zeal to research better ways to educate ELs in the United States so that they may have the opportunities afforded to her.

Dr. Kouider Mokhtari, serves as the Anderson-Vukelja-Wright Endowed Professor of Education in the School of Education at UT-Tyler University, where he engages in research, teaching, and service initiatives aimed at enhancing literacy at the school, university, and community levels.

Mokhtari's research focuses on the acquisition of language and literacy by first and second language learners, with particular emphasis on children, adolescents, and adults who can read but have difficulties understanding what they read. His research has been published in books, journals, and reports. His books include *Reading Strategies of First and Second Language Learners: See How They Read* (Rowman & Littlefield, 2008); *Preparing Every Teacher to Reach English Learners* (Harvard Education Press, 2012), and *Educating English Learners: What Every Teacher Needs to Know* (Harvard Education Press, 2014). His coauthored book *Preparing Every Teacher to Reach English Learners* was selected for the 2013 American Association of Colleges for Teacher Education (AACTE) Outstanding Book Award. The award recognizes exemplary books that make a significant contribution to the knowledge base of educator preparation or of teaching and learning with implications for educator preparation. Kouider has served in various leadership roles including service as member and co-chair of the Literacy and English Learners Committee of the International Reading Association, and coeditor of *Tapestry: An International Cross-Disciplinary Journal*, which is dedicated to the advancement of research and instruction for English language learners.

In 2014, Mokhtari received the John C. Manning Public School Service Award from the International Reading Association (IRA). This award recognizes a professor of reading education who has demonstrated their commitment to public education and has spent significant time working with public school teachers and their students in classrooms demonstrating effective approaches and techniques shown to improve reading instruction.

P.56 ... acquire a
new vocabulary Oneed to
word students
hear it 7-12 times
(Stahl (1986).

Ellis (1993) Littlewood (1984)
- El's language syllabus

Formulaic language
- Ellis (1984)
- Myles, mitchell, Hooper (1999)
Form schmidt (2001)

9 781475 818666